ISLAMIC PRINCIPLES

ISLAMIC PRINCIPLES

ZIKR-UR-RAHMAN

ANMOL PUBLICATIONS PVT. LTD.
NEW DELHI - 110 002 (INDIA)

ANMOL PUBLICATIONS PVT. LTD.
4374/4B, Ansari Road, Daryaganj
New Delhi - 110 002
Ph.: 23261597, 23278000
Visit us at: www.anmolpublications.com

Islamic Principles

First Published, 2004

ISBN 81-261-1882-2

PRINTED IN INDIA

Published by J.L. Kumar for Anmol Publications Pvt. Ltd., New Delhi - 110 002 and Printed at Mehra Offset Press, Delhi.

Contents

Preface

Every discipline has its own principles. Islam too, as a perfect code of conduct has its own principles and guidelines for its followers in particular and as an example for all the human beings, in general.

The Believers or the faithfuls, entering the fold of Islam have to abide by certain rules and regulations. Islam is a complete way of life and demands from its people, evolvement of some patterns, etiquettes and manners. Truly speaking, every human being needs to follow a course of life, either prescribed by some religion, faith or ideology or a conduct, set on his or her own.

This book, comprehensive in its unique style, exclusively covers the philosophy and ideology of Islam in nutshell. It provides a complete set of guidelines for those who wish to follow Islam and a detailed account of the same, with clarity for those, who are not followers of Islam but may desire to learn about it, for academic purposes.

This Editor is confident to be acknowledged and appreciated by scholars and common readers alike for this modest but sincere effort.

—Editor

ONE

Introduction

A firm and strong faith is such a never-drying spring, from which flow the strength for the desired activities, coveted courage and forbearance to tolerate adversities and to face dangers. It creates in man such a restless feeling and deep attachment to his ideal that if he is unable to achieve his coveted objective, he does not hesitate to partake of the drink of death.

When faith finds a place in a man's heart and takes deep roots in it, it brings out these results only. It fills a man's heart and mind with such power and strength that cover and influence all his dealings. Accordingly, when he opens his mouth, he talks with confidence and certainty. When he undertakes a work, he attends to it with full interest and sincerity. When he starts on a journey, his destination is before his eyes. If he enjoys the wealth of the correct and firm thinking, the world of the heart too is inhabited by the enthusiasm and restless courage. Hesitation and ambivalence do not find a place in his heart, and high-velocity winds do not move him from his path or make him deviate from his objective. It will not be surprising if he says to every one, in the words of an Urdu poet:

> "Come here O tyrant ! we will try our art,
> "You try your arrow, and I will try my liver (courage)."

And he may challenge the people around him thus

> "You work in your manner, I too an acting. Soon you will know who will get disgraceful punishment and who will get the everlasting punishment."
>
> (*Zumar: 39-40*)

This challenging accent, this independent spirit in action and deeds, this self-confidence in understanding truth and tradition are the qualities which make him a distinguished personality in life. He deals with the people in the light of the facts seen and experienced by him. If he finds the people on a policy which is right and truthful, he extends his hand for co-operation, and if he finds them committing errors, he withdraws himself, and leaves his conscience alive and wakeful.

> Allah's Messenger has said: 'Every one of you should desist from walking with every traveller. He should not say that he is with the people, and that if people would do good deed, he would also do the good deeds ; and that if they would do wicked deeds then he would co-operate with them. You should prepare yourself to co-operate with them if they do righteous deeds and to keep away if they do wicked deeds." (*Tirmizi*)

But one who is weak, the current customs and habits make one their slave. On such a man's conduct rule the things which are current in the society. If these customs and practices are wrong and destructive, then he carries the burden of the troubles of this world as well as of the next.

Among the people, various kinds of innovations have become customary on the occasions of celebrations and mourning. They pay more attention to performing these innovative acts than on the realities of the religion.

But a straight-going Momin does not take any interest in these things, for which there is no supportive proof in religion. He is confronted with opposition and experiences difficulties in opposing the popular and customary rituals, but it is obvious that he need not care for any condemnation from anybody in the affairs of Allah. He has to achieve his ideal. No weapon of criticism and fault-finding and no injuries from tongue can obstruct his way.

Falsehood which sometimes is successful is subsequently ruled by powerful individuals. They then destroy its position and rank. This also cannot stay for a long time with the help and support of its allies, because many enemies who are today with it, having been deceived by falsehood, tomorrow they would become the supporters of the other enemies; they approve of their aims and objects after knowing their character and pledge their support after severe hostility and spite.

Ibn Abbas has narrated that Allah's Messenger has said:

> "He who has displeased Allah for seeking the pleasure of the people, Allah is displeased with him and those people are also displeased for pleasing whom he had earned Allah's displeasure. And he who pleases Allah by displeasing the people, Allah is also pleased with him and also those people whom he had displeased for pleasing Allah, so much so that He made him splendid and his speech and acts in the eyes of others beautiful." (*Tibrani*)

A Muslim should stick to what he believes to be true, and he should ignore all the insults, fun-making, and difficulties with which he is confronted. He should adopt for himself such a policy through following which he should always try to get rewards (sawab) from Allah. If those, who believe in superstitions and absurd things, make fun of the faithful people and laugh at them, then it is necessary for a Momin to be strong and to stand his ground with firmness.

> "When they see you, (O Muhammed !) they treat you only as a jest (saying): Is this he whom Allah sends as a messenger ? He would have led us far away from our gods if we had not been staunch to them. They will know, when they behold the doom, who is more astray as to the road." (*Furqan : 42-43*)

No doubt, a Muslim must feel in his personality the strength of belief and in his heart the pressure and awe of faith. If the things around him do not influence him, then he is like a rock which is not moved by the lashing of the waves of the sea. What harm these men can inflict on a man who feels in his heart the strength of faith and belief, and on account of his relation with his Lord and steadfastness in his religion feels in himself a new determination and a fresh courage ? If all these rush and attack, they will not be able to harm him a bit.

Ibn Abbas says that he was sitting on a mount behind the Prophet. The Prophet said : "O child! remember Allah, He will take care of you. Remember Allah, you will find Him everywhere. Recognise Allah's rights in your prosperity, He will recognise you in your adversity. If you want to ask anything, ask from Allah. If you need help, seek help from Allah, for if all the men together decide to help, they will not be able to do so, if Allah has not written that for you and they have no control over it. And if all of them decide to inflict some harm on you which Allah has not meant for you, they cannot harm you a bit. The ink of the pen has been dried and the sheets have been collected."

The fact is that in a Muslim the basis of strength and power is the belief in the oneness of Allah. Similarly other virtues prevent him from accepting any disgrace and insult in this world, because a Muslim is most honoured and of high rank on account of his relationship with the heavens. In his own sphere of faith he has the power to become a whole community. These are Allah's words, speaking for him

> "Say: 'Shall I choose for a protecting friend other than Allah, the Originator of the heavens and the earth, who feeds and is never fed ?' Say : 'I am ordered to be the first to surrender (to Him). And be not you (O Muhammed!) of the idolaters'." (*An'am: 14*)

Islam has declared achievement of strength and power essential. Its one characteristic and manifestation is that you make a firm determination and a strong resolve to achieve, with the help of your nearest available means and resources, your objective. Try your utmost in achieving your goal. You should leave no stone unturned and no room for chance, and thereafter leave the outcome in the hands of destiny. There are many individuals who take Allah's shelter in order to cover their objectionable defects reprehensible negligence, inability and laziness, and grumble against luck. Islam has disapproved of this tendency.

> Auf bin Malik says that Allah's Messenger once gave a decision in a dispute of two people. When the man

> against whom the Prophet's decision was given was returning, said : "For me Allah is sufficient, and He is the best support." The Prophet said: "Allah sends curses on helplessness and weakness. You should give proof of your wisdom. When you are overpowered in any matter say : `For me Allah is sufficient, and He is the best support'." (*Abu Daud*)

It is the duty of everybody that he should make full efforts and try to the best of his ability to overcome his difficulty, till the time he achieves his objective. If he overpowers his difficulties then he has fulfilled his responsibility.

However, if after making all the efforts he fails, then at such a time the support of Allah is the best shelter for him, which would help him to overcome the sense of defeatism and frustration. In both the states he is strong and powerful. First by making efforts and working, and in the second case by relying on God he receives strength.

Islam does not like that in your affairs you should be a prey to vagueness and hesitation. You should not be undecided in the matter of selecting the advantageous alternative. Your head should not be filled up with doubts and misgivings, resulting in an atmosphere of indetermination and indecision, making it difficult for you to come to a decision. 1t does not like that due to your weakness you may not be able to strongly hold the advantageous things in your firm grip, and they should slip through your fingers and may be wasted. This restlessness and indecision does not become a Muslim.

> Allah's Prophet has said : "A strong Momin is better than a weak Momin and is more liked by Allah, and there is good in each one. Desire profitable things and seek Allah's help and be humble. If you are harmed then do not say that had you done in this way the result would have been different, but say Allah is Controller, whatever He likes He may decide, because the botheration of ifs and buts opens the door of the devil's workshop." (Muslim)

What is the work of Satan to remind of the troubles and the difficulties of the past, which would create a sense of heart-breaking disappointment and deprivation. Man thinks about the prospects of his present and future. As regards shedding tears on the defeats of the past, to bring back the memory of the past sadness, to think of old enmities and to be entangled in the net of ifs and buts, are inclinations which do not suit the conduct of a Muslim. Quran has listed them with sorrow and frustration in those manifestations which are generated in the hearts of the infidels:

> "O you who believe! Be not as those who disbelieved and said of their brethren who went abroad in the land or were fighting in the field: If they had been (here) with us they would not have died or been killed; that Allah may make it anguish in their hearts. Allah gives life and causes death and Allah is Observer of what you do." (*Ale Imran: 156*)

One hadith has it: "One who wants to be strong among men, should rely on Allah."

Trust in Allah which makes a man powerful is a kind of confidence in Allah, which saves a man from destruction at a time when he is surrounded on all sides by harrowing difficulties, and when he is unable to get help from any one else, nor is there any hope of getting it from elsewhere.

Accordingly he becomes a mountain of strength at the time of confrontation with the enemy. If the reliance is on Allah, then inspite of the shortage of weapons and war-equipment and insufficient number of supporters, he feels that he has a strong support. From this trust in Allah he .receives encouragement and support to be steadfast. He sticks to his job till in the dark and frightening atmosphere the glad tidings of victory are heard by him. The holy Quran says that trust is such an eternal food for war that with its help prophets and their followers have bravely and successfully faced the tyrants of their time:

> "How should we not put our trust in Allah when He has shown us our ways ? We surely will endure that hurt you do us. In Allah let the trusting put their trust." (*Ibrahim : 12*)

The faithful and their supporters stand their ground, sticking to their mandate. They have expectations of well-being in the future. They have full confidence that their present weakness will be converted into a powerful victorious force, but the wicked and evil rulers and their disciples term this determination and trust of the faithful their pride and madness

> "When the hypocrites and those in whose hearts is a disease said: `Their religion has deluded these. Whosoever puts his trust in Allah (will find that) surely, Allah is Mighty, Wise." (*Al-Anfal : 49*)

For becoming strong and powerful a Muslim should take care that he keeps away from the life of wickedness and evil, loves the policy of cleanness and steadfastness. A man who is ill-mannered, and bereft of decency and consideration, cannot attain strength. He should put on the hide of the beasts and walk in the wake of the kings as a servant.

Allah informed the nation of Hud, that was tyrant and rebellious against Allah, the correct and profitable causes of strength:

> "Ask forgiveness of your Lord, then turn to Him repentant; He will cause the sky to rain abundance on you and will add to you strength. Turn not away, guilty. (*Hud : 52*)

The kind Prophet wanted to present the worship to the people in a beautiful form and to persuade them to perform it. When a man performs a righteous deed, he opposes the Satan and tries to rise towards the angels. At that time how great becomes his sanctity and magnificence! To focus attention on this the Prophet has explained it by giving an example:

> "When Allah created the earth, it tilted and was unsteady. Accordingly Allah put the stakes (nails) of mountains in it, and it became steady, and stood in one position. The angels were amazed by the strength of the mountains. They asked the Creator : `Our Lord ! Have you created anything harder than the mountains

?' He replied: 'Yes, Iron is harder than this.' The angels again asked 'Is anything harder than iron ?' He said : 'Yes, Fire has more power.' They asked : 'Is there anything more powerful created by you than fire ?' He said : 'Yes, Water is more powerful than this.' The angels asked : 'Does anything among your created things exist more powerful than water?' He said 'Yes, air has more power than this.' They asked 'Have you created anything more powerful than air?' He said : 'Yes, Adam's sin is more powerful, provided he gives charity from his right hand without letting his left hand know it." (*Tirmizi*)

Man is the strangest creature of the universe. The day his personality attains greatness and excellence of moral character he becomes the hunter of the universe. He brings under his control the hardest and the most powerful things of the universe, and derives benefit from it. But the day when his personality declines, he earns the curses of the inhabitants of the heavens and the earth, and the particles of dust carry him with them in their flight.

In the *hadith* quoted above the value and importance of such a virtuous man has been mentioned who tries to forge ahead in the field of righteousness and who tries to touch the heights of excellence and decency.

One factor of strength is that a Muslim should be in the habit of stating the truth unhesitatingly. He should meet people with an open heart, and on the basis of righteous values and principles. He should not compromise in the matter of truth, so that his decency and his companions' character may not be tarnished. He should consider his strength a direct outcome of his belief which he represents and for which he is alive. He should never waver in unhesitatingly and courageously proving a reality.

It is reported that when the Prophet's son Ibrahim died, the sun went into an eclipse. The people said that the eclipse was due to the death of Ibrahim. Allah's Messenger gave a sermon to the people, and said:

"The eclipse of the sun and the moon are not on account of the death or life of some person, but they

> both are the signs of Allah, which He shows to His slaves. So when you see the eclipse of the sun or the moon, you run for offering salat." (*Bukhari*)

A man who breathes in the atmosphere of realities, does not compromise with falsehood and absurdities. He is always indifferent to such things, and his uncompromising words point to the vast treasure of greatness and nobility, whose owner does not derive any benefit from deception and his character stands on the rock of excellent moral character.

The performance of the duty of ordering the righteous thing and preventing the commitment of the forbidnen thing comes from the personal excellence, because it results from the courageous talk of the sincere people who want to earn Allah's reward by ending their own egoist leanings.

In our other books we have explained the social and political objectives which is related to the performance of the righteous and the forbidding of the forbidden. (Author's Arabic book)

Here what we want to emphasise is that a Muslim must necessarily straight away criticise the general evils, should be courageous in attacking them, neither the fear of a big man nor the consideration for a relative should prevent him from doing the right thing, and in the path of Allah no condemnation from any source should block his way.

Islam has disliked that a man should feel weak in the presence of wicked and evil persons, and should address them in a respectable way. Allah's Messenger has said: "When a man addresses a hypocrite as 'Ya Sayyedi' (My master), he makes Allah very wrathful."

This is a double crime that a man should not respect Allah's commands about forbidden things, and then he should only listen to those who think him respectable and should not care for those who consider him mean and humble

> "He whom Allah scorns, there is none to give him honour. Surely, Allah does what He wills." (*Hajj: 18*)

Islam has declared backbiting as haram, so that man's life may continue and the factors of strength may remain in it, for the man who states the defects of a person in his absence and derives satisfaction from it, is undoubtedly very mean and low.

But the man who has the strength to respond to the motivation and call of truth, he stops those whom he likes, in whatever manner and words he thinks proper he criticises them. He does not keep anything hidden in his heart for condemning anybody behind the scene.

However it does not mean that we may address anybody whom we like in an insulting way. If we find any defects in persons, we may fix up certain norms about dealing with them.

If his defect is limited to his own person or if it is not in consonance with his position, then it would be foolish to castigate him in his presence or in his absence.

And if his steps are slipping towards a sin, and he does not seem to be in a mood to give it up-like a horse who flounders and falls on his face-then to defame such a person among the people is meanness.

However, if he is a blatant sinner, and he openly breaks the rights of Allah and usurps the rights of his fellow men, then it is necessary that he should be opposed with the words of truth and without caring for anybody he should be properly warned.

Since this dialogue has to be straight, it is necessary that curses and abuses should be avoided and physical hurt should be averted. The purpose should be to change the bad habit and to reform the individual and the society. It does not mean that his mention before his enemies should be in demeaning words, so that you may get closer to their hearts, or may derive some benefits or may claim yourself to be innocent of those sins.

> Allah's Messenger has said : "He who has eaten food in exchange for the honour of a Muslim, Allah will feed him fire of hell in compensation on the Doomsday; and he who put on clothes in exahange for dishonouring a Muslim, Allah will clothe him in

compensation with the cloth of hell fire: and if he who earned respect and fame by playing with the chastity of a Muslim, Allah will make him taste fully for this on the Doomsday." (*Abu Daud*)

Backbiting is the policy of the weak persons, and "only those people try to indulge in backbiting who are unable to strive for themselves."

Islam dislikes those persons who become merely supplement of other people, those persons who live on the charity of others, those who want to live like foxes that is content with eating the remnants of a Lion's prey.

A Muslim is much above this kind of living, to maintain himself in this superficial way on the support of others. It is necessary that he should shun all places or situations of insults and ignominy, and should go to the end of the world in search of a life of honour and dignity.

Allah's Messenger has talked of the people of the Paradise and their companions, and the people of the hell and their companions. Accordingly he has mentioned in the first group the good qualities and advantages of strength, decency and morality, while in the other group he has mentioned the infamy, ignominy, helplessness and immoral enjoyments.

"People of paradise will be of three kinds. First that powerful man who was just and balanced in his dealings, who popularised the practice of charity and virtue, and adopted the attitude of softness and rightness. Second will be that person who was kind, who was soft hearted for every relative and every Muslim. Third will be that person who having a wife and children, yet was able to save himself from the forbidden things. In the people of the hell will be that dishonest person whose greed will not be discernible, but he would be indulging in misappropriation, that man who may deceive you every morning and evening in connection with your property and your family. And the Prophet talked about miserliness, falsehood, speaker of vulgarity and illmannered person, and said:

> "Allah has inspired me to say that you should be humble and none should feel proud, nor should any one oppress others." (*Muslim*)

Although many occasions come when a Muslim is caught in dilemmas and sometimes he feels mean in his own eyes, if he is bound by these melancholic handcuffs. Accordingly the fear of individual infamy and social ignominy sometimes compel a man to be inactive. He thinks on wrong lines and considers these misfortunes as bad omen. His productivity in the field of life reduces considerably. But it is the responsibility of a Muslim that he should break all these chains of sorrow and adversities and should strive fully to extricate himself from these crippling curbs.

The last Prophet of Allah used to pray for shelter under his Lord from all these adversities:

> "O Allah ! I seek shelter through you from sorrow and hardship. I seek shelter from humility and laziness, and through you seek shelter from cowardice and miserliness, from the defeat of the religion and from the cruelty and tyranny of oppressors. (*Abu Daud*)

Patience and hope are the weapons of the present and the future. In their company man is able to bear the severest of the hardships and is not disgraced, and all sides of his life become more safe from evils, and he rises above the mischief and trials, because he is a Momin-a faithful slave who begs and supplicates in humbleness before Allah only.

TWO

High Morality

The holy Prophet has stated the foremost purpose of his being sent down in this world and the method of his call to the people in these words :

> "I have been sent only for the purpose of perfecting food morals." —*(Al-Muta)*

That great message which has left an indelible impression on the history of life,and for propagating which and for bringing people under whose influence Prophet Muhammed (P.B.U.H.) worked ceaselessly. Its purpose was nothing else but to strengthen the moral character of the people so that the world of beauty and perfection may be illuminated before their eyes and they may try to achieve it consciously and with knowledge.

Worshipping has been made compulsory in Islam, and it has been included in the basic pillars of faith. But the Islamic forms of worship are not some sort of mystic exercises that link men with some unknown, mysterious and which subject men to perform useless acts and meaningless movements. All the Islamic compulsory forms of worship are designed as exercises and training to enable people to acquire correct morals and habits and to live righteously, and to adhere to these virtues till the end, whatever be the changes in their circumstances.

Prayer prevents commits of Evil: Salat(prayer) is a compulsory form of worship, which is like an exercise towards which man is attracted with interest and willingness. He offers it continually, so that his life may be free from all diseases and the body may be healthy and strong.

The holy Quran and the Sunnah of the Prophet both are the open proofs of these realities.

When Allah commanded the compulsory prayers to be established, He stated its wisdom in this way:

"Prayer prohibits obscenity and erg."

To keep away from evil, wickedness and to purify from bad deeds are also realities of the prayer. In a Hadith-e-Qudsi it is stated:

"I accept the prayers of the person who adopts the policy of humility with it on account of My greatness, obliges My creatures, does not insist on sinning against Me, spends his day in remembering Me, and is kind to the poor, travellers, weak and the suffering people."

Zakat is a means of purification : Zakat has been made compulsory on the eligible 'scheduled'(sahibe Nisab) persons. It is not merely a tax that is collected from the pockets of the people, but its foremost purpose is to sow the seeds of kindness, sympathy and benevolence, and to provide a chance of introduction among the various sections of the society and to establish the relationship of love and friendliness.

The purpose of paying Zakat has been stated in the Quran in the following words:

> "O Prophet! Take charity from their property so that it may clean them and purify them." —(*Tauba : 103*)

To clean the self of the worldly impurities and to raise the standard of the society to the heights of decency and purity are the wisdom behind the levy of Zakat.

For this reason the Prophet (S.A.W.) has taken it in a very wide sense, and to pay Zakat has been made compulsory for every eligible Muslim. The Prophet (S.A.W.) has said:

> "To smile in the company of your brother is charity. To command to do good deeds and to prevent others from doing evil is charity. To guide a person in a place where he can go astray is charity. To remove troublesome

things like thorns and bones from the road is charity. To pour water from your jug into the jug of your brother is charity. To guide a person with defective vision is charity for you." —*(Bukhari)*

The environment of desert and the Bedouin life—an environment which had its basis on internal bickerings and fights—in such an environment the teachings of Islam were presented to the world and they show what aims and purpose these teachings had, and it shows where these teachings led the Arabs in that dark and dismal environment.

Fasting is a stepping stone to Righteousness : Similarly Islam has made fasting compulsory. But it is not envisaged that men should keep away from their carnal desires and other prohibited things for a fixed period only. The Prophet (S.A.W.) has said:

"Fasting is not the name of merely keeping away from eating and drinking, but it is keeping away from wicked and obscene things. If in the state of fasting, someone abuses you or picks up a quarrel with you, say : "I am fasting."

Quran states the purpose of the imposition of fasting in these words:

"Fasting has been made compulsory for you, as it was made compulsory for those (followers of earlier prophets) who preceded you, so that you may become righteous." *(Baqarah : 183)*

Hajj is a compulsory pilgrimage to weaken the love for the world : Sometimes man thinks that to travel to the holy places and to perform pilgrimage, which has been made compulsory for every rich Muslim, and which is included in the basic pillars of Islam, is merely a form of worship that has no relation with the world of morality and character. This is a clear misunderstanding. Giving commands about this compulsory worship, Allah states:

"The months of Hnjj are well-known. In these months whoever intends to perform Hajj should not indulge in sexual act, wicked act, and fighting during the Hajj. Whatever righteous act you will perform will be known to Allah. Take

with you provision for the journey (for Hajj), and the best provision is righteousness. So fear me, O men of understanding!" —*(Baqarah:197)*

This is merely the main outline of the forms of worship which are well known and generally practised in Islam and they are its basic pillars. They show us what a deep relationship is there between religion and morality and how strong and lasting is this relationship.

How varying are these forms of worship in their spirit and appearance from one another, but in those aims and purpoes how close they are, which the holy Prophet (S.A.W.) declared is main objective.

Therefore, salat (prayer), sawm (fasting), zakaf, Hajj and other forms of worship like these are the stepping stones for real perfection, and are the means of cleanliness and purity that make life secure and magnificent. On account of high attributes and noble qualities that are the inalienable parts and the consequences of these forms of worship, they have been given a very high and important place in Allah's religion.

If these forms of worship do not purify the hearts of men, if they do not nourish best qualities in those who observe them, and if they do not improve and make firm the relationship between Allah and His slaves then there is nothing left for men but destruction and devastation.

Allah says :

"Surely, he who appears before his Lord as a criminal, there is hell for him, in which he will neither die nor will he live. And he who will appear before Him as a faithful, who has performed good deeds—for all such people there are high positions, ever green paradise, beneath which canals will be flowing; they will live in them for ever. This is the reward for him who adopts purity." *(Taha: 74-76)*

Moral Defects

Faith is such a power that it keeps men away from low

attributes and mean acts, and encourages him to achieve high attributes and clean morals. That is why whenever Allah called his slaves towards virtue or whenever He wanted them to hate evil, He declared it as an essential requirement of the Faith in their hearts. For example when He, in Surah Taubah, commands men to adopt righteousness and to speak truth, He addresses them as "O you who have faith"(or "O you who believe"):

> "O you who have faith ! Fear Allah and be with the truthful people." (*Taubah : 119*)

Allah's Messenger has nicely explained it that when faith is firm and belief is strong, then strong and lasting moral will be developed, and if the moral character is low then faith will accordingly be weak.

A man, who is immodest and ill-mannered and who adopts bad habits without caring for others, is like the person about whom the holy Prophet (S.A.W.) has said :

Once the Prophet (S.A.W.) passed by an Ansari who was scolding his brother about his immodesty. The Prophet advised him to let him go as modesty was a branch of faith.

A man who harasses his neighbour and makes him suffer any kind of damage is called cruel and stonehearted by the religion. In this connection the decision of the Prophet is:

"By God, he cannot be a Momin; by God, he cannot be a Momin ; by God, he cannot be a Momin. He was asked: 'who'? He answered, "He from whose misdeeds his neighbour is not safe." —(*Bukhari*)

The holy Prophet advises his companions to keep away from the talk that is trash, the acts that are wicked, and the deeds that are senseless. He says :

"A person who believes in Allah and the Hereafter should speak about good things or else should keep quiet." —(*Bukhari*)

In this way through the truth of faith and by means of its perfection noble qualities are nurtured and developed and they are guarded and kept secure till they bear fruits.

Rows disrupted, hearts sad, prayers tasteless : However, you will also find such people, who will be calling themselves Muslims, yet they will be lazy in offering comulsory prayers, and will be posing in the public as if they were very keen on establishing these prayers. But they will not lag behind at the same time in acting in such a way that will be contrary to the demands of the noble character and perfect faith.

Such people have been warned by the holy Prophet (S.A.W.) and the Ummah has been asked to be careful of them.

A man who commits the mistake of performing the various forms of worship without understanding their significance can only be a man who had not understood the spirit of the worship or has been unable to rise to that standard.

Many times even a child can copy the movements of salat and is able to repeat what is recited during the prayer. Sometimes an actor also offers prayer with all humility and concentration, and performs all the necessary rites.

But these kinds of movements do not benefit belief or meet the purpose. There is only one way of offering prayers in the best manner or performing other forms of worship that will never bring out wrong results, and that is : high moral character. Any person who has this attribute in him, his prayer is useful. But one who is deprived of this attribute, his worshipping is useless.

It is narrated by Imam Ahmed : One person asked the Prophet (S.A.W.), "O Messenger of Allah ! a certain woman is very famous for her prayers, fasting and many charities. but she talks rudely with her neighbours. Tell me, what will be her fate ?" He replied that she would go to Hell." Then that person asked : "O Messenger of Allah ! Another woman does not do much by way of prayers and fasting ; gives pieces of cheese in charity and does not harm her neighbours." He replied: "She is of the Paradise."

This reply gives an idea of the high value attached to good character. It also shows that charity is a collective prayer whose benefit reaches the society. For this reason there is no room for any reduction in them. As salat and fasting are apparently individual forms of worship, a little relaxation — to a very little extent—is allowed in not making very elaborate arrangements about them.

The holy Prophet (S.A.W.) did not merely answer a casual question that explains the relationship between morality and the religion, shows its connection with the correct forms of worship, and forms the basis of reform and improvement in the world and salvation in the next world.

The problem of morality was much more important. It was necessary that he should have continually provided guidance to his followers. He should have persisted in giving good advice to them so that its importance takes root in the mind and heart and it becomes quite clear that faith, goodness and morality are all dependent on each other. They are connected with each other and none can separate them.

Who is poor ? One day the Prophet (S.A.W.) asked his dear companions whether they knew who was poor. They answered that poor was one who had no *dirham* or *dinar* (money). He said:

> "In my *Ummah,* the poor is that man who would appear on the Day of Judgment who had paid zakat ; had observed fast ; but he would have abused somebody, he would have falsely accused some one ; he would have unauthorisedly taken some one else's property ; he would have murdered some one ; would have hit some body. All his virtues would be given to his victims. If his virtues are finished before his wicked deeds are finished, then the errors and sins of the victims would be given to him and he would be thrown into the Hell."
>
> (Muslim)

Such a man is really poor. His condition is like that trader who has goods worth one thousand rupees but he is a debtor for two thousand rupees. How can such a man be called rich ?

A religious man who offers certain prayers or performs certain forms of worship, but even after that performs certain evil deeds, behaves rudely with the people, treats poor and helpless people cruelly, how then such a man will be called righteous ?

The Prophet has explained by quoting an example. He said that the best moral character melts errors like water and bad morals spoil man's record as vinegar sopils honey.

Identification of a hypocrite : When wickedness is nourished in the self, and the loss caused by it has become manifest and the danger has increased, then that man has come out of his religion like a nude who has come out of his garments. At that time his claim of righteousness or faith would be false. What will be the value of religiousness without good morality? How is it possible that a man should belong to Allah and at the same time should be a victim of corruption?

This relationship between faith and morality is clearly shown in the hadith of the holy Prophet (S.A.W.):

> "The man who has these three habits is a hypocrite even if he observes fast, offers prayers, performs umra (pilgrimage), and calls himself a Muslim : when he talks he speaks untruth, when he makes a promise he does not keep it, and when he is given something in trust, he commits dishonesty." (Muslim).

In another tradition, he (S.A.W.) has said:

"There are three signs of a hypocrite: when he talks he speaks untruth, when he makes a promise he does not keep it, and when he makes a contract he deceives, although he may be offering prayers, observing fast and calling himself a Muslim."

He has also said:

> "There are four habits, in whosoever they are found, he will be a complete hypocrite. If any one of these habits is found in a man, he will have one habit of disruption till he gives it up, when something is given to him in trust he commits dishonesty, when he talks he tells lies, when he makes a contract he deceives, and when he quarrels he starts abusing. (Bukhari).

Traditions on Morality

These teachings show that Islam had come to illuminate the lives of the people with the light of virtue and good manners, to create in them brightness of character, and to fill their laps with the pearls of good conduct. It made the stages that came in the process of achieving this great objective as an important part of the prophethood. Similarly, it declared all attempts to create disruption in these stages as an expulsion from the religion and equivalent to throwing away the yoke of faith from one's neck.

The position of morality is not like that of the means of pleasures and luxuries, from which indifference may be possible. But morality is the name of the principles of life which the religion must adopt and must care for the respect of its standard-bearers.

Islam has enumerated all these virtues and principles and has encouraged its followers to make them parts of their lives, one after another.

If we collect all the sayings of the holy Prophet about the importance of good moral character, then a voluminous book will be prepared, about which many of the great reformers will be ignorant.

Before we enumerate these virtues and state their details, it will be proper if we quote some examples of how strongly and emphatically Islam has called upon the people to adopt good moral character.

Usama bin Shareek says : "We were sitting in the presence of the Messenger of Allah (S.A.W.) so quietly as if birds were perched on our heads. Nobody had the courage to open his mouth. In the meanwhile some people came and asked : "Amongst the slaves of God who is the dearest to Him."

> The Prophet (S.A.W.) replied : "One who has the best moral character." (*Ibn Haban*)
>
> Another tradition has it : "They asked what is the best thing given to man ?" He replied : "Best moral character." (*Tirmizi*)
>
> The Prophet (S.A.W.) was asked : "Which Muslim has the perfect faith ?" He answered : "He who has the best moral character." (*Tibrani*)

Abdullah bin Amar has reported : "I have heard the Prophet as saying : 'Should I not tell you who amongst you is the most likeable person to me? And who will be the nearest to me on the Day of the Judgment ?' He repeated this question twice or thrice. The people requested him to tell them about such a person. He said :

> 'He who amongst you has the best moral character.'
>
> (*Ahmed*)

In another hadith, he (S.A.W.) has said : "On the Day of the Judgement there will be nothing weightier in the balance of a momin than the goodness of character."

> Allah dislikes an abscene and a rude talker and the bearer of a good moral character reaches to the level of the observer of the prayer and fasting, on account of his character." (*Imam Ahmed*)

There would be nothing surprising if such teachings were to come from a philosopher who was busy in his campaign of moral-reform. But the great surprise is that these teachings come from a man who strived for establishing a great new faith, when all other religions turn their attention first only towards the performance of worship and such other religious rites.

The last Prophet (S.A.W.) gave a call for the performance of various forms of worship and for the establishment of such a government that was involved in a long-drawn war with its large number of enemies. Inspite of the expansion of his religion and the immense increase in the various tasks of his followers, the Prophet (S.A.W.) informs them of the fact that on the Day of the Judgment there will be nothing weightier in their balance than their good moral character, then definitely this reality is not hidden from him that in Islam the value of morality is very high.

The fact is that if religion is the name of good conduct between man and man, then on the other hand in its spiritual sense it is also the name of the best relationship between man and his God, and in both these aspects there is the same reality.

There are many religions which give this glad tiding that you may embrace any belief, your sins will be washed away and offering fixed prayers of any religion will cancel your mistakes.

But Islam does not believe in this. According to it, these benefits will be available only when the axis and centre of belief is a conscious step towards virtue and payment of the compulsory dues, and when the proposed worship can become the real source of washing away the sins and generating the real perfection. In other words, evil can be removed by those virtues which man makes his own and by which he is able to reach high and lofty standards.

The holy Prophet (S.A.W.) has very forcefully emphasised these valuable principles so that the Ummah may understand it very clearly that the value of morality may not go down in its eyes and the importance of mere forms and shapes may not increase.

> Hazrat Anas has reported : "Allah's Messenger has said : "A slave achieves, by means of the goodness of his character, great position and high honour in the Hereafter, though he may be weak in matters of worship ; but on account of his wickedness of character he is thrown in the lowest recesses of the Hell." (*Tibrani*)

Hazrat Ayesha narrates

> "I have heard the Prophet (S.A.W.) as saying : 'Momin, by goodness of his character, achieves the high position of the one who observes fast and offers prayers." (*Abu Dawood*)

> Ibn Umar is (R.A.A.) reported to have narrated : "I have heard the Prophet (S.A.W.) as saying : "A Muslim who observes moderation in matters of worship, on account of the goodness of his character and decency achieves the position of that man who observes fast and recites Allah's verses during prayers in the night." (*Ahmed*)

> Abu Huraira has (R.A.A.) quoted the Prophet (S.A.W.) as saying "A Momin's nobility is his religiousness, his tolerance is his intelligence, and his lineage is his goodness of character." (*Hakim*)

> Abuzar (R.A.A.) has narrated : "Successful is the man who had purified his heart for faith, kept his heart on

the right lines, his tongue was truthful, his self was content, and his nature was on the right path."

(*Ibn Haban*)

Prophet's excellent example : Mere teachings and commands of Do's and Dont's do not form the foundation of good moral character in a society, because only these things are not sufficient for developing these good qualities in the human nature; a teacher may merely order to do such and such things and not to do such and such things, and not to do such and such things, and the society becomes a moralist society. The teachings of good conduct which is fruitful requires long training and constant watchfulness.

The training cannot be on the right lines if the example before the society is not such that commands full confidence, because a person having a bad moral character cannot leave a good impression on his surroundings.

The best training can be expected only from such a man whose personality, by the force of its Morality, would create a sense of admiration in the beholders. They would sing praises of his nobility and feel the irresistible urge to benefit from the example of his life. The world would spontaneously feel the urge to follow his footsteps.

For nourishing and developing more and more excellent good character among his followers it is necessary that the leader must possess higher and nobler character and attributes than his followers.

The holy Prophet (S.A.W.) himself was the best example of the good moral character, to emulate which he was giving a call to his followers. Before advising them to adopt a moral life by giving sermons and counsels, he was sowing the seeds of morality among his followers by actually living that kind of life.

Abdullah Ibn Amar (R.A.A.) says : "The Messenger of Allah (P.B.U.H.) was neither ill-mannered nor rude. He used to say that the better people among you are those who are best in their moral character. (*Bukhari*)

Anas (R.A.A.) says : "I served the holy Prophet (S.A.W.) for ten years. He never said 'Uf ' (expressing dissatisfaction), nor did he ever ask me why I did this or did not do that." (*Muslim*)

It is also reported by him : "My mother used to hold the Prophet's hand and used to take him wherever he wanted. If any person used to come before him and shake his hand, the Prophet (S.A.W.) never used to draw away his hand from the other person's hands till the latter drew away his hands, and he never used to turn away his face from that person till the latter himself turned away his face. And in the meetings he was never seen squatting in such a way that his knees were protruding further than his fellow-squatters." (*Tirmizi*)

Hazrat 'Ayesha (R.A.A.) says : "If there were two alternatives, the holy Prophet (S.A.W.) used to adopt the easiest alternative, provided there was no sin in it. If that work was sinful, then he used to run away farthest from it. The prophet (S.A.W.) did not take any personal revenge from any body. Yes, if Allah's command were to be disobeyed, then his wrath was to be stirred. Allah's Messenger did not beat anybody with his own hands, neither his wife nor a servant. Yes, he used to fight in the wars in the cause of Allah." (*Muslim*)

Anus (R.A.A.) has narrated : "I was walking with the Prophet (S.A.W.). He had wrapped a thick chadar round his body. One Arab pulled the chadar so forcefully that a part of his shoulder could be seen by me, and I was perturbed by this forceful pulling the chadar. The Arab then said : 'O Muhammed ! Give me some of my share from the property which Allah has given you.' The Prophet (S.A.W.) turned towards him and laughed, and gave orders for a donation being given to him." (*Bukhari*)

Hazrat 'Ayesha (R.A.A.) has reported that Allah's Messenger (S.A.W.) has said : "Allah is soft-hearted. He likes softheartedness. And the reward which He

> gives for soft-heartedness does not give for hardness, nay, such a reward He does not give for any thing." (*Muslim*)

In another tradition it is stated: "Softness in whichever thing it may be, will make that thing beautiful. And from whichever thing softness is taken out, it will become ugly."

> Jarir (R.A.A.) narrates that the Prophet (S.A.W.) has said : "The reward which Allah gives for soft-heartedness He does not give it for folly ; and when Allah makes any slave His favourite, He gives him softness. Those families that are devoid of softness become deprived of every virtue." (*Tibrani*)

> Abdullah bin Harith (R.A.A.) has reported that he did not see anybody smiling more than the Messenger of Allah (S.A.W.) (*Tirmizi*)

> Hazrat 'Ayesha (R.A.A.) was asked what did Prophet (S.A.W.) do at home ? She replied : "He used to be in the service of his home people ; and when the time of prayer came he used to perform ablutions and go out for prayer." (*Muslim*)

> Anas (R.A.A.) has narrated : "Allah's Messenger had the best manners of all the persons. I had an adopted brother, whose name was Abu Umair. He had a sick sparrow, who was called 'Naghee'. Allah's Messenger (S.A.W.) used to be playful with him and ask him : 'O Abu Umair ! what has happened to your Nagheer'." (*Bukhari*)

Of the habits and traits of the Prophet (S.A.W.) one trait was very well known that he was extremely philanthropic. He was never miserly in anything. He was very brave and courageous. He never turned away from Truth. He was justice-loving. In his own decision he never committed any excesses or injustice. In his whole life he was truthful and an honest trustee.

The same Quran : Allah has commanded all the Muslims to follow the excellent habits and the best traits of the Prophet (S.A.W.) and to take guidance from the holy life of the holy Messenger.

> *"Surely there is in the person of Allah's Messenger an excellent example for you for every person who has hope in Allah and the Hereafter and remembers Allah, reciting His name many times."* (*Ahzab* : 21)

Qazi A'yaz says that the Prophet (S.A.W.) was the most excellent-mannered, most philanthropic and the bravest of all. One night the people of Medina were terribly frightened. Some people proceeded towards the sound (which was probably the cause). They saw that the Prophet (S.A.W.) was coming from that direction. He had rushed before all others to find out what was the trouble. He was riding the horse of Abu Talha, (R.A.A.) without a saddle, and a sword was hanging from his neck, and he was comforting the people not to be afraid saying there was nothing to worry.

Hazrat Ali (R.A.A.) says that in the battles when fighting started, we used to worry much about the Prophet (S.A.W.) because nobody was nearer to the enemy in fighting than the Prophet (S.A.W.) .

Jabir bin Abdullah (R.A.A.) says that whenever anything was requested of him, he never said : No.

Hazrat Khadija (R.A.A.) had told him when he was first blessed with the Divine Revelation

> "You carry the loads of the weak people, you earn for the poor, and help a person if any trouble comes to him in following the Truth."

Once he received seventy thousand dirhams. They were placed before him on the mat. He distributed them standing. He did not refuse a single beggar till he finished the entire amount.

A man approached him and requested for something. He said : "At present I do not have anything, buy something in my name, and when we will get some money we will pay for it." Hazrat Umar (R.A.A.) stated : "Allah has not made it compulsory for you to do a thing on which you have no power or control." This saddened the Prophet (S.A.W.). One Ansari said : "O Messenger of Allah! Spend and be not afraid of the straitened circumstances imposed by Allah." The Prophet (S.A.W.) smiled and his face shone resplendently. He said : "I have been commanded to do this only."

The holy Prophet (S.A.W.) used to love his companions. He did not hate them. He respected every respectable man from any other nation and he used to appoint him as a responsible officer over them.

He used to be in search of his companions and gave them their shares. No companion thought that any other person was more respectable in the Prophet's eye than the companion himself.

Any person who adopted his companionship or anybody who came to him for his need, he used to advise him to be patient, till he was satisfied.

If anybody asked anything from him, he gave it to him or else talked to him so lovingly that he came back satisfied. The river of his kindness was flowing for every body. For his companions he was a guardian, and in matters of Truth all were equal in his eyes.

He was good-looking, decent, humble and softhearted. He was not a narrow-minded and a hard person. Quarrelling was not his habit. He never spoke obscene words. To condemn others or to praise someone excessively was beyond the pale of his character. He expressed indifference towards unnecessary things, but ha was never given to pessimism.

Hazrat Ayesha says that there was none who possessed a better moral character than the Prophet. Whenever his friends or his home people called him, he readily responded.

Jarir bin Abdullah says : "Since the time I became a Muslim, the Prophet did not prevent me from entering (the house); whenever he looked at me, he smiled."

He used to exchange repartees with his companions, mix up with them freely, and tried to be nearer to them. He played with their children and took them in his lap.

Invitation from free men, male or female slaves, or poor persons were acceptable to him. He visited the ailing and invalid persons in the far-flung areas of Medina. He accepted the excuses of the really helpless people.

Hazrat Anas says that if any person who whispered anything into his ears, he never removed his ear from his mouth unless the whisperer himself withdrew his mouth. Whenever anybody held his hand, he never tried to withdraw his hand unless the other man withdrew his. He always used to be the first to salute any one who met him or to be first to shake hands with his companions. He never stretched his legs in the midst of his companions so that they may be inconvenienced.

Whoever came to him was duly respected by him. Many times he used to spread his cloth for the visitor, and used to place the cushion which was in his use behind the visitor's back. If the visitor was reluctant to sit on the cloth, he used to insist.

He gave new family names to his companions. In their honour, he used to call them by beautiful names. He never used to interrupt anybody's talk till the speaker either stopped or stood up.

Hazrat Anas narrates that if anybody brought a present to the Prophet he used to ask him to take it to a particular house because she was a friend of Hazrat Khadija and loved her.

Hazrat Ayesha says : "I was not jealous of any woman, nor did I feel any ill will towards Khadija, as I used to hear of her repeatedly from the Prophet. If any goat was slaughtered, he used to send it to her friends' houses as a present. Once her sister asked for permission to come in. He was very pleased to see her. A woman came to him and spoke endearingly of Khadija and enquired about her lovingly. When she went away, he said: 'This woman used to come during Khadija's time. Good relationship is a sign of faith."

He treated his relatives kindly, but he did not give them preference over better persons.

Abu Qatada has reported that when a delegation of Najashi came to the Prophet, he rose for serving them. His companions told him that they were sufficient to serve them. He replied : "They had honoured our companions, therefore I personally want to serve them."

Abu Usama has narrated that once the Messenger of Allah went among his companions leaning on a cane and his companions stood up. The Prophet said: "Do not stand up. Do not adopt the system of these NonArabs who stand up to pay respect to one another."

He said : "I am a slave of Allah ; I eat as other people eat, and I sit as other people sit." When he rode a mule, he allowed some one else to ride behind him. He used to visit poor invalids. He allowed the beggars to sit in his meetings. He mixed up freely with his companions. Where the meeting was over, he used to sit there.

The Prophet once performed Hajj on a cheap Kajawa on the back of a camel on which an old, torn chadar was spread, whose cost could be at the most four dirhams. He said: "O Allah! This is my Hajj in which there is neither hypocrisy nor show."

When Makkah was conquered and the Muslim soldiers entered the city, the Prophet was riding a camel and his head was vowed down in humility, so much so that it appeared that his head was touching a part of the *kajawa*.

He was of a quiet nature. He never talked without necessity. And if anybody talked with a wry face, he used to be indifferent to him and ignored him.

His smile was his laughter. His talk was straight and direct, in which there was no excess. His companions, in his honour and in following him, considered it sufficient to smile in his presence.

His meetings manifested a spirit of tolerance, trusteeship, honesty, virtue and righteousness. Voices were not raised there and no back-biting was allowed therein.

Whenever he opened his mouth to speak, his companions (R.A.A.) used to keep silent, as if birds were perched on their heads.

When he walked, it was with a balanced gait. There was neither fright nor haste in his gait, nor was there laziness.

Ibn Abi Hala (R.A.A.) says : "His silence was on account of tolerance, far-sightedness, estimation and thinking and contemplating."

Hazrat Ayesha says that he talked in such a way that if anybody wanted to count the words, he could do so.

The Messenger of Allah liked fragrance and used perfumes many times.

The world was presented to him with all her allurements and amusements. Victories were won by his armies, but he was indifferent to luxuries and pleasures. He died in such a condition that his armour was pledged to a Jew.

THREE

Simplicity

Modesty is the true symbol which indicates human nature. It gives an idea of a man's faith, virtue, etiquette and morals. If you see a man hesitating or restive at the time of performing some improper act, or he is sorry on doing some wrong work and the colour of his face is changing, then you can consider him to be a man with a living conscience. He is a man of simple nature and right temperament. But if his face does not show any colour, no trace of modesty or shame is seen on it, his mind does not take any notice of the wrong act being performed by him, he is totally careless about what he is taking up and what he is leaving, then there is no virtue in him, there is not an iota of modesty and shame in him which can prevent him from committing sin and from living a sinful life.

Islam has taught its children modesty, and it has considered it its most distinguishing quality. Allah's Prophet (S.A.W.) has said:

> Every religion has its moral, and the moral of Islam is modesty. (*Malik*)

In the time of Prophet Moosa (Moses)(A.S.) the special element of the Jewish teachings was courage and bravery. In the time of Issa (Jesus) (A.S.)the Christian teachings gave a special place to charity and generosity. And the distinguishing feature of Islam is modesty and sense of shame, when all religions and nations give importance to all the good qualities and take a reckoning of them.

The sense of loving virtue and hating wickedness found in a Muslim has been said by the Prophet (S.A.W.) to be the foundation of adopting virtues and rejecting evils, in order that before the final requital the feeling of love for the good and hate for the evil should be generated in every man. How truly Ibn Qayim has said:

"Suppose the Messenger of Allah (S.A.W.) had not brought Allah's Message and the fire of Hell had not been kindled, then was it not incumbent upon the slaves to display modesty before their Benefactor."

The Prophet (S.A.W.) was the softest of men, most virtuous, decent and the most considerate for giving the dues of Allah and others. He was the farthest away from evil.

> Abu Saeed Khudri (R.A.A.) says : "Allah's Messenger was (S.A.W.) more modest than the maiden staying behind the veil. If he saw any unpleasant thing, we could see its sign on his face." (*Muslim*)

Modesty and faith : Faith, in fact, is the name of the best relationship between the slave and his Lord. It affects the human life primarily in this way that it purifies the self, morals are improved, and actions are corrected. This so happens when there is an awakening in the self which would keep it away from errors and induce man to hate even the smallest of sins. If a man does not keep away from small errors and goes on committing them without any care, then it is the symbol of the fact that there is no modesty in him and his faith has been shaken.

> Allah's Messenger (S.A.W.) has said : "Modesty and Faith are one another's companion. If one goes, the other will also not remain." (*Hakim*)

The reason for this is that when a man gives up modesty, he gradually moves from a smaller coil to a deadly evil and from a smaller sin to a bigger sin, till he reaches the lowest of the low. One hadith of the Prophet (S.A.W.) takes off the veil from this fall of man. It begins with lack of modesty and consequently reaches the worst of the sins.

> "When Allah wants to destroy a man, He takes away modesty from him. When he is deprived of modesty, he becomes the most detestable man. And when he becomes detestable, he loses trust. When he loses trust and honesty, he becomes extremely fraudulent. Allah's blessing is snatched away from him. He becomes extremely cursed, and when he becomes reproachable,

then the yoke of Islam comes out from his neck."

(*Ibn Majah*)

The explanation of the psychological sickness and how it advances, stage by stage, has been very dexterously shown. It has been explained how an evil progressively leads to the commitment of the worst sin. When a man tears the raiment of modesty and does not keep an account of his acts, nor does he care for she reproaches of others, then he extends his hand of aggression to others, he subjects his subordinates to tyrannies. A man of such a character cannot show mercy to any one. He will nourish rancour and jealousy in his heart and will encourage them.

A man who becomes so aggressive with the public, can a quality like modesty prevent him from sins ? When a man falls so low, he cannot be trusted with people's valuables in his trust. How can he be made a trustee, when he is not ashamed in misappropriating the property of others or how can he be considered a watchdog of honour, when he is ever ready to make an assault on any body's honour, or how can his promises be relied upon when he does not care to keep his promises ? No responsibility can be entrusted to him, as the fear of negligence and defection will always be there. Nor can he be given a high office, because there is no guarantee against deception and trickery.

When a man loses his modesty and is deprived of trust and honesty, then he is like a mad dog and runs after his desires and in his way tramples upon the righteous and pure feelings. Then he misappropriates the wealth of the poor and the beggars, and no softness is felt by him in his heart for those unfortunates ; he observes the weak and the meek, but no waves of kindness is generated in his heart. And if at all some delicate feeling is engendered in his heart, he blindfolds himself. Then he seeks knowledge about those things,which go on throwing him in further darkness and misguidance. When a man falls down so low, then be sure that he has become free of the restrictions of the religion and he has thrown away the yoke of Islam from his neck.

There are different occasions when modesty is desirable. In conversation decency demands that man sbould avoid obscene talk, back-biting and fault-finding of others, and he should avoid touching upon the personal matters of the people. It is extremely disrespectful that a man should irrelevantly blurt out obscene and lewd words.

Allah's Messenger (S.A.W.) has said :

> "Modesty is faith, and the faithful will go to Paradise, and obscene talk is tyranny and the place of a tyrant is Hell." (*Ahmed*)

It is also included in modesty that Muslims should talk in a balanced way in their gatherings. Some people have the habit of making lengthy speeches in big meetings; they fret and fume and their saliva drips from their mouths, but they are not ashamed. Islam has disliked this bad habit.

The Prophet (S.A.W.) has said:

> He who has learnt the art of conversation for the purpose of turning the hearts of the people, then on the Day of Judgment Allah will not accept his eloquence." (*Abu Daud*)

In another tradition he has said:

> Allah does not like those eloquent men who move their tongues as cows chew the cud. (*Tirmizi*)

The reason for Allah's dislike and hatred of these people is on account of the fact that their talk is full of exaggeration and falsehoods, their affairs are never devoid of hypocrisy and exhibitionism, their gatherings are a prey of various moral diseases. If these people adopt modesty, then they can get rid of all these diseases completely. For this reason in some hadith it is mentioned that weakness and helplessness is better than eloquence. Here helplessness is of the tongue and not of the heart.

Modesty also demands that a man should feel ashamed if he is adversely criticised any where ; he should be desirous of being introduced as a person who shuns sins and keeps away from evil.

It is forbidden (haram) to speak ill of those absent persons whose defects are hidden, but those who display their own faults and themselves show their own evils, then other people cannot spread it so speedily as they themselves spread it far and wide. Therefore, the Prophet (S.A.W.) has said that one, who has committed sin, walks hiding from the people.

When the companions of the Prophet (S.A.W.) saw him with one of his wives in a corner of the mosque, he stopped them and told them that he was not with any strange woman.

There is a man who wants, more than anything else, name and fame, and there is another man who turns away the eyes of others from his fame. Their difference is quite distinct.

The meaning of a Muslim's hiding from the people is not that he should indulge in the evil of hiding his evil and displaying his good points,but it means that he should not go on advertising his defects and evils and that he should feel ashamed of committing any sin openly.

A man who feels ashamed to disclose his defects has some element of good in him, and the man who feels proud to show his good points has some element of wickedness in him. As a man feels ashamed in the presence of others, he should have the similar feeling of being ashamed even from himself. If he dislikes that others should find any defect in him, then he should also feel hateful towards having any defect in himself. There is a well-known saying : "Whoever has done a thing secretly which he would have been ashamed to do openly, he has no respect for himself in his own eyes." Therefore it is essential for every Muslim that he should be free from all sins, open or secret, whether they may be known to him only or disclosed to all the people.

A well-known saying is: "Adopt a thing which both your ears may like to hear, and keep away from the thing which your ears may not like to hear."

Pious Ways

> Modesty is the foundation of virtue. This is the only criterion of decency in all acts. Allah's Messenger (S.A.W.) has said : "The thing, which has obscenity in it, will be spoilt by it, and the thing in which there will be modesty, it will adorn it." *(Tirmizi)*

If a man puts on the raiment or modesty, he becomes the symbol of welfare and goodness. Hazrat Ayesha (R.A.A.) narrates that the Prophet (S.A.W.) has said:

> "If modesty were to appear in the form of a man, then it would have appeared in the form of the best and virtuous man, and if obscenity takes the form of man, it would be of the worst man." *(Tibrani)*

> Modesty also demands that man should pay the rights of the right claimants and should give them their proper place. He should treat every man of talent in a respectable way. The relationship of the slave with his master and of the student with his teacher is that of respect and honour. It is not proper that they should raise their voices in their presence, or should walk ahead of them. In a hadith it is written : "Treat them well from whom you learn." *(Tibrani)*,

> "O Allah! Do not show me the time when the learned men of the religion are shunned and men of tolerance and forbearance are not treated with modesty." *(Ahmed)*

Abdullah bin Yasar (R.A.A.) says:

> "I have been hearing a hadith for a long time:'When you go to a nation, and from their faces you realise that there is none among them who is afraid of Allah, then know that the matter is extremely delicate'." *(Ahmed)*

Modesty is not cowardice. A modest and respectable person would rather sacrifice his life than tolerate disgrace and immodesty.

Sometimes an element of fear creeps in modesty, but this fear is for safeguarding the honour lest morality and modesty may suffer in the straitened circumstances. The borders of modesty meet the limits of bravery and valour, which is praiseworthy. When the Jews avoided taking up cudgels against the invaders of the holy land

> Then outspoke two of those who feared (their Lord, men) to whom Allah had been gracious : Enter in upon them by the gate, for if you enter by it, surely you will be victorious. (*Maida* : 23)

These people feared Allah. They feared disgrace and infamy. They were ashamed to take the course of running away. If there were fighting, then these people only led the people in the fight and brought victory nearer.

Undoubtedly perfect modesty is given to man by nature, while there are some people in whose very nature there is shamelessness and immodesty. On the other hand there is no dearth of the people in whom the substance of modesty, sense of shame and consciousness for honour is much more. But in spite of the fact that shyness is a distinct element of modesty, it is displayed at both good and bad occasions, and sometimes a shy person commits a very serious mistake. Modesty appears within the religious limits only. A man who is cowed down by the threats of the followers of Falsehood can not be called modest or respectable. Modesty or respect will not be displayed before falsehood, and it is not required to be shown before the people who have gone astray, when helping Truth and giving assistance to the right is the need of the time. The polytheists accused Islam that its followers were abusing their gods, saying that they have no power to create anything, that they are unable to whisk away flies from their faces. They said that it is not modesty that their gods should be so insulted. This was answered by Allah thus:

> Allah does not feel shy of using similes of the lowly things, be it a mosquito or a still lower being. Those who are believers know that it is truth from their Lord. But these who are rejectors of Faith, they say: What does Allah mean by such a simile? (*Baqarah*: 26)

The picture drawn of the false gods is correct and Allah has no shyness in saying what is true, and a Muslim should not be afraid of proving what is truth and what is falsehood, nor should he care about it.

Submission to God

The highest peak of modesty is to be modest before the Lord Almighty, Allah, the Creator of the Universe. We eat from the provision given by Him. We breathe in His air. We grow up on His land, and we are under the shadow of His blue umbrella, the vast sky. A man does not pay his fellowman for his kindness and favour by some evil or unkind act. But it is surprising how his dealing with God is different while he is under his obligation and burden of favours from the cradle to the grave, and even after this his life is at the mercy of the Gracious Lord.

Allah has great rights on his slaves. If people appreciate this, they will rush towards righteousness and virtue without any pressure or delay, and will run away from evil and shameless acts.

Hazrat Abdullah Ibn Masood (R.A.A.) has narrated that the Messenger of Allah (S.A.W.) has said:

"Be modest before Allah as it is proper to be modest." We said : "We are modest before Allah, and for this we thank Him." The Prophet (S.A.W.) said:

> "This is not modesty. The modesty that should be before Allah demands that you keep your head and all the parts safe from falsehood, keep your belly and your foods safe from the forbidden things, and remember the condition of death and that of the grave ; and he who wants to love the life of the Hereafter, he should give up the embellishments and grandeur of the worldly life, and should prefer Hereafter to the world. He who has done so, he has, as if, fulfilled the right of being modest before Allah." (*Tirmizi*)

This advice contains a majority of Islamic principles of etiquette and virtues. 1t is the responsibility of a Muslim that he should not let any wrong word to come out from his mouth, his eyes may not be directed towards any forbidden thing or things exciting sexual feelings, his ears should not hear wrong things ; he should not accustom his stomach to accept forbidden food, but that it should be content with permissible and clean things. Then it is also his duty that he should spend his time in seeking Allah's pleasure, and should employ all his efforts and resources and capabilities in earning sawab (reward). Carnal desires should not misguide him.

If he does all these things with the consciousness that Allah is watching him, and if he hates to be lax and defective in matters concerning Allah, then he has fulfilled the right of being modest before Allah.

In this sense modesty comprises the whole religion. When it is applicable on so many acts then it has become a part of faith.

The Messenger of Allah (S.A.W.) has said:

> There are more than seventy aspects of faith. The highest among them is the confirmation of the words that there is no god, except Allah, and the lowest is to remove some harmful thing from the road, and modesty is an aspect of faith. (*Bukhari*)

Man tries to display good conduct and behaviour in the presence of those whom he considers great and whom he wants to please. Before them he speaks only when necessary. Every step that he takes before them is with caution and fear. A Muslim, whose religion teaches him that he is never away from the sight of Allah, because he is in his presence day and night, feels more awe from the wrath of Allah, and he should be very cautious and careful in obeying His commands. The meaning of this hadith is also the same: "Be modest before Allah, as you are in the presence of the powerful people of your nation."

> On some occasions a man's feeling of hesitation and the changing colour of his face is the proof of the fact that there is a streak of virtuousness and purity in him, and "modesty is the name of perfect virtue." (*Muslim*)

If the colour of modesty goes out from the face, then life becomes free to adopt a sinful line, and becomes the fuel of the hell. For this reason it is said: "If you have no modesty, do whatever you like."

FOUR

Significance of Honesty

The motivations and the factors which prompt a man to do a job in a better way, to strive hard and bear all the trials and tribulations and induce him to sacrifice his property and life for a thing, are many and varied.

One motivation is such that it manifests itself with the man's interest and involvement in his work, while there is another motivation which remains hidden in the interior recesses of the heart and cannot be discerned from outside.

Many times the man who performs the act does not recognise it although he is influenced by it and the secret of his acceptance or non-acceptance of a thing is hidden in that.

The normal human nature decides what are the general rules of treatment in certain cases. You can very easily determine what are the motivations of a particular person in acting in a certain manner by looking at his work. He will be seen either involved in self-love and self-preservation or greed for more wealth would be troubling him, or the feelings of pride and self-importance would be giving him sleepless nights, or hypocrisy, and desire for fame would be inciting him to advance forword.

Hear what the people talk about. Take a survey of their daily activities. You will not find anything else the axis of their talk and efforts but their feelings of joy and hatred, pride and conceit.

Islam judges the acts and deeds, and decides about their importance on the basis of the intentions, feelings and sensations behind them. For Islam the value of an act depends on the nature of the motivation which prompted the act to be performed.

Sometimes a man gives costly donations and gifts so that through these good acts people should be attracted towards him and should talk about his generosity, and sometimes his purpose is to give valuable presents to that person who had treated him in a commendable way and had obliged him.

Both these acts are of charity and generosity, which were guided by, as pointed out by the psychologists, by the man's consciousness directly or indirectly. But Islam does not give importance to charity if it is given in a hypocritical way or for attaining fame, and unless it is given entirely for seeking the pleasure of Allah:

> "We are feeding you for the sake of Allah. We do not expect from you any compensation nor thanks."
>
> (*Dahr : 9*)

> "Those who spend their wealth for increase in self-purification, and have in their minds no favour from any one for which a reward is expected in return, but only the desire to seek the pleasure of their Lord, Most High, and soon will they attain (complete) satisfaction."
>
> (*Al-Lail: 18-21*)

To correct the inclinations of the heart and to keep it away from the superficial due, the Prophet has said:

> "The acts depend on intentions. A man will get whatever he had intended for. So the man whose migration will be for the sake of Allah and His Messenger. But if anybody migrates with the intention of earning the world or to marry a certain woman then his migration will be counted for the purpose for which he has left his house." (*Bukhari*)

The distance between Mecca and Medina is traversed by thousands of travellers for different purposes, but the purpose of assigning supremacy to the religion and to keep oneself alive is the thing which distinguishes between Mahajir (refugee) and a common traveller, although the ads of both the person are the same.

The man who left Mecca to go to Medina so that he may save his religion from the various dangers, and that ,he may form a new government in a new city, was called a Mahajir (refugee), but another person who travelled for another purpose he has no connection with the *hijrat* (migration).

Pious Goals

The rightness of intention and sincerity are the two things which enliven a man's worldly action and make it a prayer that is answered.

But if there is perversion in the intention and corruption in the heart, a man, inspite of offering prayers, is degraded. He commits sins and inspite of his showing interest in and taking pains for performing worship is doomed to failure and loss.

But as against this many times a man builds high and lofty palaces, constructs broad and spacious buildings, lays out a beautiful garden full of fruits, and starts living in this paradise, and he is called a king. But since in his efforts and labour of building these high and lofty palaces, etc. the purpose was to benefit humanity, then for these acts he will be a recipient of an unending reward (sawab).

Allah's Messenger has said:

> "Anybody who, without subjecting another person to cruelty or aggression, builds a magnificent building, or plants saplings without indulging into cruelty and rancour, he will be getting reward for that till the time Allah's creatures would be benefitted by them."
>
> (*Ahmed*)

> In another tradition it is stated : "If a Muslim lays a garden or does farming, and if a bird or a man eats something from it, then he will get a virtue (neki) in its place." (*Muslim*)

Even carnal pleasures are also counted as acts of prayer, if behind them there is righteous intention and clean purpose. When a man goes to his wife so that he may be able to save his chastity, and protect his faith, he gets a recompense for this act.

Whatever he feeds his body, or whatever he does to sustain his wife and children, for that also he gets reward, provided there is goodness and righteousness in his intention.

Sa'ad Ibn Abi Waqas narrates that the Messenger of Allah has said : "If you spend even an ordinary thing for seeking the pleasure of Allah, you get its reward, so much so that even putting a morsel of food in the mouth of your wife is a virtuous act."

Another tradition has it:

> "Whatever you feed your father, it is a charity from you. Whatever you feed your child it is a means of reward for you, and whatever you feed your servant, it is also a charity from you." (*Ahmed*)

The fact is that as long as man keeps himself as an obedient slave of Allah and his intention is pure and sincere, then all his acts and movements, his sleep and and his waking are considered to be for seeking the pleasure of Allah. And sometimes it so happens that a man wants to perform a righteous act, but on account of his poverty he is unable to do so, then Allah, who knows the secrets of hearts, gives the man desirous of reform the honour of a reformer, the man desirous of fighting in the cause of Allah the honour of a Mujahid (the fighter in the cause of Allah), because for Him high courage and righteous intention is more appreciable than the want of resources.

During the days of scarcity and poverty a battle was to be fought. Some people came to the Prophet with a view to joining his forces and offered themselves to be sacrificed in the cause of Allah. But Allah's Messenger did not allow them to take part in the jihad because of their incapability. They returned with a heavy heart and sorrowfully. They were very much grieved for not being allowed to participate in jihad. About them the following verses were revealed:

> "Nor (is there blame) on those who came to you to be provided with mounts, and when you said: `I can find no mounts for you,' they turned back, their eyes steaming with tears of grief that they had no resources wherewith to provide the expenses." (*Tauba: 92*)

Do you think that a firm and strong faith and belief would be wasted? And this burning desire for sacrifice would be just lost? No, never. For this reason the Prophet appreciated their faith, and said to, the soldiers going with him:

> "There are some people whom we have left behind in Medina ; in whatever place or valley we may camp, they will be with us. For them their excuse is enough."
>
> (*Bukhari*)

As their intentions were honest, they were the recipients of the reward (sawab) of the mujahedeen (fighters), because they had stayed in Medina against the wishes of their hearts and with great unwillingness.

If this is the achievement of the honest intention that the person having it is so favoured, then the dishonest intention also earns the punishment reserved for the bad deed, although apparently the act was righteous. Such a hypocrisy has been condemned:

> "So woe to the worshippers who are neglectful of their prayers, those who (want but to be seen (of men), but refuse (to supply) (even) neighbourly needs."
>
> (*Al-Ma'un : 4-7*)

The prayer based on hypocrisy is considered a sin, because after losing the essential sincerity it has become dead, and is, therefore, useless. Similar is the case of zakat. If it is paid merely to seek Allah's pleasure then it can be acceptable to Allah, otherwise it wilt be a waste:

> "Waste not your charity by reminders of your generosity or by injury—like him who spends his wealth to be seen by men and believes not in Allah and the Last Day. His likeness is the likeness of a rock on which there is (some) dust of earth ; on it heavy rainfalls, which leaves it a bare stone. They will be able to do nothing with anything they have earned."
>
> (*Baqarah : 264*)

The heart which is bereft of sincerity cannot be acceptable, as the rock with some dust on it cannot grow any grain when rain falls on it.

If the kernel is rotten, beautiful outer skin will not be of any use.

However, if the self is full of sincerity, then its blessing helps to make an ordinary thing as weighty as a mountain. If it is devoid or sincerity, then what reward can mounds of chaff and husks achieve from Allah ?

That is why Allah's Messenger has said:

> "Make your faith pure ; a little (righteous) act will be sufficient to save you from hell." (*Al-Aakim*)

In the *hadith* the reward for virtuous acts has been mentioned to be from ten times to hundred times, depending on the performer's intention and sincerity hidden in his heart, which is known only to that Being who knows about all the manifest as well as hidden things. Accordingly the reward increases according to the sincerity and honesty of the intentions.

The external acts of man can neither achieve the pleasure of Allah nor the grandeur of the worldly life. Allah gives his attention to his faithful and sincere slaves accept only those of their acts which bring them nearer to Him. As regards the worldly show and human trappings, they have no importance and no value.

The Prophet has said:

> "Allah does not see your bodies nor does he look at your faces, but he sees your hearts." (*Muslim*)

It is mentioned in the hadith

> "When Doomsday would occur, the deeds done in the world will be presented to Allah. From them the acts performed for Allah will be separated. And the other acts performed for other purposes will be thrown into the fire of hell." (*Baihaqui*)

One who would adopt these realities in one's life would experience relief and comfort in this world and would also achieve eternal bliss in the Hereafter. He will not be harmed by the loss of anything nor will he grieve for any act.

The Prophet has said:

> "The man who has left his world in the condition that he had performed acts sincerely for the one and only Allah, had established prayer and had paid zakat, then Allah is pleased with him." (*Ibn Maja*)

This hadith is in conformity with these words of Allah:

> "And they have been commanded no more than this; to worship Allah, offering Him sincere devotion being true (in faith) to establish regular prayer ; and to practise regular charity; and that is the religion, right and straight." *(Baiyina :5)*

Sincerity, the desired thing : In the times of scarcity and adversity the rays of sincerity throw their light with full force. At such times man separates himself from his carnal desires and yearnings. He severs his relations with their defects and errors. He repents before Allah and weeps and wails and prays for His blessings. He shakes from the fear of Allah's wrath.

The holy Quran has drawn a very fine picture of such a man, who is surrounded by adversities, and is appearing to his Merciful Lord so that He may lift him out of this mire:

> "Say: 'Who is it that delivers you from the dark recesses of land and sea, when you call upon Him in meekness and silent terror; if He only delivers us from these (dangers), (we vow) or shall truly show our gratitude ?'
> "Say : 'It is Allah that delivers you from these all (other) distresses ; and yet you run after false gods' ?"
> *(Al An'am : 63-64)*

This sincerity is temporary. Those conditions which befall a man and sometimes do not befall, how can they be called moral conduct? Allah wants that He should be truly and correctly known and recognised and should be respected and honoured in good or bad condition, as deserving of Him. People should give their due place to honest and sincere intention and good conduct in their lives. Their attachment to these qualities should be strong and should not break at any time, and they should not make any other thing but selflessness and Allah's pleasure as an ideal to follow in their life.

This heat of sincerity dies down gradually as passion for greed for wealth, self-love, egotism, hunger for position and office, hypocrisy and desire to be famous increases. But to Allah only that act is desirable which is free from all these undesirable impurities:

"Surely, pure religion is for Allah only." (*Zumar : 3*)

The example of the superior nature is like that of a ripe fruit, which requires to be protected from diseases and mishaps in order to preserve its sweetness and cleanness.

For this reason Islam has considered hypocrisy in righteous acts as most abominable and has declared it as, shirk, associating some one else with Allah.

The truth is : this hypocrisy destroys all acts as white ants destroy slowly all things they come in contact with. When the habit of hypocrisy takes roots in any man's dealings, as germs of an infectious disease spread in the society, then it becomes a sort of idolatry and throws its practitioner into the fire of hell.

> The Prophet has said : "A little hypocrisy is also polytheism. He who is hostile to Allah's friends, he openly declares a war against Allah. Allah likes those who are righteous, who fear him and who pray secretly, those who would not be missed if they disappear and would not be recognised if they are present. Their hearts are the lamps of guidance. They remove darkness from every piece of land." (*Hakim*)

Ibn Abbas narrates that one man asked the Prophet : "O Messenger of Allah ! I take up a stand with the intention of seeking Allah's pleasure, and I wish that the people of my country should see it. What do you think of it?" The following verses were revealed before the Prophet gave an answer

> "Whoever expects to meet his Lord, let him work righteousness, and in the worship of his Lord, admit no one as partner." (*Kahf : 110*)

The severe criticism and attacks which Islam has unleashed on the evils emanating from hypocrisy and want of sincerity is because it is a kind of corruption that is not discernible, and keeps the carnal desires and the wicked wishes of the self hidden.

The evils which can be seen give rise to other evils and increase the rate of corruption of the society considerably. Such evils are considered very low and mean, and on account of this consciousness and feeling it is quite possible that the man who commits them may give them up sooner or later, and may turn a new leaf.

But that sinning which puts on the garb of worship has its evils hidden from the sight of the sinner himself and the society is also not able to recognise it.

It is so because such a criminal remains absorbed in the ramifications of his acts. He is under the impression that he is also working for the pleasure of Allah, then how can he realise that he has committed a sin? And how can he turn away from a thing which he considers righteous ?

As regards the general society, it is harmed more by the learned (ulema) hypocrites than by the poor and needy people, who are the habitual criminals of this type.

Want of sincerity in the talented people makes their ability a curse for the country, and such a society suffers a set back instead of making progress.

It is also true that to pollute a virtue with the impurities of the self is to downgrade its value. This is another crime which is committed for want of sincerity. The man wants to please other men and is neglecting to seek the pleasure of his Lord ; he does not understand, on account of his foolishness, as to what his sin signifies. He is turning away from the Being who is Most Powerful and who is Independent of everything, to those beggars who have neither power, nor riches. That is why Allah's Messenger has said:

> "When on the Day of Resurrection, about the occurrence of which there is no doubt, Allah will gather all the people who came first and last, a caller will give a call : "Whoever has associated another with Allah in his acts should seek his reward from that partner because Allah is more free from partnership than all the partners." (*Tirmizi*)

Soldiers should prove sincerity : Whether it may be a common soldier or a commander, the soldiers should keep their jihad free from all the impurities of worldly show and trappings, because they have attached their life and death with a sacred duty, compared to which ranks, medals, honours, salaries, etc., have no value..........They should give preference to whatever is with Allah, and should sacrifice their desires for pure devotion and sincere submission.

It is narrated by Abdullah bin A'mar bin A'as that he said:

> "O Messenger of Allah! show me the difference between jihad and battle." The Prophet replied: O Abdullah bin A'mar! If you fight displaying patience and for seeking the pleasure of Allah, then He will lift you in the same state ; and if you fight with pride on the largeness of your numbers and to show to the people, then Allah will lift you is the same state. O Abdullah bin A'mar ! In whatever condition you fight or you are killed, Allah will lift you in that condition." (*Abu Daud*)

Employees in the cause of Allah : The writing work that the employees do in their offices, the accounts that they maintain, the intellectual energy that they spend, the manual work which they do with their hands, all these activities should be conducted by them is the interest of their country and for seeking the pleasure of Allah.

An animal labours for the whole day for its fodder. The efforts and labour of a common man has the value of an animal's labour, and all his work and labour are in proportion to his salary, and that is his purpose and centre of activity.

But an intelligent and wise man knows the value of his ideas and his acts and employs them in the cause of some great objective.

It is very regrettable that the general employees are suffering from this disease. They do not understand anything else but wealth, ranks and promotion. They consider their world and their religion also limited by this circle only, and they think that it is the axis of their happiness and sorrow, action and inaction, desire and ambition, and their lives revolve round that only.

Allah's Messenger has said : When the last period would come, there would be three sects in my Ummah. One sect will sincerely worship only Allah. The second sect will worship as hypocrites.

The third sect will worship so that they may defraud others of their wealth. When Allah would gather them on the Day of Judgment and say to the last sect : 'By My honour and grandeur, what did you expect to get from My worship? He would answer: 'By Your honour and grandeur, I was fraudulently taking others' property by that.' Allah would say that whatever he had collected was of no use to him and would command him to be sent to hell. Then He would address the sect whose worship was governed by hypocrisy: 'By My honour and grandeur, tell Me what was your purpose? He would say : 'By Your honour and grandeur, the purpose was to show to the people.' Allah would say: 'Nothing from it has reached me. Take him away to hell.' Then the Almighty Allah would ask the sect that was sincerely worshipping Him: 'By My honour and grandeur, what did you expect to get from My worship? He would answer: 'By Your honour and Your grandeur, You are better aware of the condition of the person who sought Your words and Your pleasure.' Allah would say:

> 'My slave has spoken the truth. Take him to Paradise':"
>
> (*Tibrani*)

In the Path of God

In the fields of learning and culture deep sincerity is extremely necessary. Knowledge is such a pure and high thing that on its basis Allah granted superiority to man over all the other creatures. Therefore it would be a very mean thing if it is utilised in furtherance of human motivations and if it is reinforced with mischief, corruption, and carnal desires. The world received a great setback at the hands of those learned men who did not possess good moral character, and were deprived of purity and loftiness.

Islam has made it compulsory for the teacher and the taught to give proof of sincerity in the matter of knowledge, and should give preference to high values and public interests over all other things. This activity of learning and teaching is however undertaken with the purpose of merely earning wealth. This limits its utility to individuals only. In this way this valuable treasure is wasted, as is seen in the case of lakhs of people. In fact, it amounts to depreciate the value of learning and to waste this great message.

> Allah's Messenger has said : "Any one who has obtained a learning by which Allah's pleasure could be obtained, but his purpose was merely to achieve success in the world, then on the Day of Resurrection he will not be able to smell the fragrance of Paradise." (*Abu Daud*)

Islam severely disapproves that a man should attain learning and when he gets proficiency in that line, he should start impressing others of his learning and his greatness, and open a battle-field of debates and controversial discussion.

> It is mentioned in the *hadith* : "Do not attain learning in order to express pride before the ulema, nor by its help quarrel with the foolish people, nor through it try to overwhelm the meetings, but he who does so, his destination is fire." (*Ibn Maja*)

These religious and worldly learning which are flying their banners over the world have reached this position when they were seekers of truth, and avoided mean purposes. But it does not mean that the ulema and students must necessarily face trials and tribulations and have definitely to pass through hard times. No, its meaning is never this, for it is not an inevitable demand of the honest intention that the sincere people should be subjected to difficulties and be confronted with adversities.

The diseases that are generated for want of sincerity are many. When these diseases grow, they destroy faith ; and when they are less in number then they bore holes in it and give a chance to Satan to enter through them.

The Almighty Allah is displeased with the slaves of wealth and position because it is determined for a Muslim that he would sacrifice all interests, relations and ambitions in the cause of Allah, and it is not for him that he should go after them and forget his Lord and His pleasure.

The magicians of Firaun (Pharaoh) established a perfect example of true belief and high sincerity, when they rejected all the threats of Firaun, and trampled below their feet the love of wealth and position, and replied to that tyrant king's challenge in these words:

> "So decree whatever you desire to decree ; for you can only decree (touching) the life of this world. For, we have believed in our Lord; may He forgive us our faults, and the magic to which you did compel us ; for Allah is Best and most Abiding." (*Taha : 72-73*)

What a great difference between these two groups! One group disdainfully kicks at the material world, and the other group, in order to reach up to some big personality or to achieve some small gains, makes fun of its own religion and faith and sacrifices it for achieving success in the world.

FIVE

Truthfulness

Allah has created this whole universe on the basis of love, and has demanded of the people that they should build up their life on the foundation of truth, to make truth and straight dealing a practice of their life, and should give place to truth only in their talks and dealings.

When this clear sense is lost sight of by people, and false stories, superstitions and absurd beliefs rule their self, ideas and thoughts, then hardness and harshness are generated in them, they move away from the right path, and they totally give up those realities, the adoption of which was necessary.

For this reason the strong and firm pillar of a Muslim's character is straight dealing. It is his duty to be attached to truth in every matter and to see every problem and affair through the glasses of truth. To keep it before him in every decision is the clearest manifestation of his dealing and treatment. Similarly the construction of the society in Islam is made on this foundation that mere conjectures and superstitions should be opposed, baseless things and imaginary stories should be thrown out, doubts and misgivings should not be encouraged, because strong and firm realities only deserve to be manifested ; they should have their imprint on the society , and their help should be taken in strengthening various relations.

Allah's Messenger has said:

> "Keep away from ill-thinking, because ill-thinking is the greatest falsehood." (*Bukhari*)

Another *hadith* says:

> "Leave alone doubtful things, follow those matters in which there is no doubt, for truth is a means of satisfaction and falsehood is the cause of doubts and misgivings." (*Tirmizi*)

Quran has expressed condemnation of those communities who follow conjectures and superstitions that have filled their brains with absurdities and has staked their present and future, with the help of the false stories, on the gamble of corruption and disruption:

> "They follow nothing but conjecture and what their own souls desire, even though there has already come to them Guidance from their Lord." (*An-Najm : 23*)

> "But they have no knowledge therein. They follow nothing but conjecture; and conjecture avails nothing against Truth. (*An-Najm : 28*)

Since Islam respects truth most strongly, it turns away liars very harshly. It admonishes them very severely. Hazrat Ayesha narrates:

> "Allah's Messenger did not hate anything as strongly as he hated falsehood. If he received information that a particular man has told a lie, he used to throw away that man's respect and honour from his heart till the time he was not informed that he has repented for it." (*Ahmed*)

Another narration by her states:

> "For the Messenger of Allah falsehood was the worst habit in a person. If any man told a lie in his presence, that man's thought always troubled him until the time he was informed that he has repented." (*Ibn Habban*)

This habit of the Prophet is not at all surprising. This was the policy of our forefathers. Their relations were formed on the basis. of righteousness and good moral character. They knew each other. If any one had blemishes in his character, and if he could be singled out on account of his misdeeds, then his position in that society would be like the position of a man suffering from an infectious itching disease in a healthy society, and he was not considered deserving of any respect until he was not cured of that defect.

The distinctive characteristic of the Muslim society in its first period was truth, discipline, tolerance and cautious manner of speaking. Falsehood, breaking of promises, false accusations, and baseless things are the signs of disruption or of breaking away relation from religion. Or if they are to be termed having relation with the religion, then it would be called the religious business of the false accusers, deceivers and tricksters, or the religiosity of liars and promise-breakers.

Falsehood is a great curse : Falsehood is such an evil that discloses the internal corruption and wickedness of the liar; and this is a name of the wrong dealing which only acts in spreading evil, so much so that even without the needs that are troublesome or the forcing inclinations it leads persons to committing sins.

Some evils are such that a man is involved in them totally. They are like diseases which require a very long-drawn treatment; they are like fright and cowardice, which always hinder the progress of a coward and a frightened man, or like greed which makes men miserly and stingy.

When some people come out for jihad to accompany the soldiers, they are shivering in their boots. Or some other people who are terrified when they work out the amount of zakat that they have to pay. What is the comparison of these coward and miserly natures with those brave and generous natures which rush towards death laughing and which spend their wealth in the cause of Allah most willingly!

Here some excuse can be found for such persons as they become a prey of their fears and doubts wher called upon to offer sacrifices.

But there can be absolutely no excuse for those who make lying their habit and who for the whole of their life go on deceiving people by their falsehoods.

Allah's Messenger said:

> "All the evils can be found in a momin, except dishonesty and falsehood." (*Ahmed*)

> The Messenger of Allah was asked whether any Muslim could be a coward. He answered : "Yes." He was asked : "Can a momin be a miser ?" He said that yes, he could be a miser. He was again asked : "Can a momin be a liar ?" He replied :"No." (*Malik*)

The replies of the Prophet show that these factors of deficiency and weakness enter some persons' nature and when they are called upon to do their duty or pay the dues of Allah and His slaves, then these factors adversely influence them. But this does not mean that miserliness is tolerated and cowardice is a lesser evil. How is it possible when nonpayment of zakat and running away from jihad are acts which touch the borderline of infidelity (kufr)?

The extent to which a liar and a defiant person may spread falsehood — and however wide this extent may be — his sin, before Allah will be to the same extent. Journalist, who misguide the people by false news, politicians who misrepresent important public problems and slaves of selfishness who cast aspersions against eminent persons and ladies of good character — all these sections commit terrible crimes and their punishment is very severe.

> Allah's Messenger said : "One night I saw two men. They came to me and said :"Any man whom you see talking by widening his jaws, consider him a liar. He tells a lie which is copied through his medium, till it is talked of in the whole world. He goes on doing this till the Doomsday." (*Fathul Bari*)

> Making false promises to their subjects by the rulers also comes in this category, because the falsehood spoken from the pulpit spreads to the four corners of the world.

> It is in the Tradition that "Three persons can never enter Paradise. First the old man who commits illegal

> sex, second the man who tells lies and third that poor man who indulges in pride." (*Al Bazzar*)

To invent lies against Allah's religion is the worst evil. One who has the slightest relation with Allah and His Messenger will never indulge in this kind of activity.

This is the worst kind of liar, and the consequences which he will have to face are terrible.

> The Prophet has said : "The consequence of inventing falsehood against me is not as bad as it is for inventing falsehood against anybody. Let the man who purposely and wittingly makes a false statement about me make his destination Hell." (*Bukhari*)

In the list of false charges and accusations are included all those inventions and absurdities which the uneducated have fabricated against Allah's religion, which have no place in the faith. The general public has taken them to be the religion, though they have nothing to do with it. In fact they are nothing but mere pastime and plaything.

Allah's Messenger has warned his followers against the sources of these invented absurdities, has admonished them to be wary of adopting other ways than those directed by the Quran and the Sunnah. He has said:

> "In the last period of my Ummah there will come people who will be deceitful, liars. They will tell you things which you would never have heard, nor have your forefathers heard them. Be wary of them ;let them not misguide you and let them not involve you in corruptions." (*Muslim*)

Children should be Truthful : Islam commands that in the hearts of the children the seeds of the greatness and importance of truth be sown, so that they may grow up and develop on truth and may become young in its lap; and they may give it its due place in their talks.

> Abdullah Ibn A'amir says that once my mother called me when the Prophet was present in my house. My

mother asked me to come and said that she would give me a certain thing. He asked what did she want to give ? She said that she wanted to give me a date (fruit). The Prophet said : " If you had not given him this date, then the committing of a falsehood would have been entered into your record of deeds."

(*Abu Daud*)

Abu Huraira says that the Prophet has said:

"Anybody who called a child saying that he would give him a certain thing. and did not give it, then it is a lie." (*Ahmed*)

It is worth noting that in what a wise way the Prophet has instructed his followers to train their children in such a manner that they should consider truth and straight dealing respectable things and should avoid telling lies. Had the Prophet ignored these things and had not emphatically reminded about them, then there was a danger that the children on growing up would not have considered telling lies as sin.

Adoption of straight dealing and telling the truth has been very strictly insisted upon, so much so that it has been enjoined upon to take care about this in even small household matters.

Alma Binte Yazid narrates that she once asked the Messenger of Allah:

"If some one of us women stated that she had no desire to have a certain thing even though she had that desire, then would it be considered a lie ?" He replied : "Falsehood is written as falsehood, and a small falsehood is written as a small falsehood."

(*Muslim*)

Prohibited to tell a Lie even in a Joke : The Establisher of the Shariah (P.B.U.H.) has warned of all the occasions where falsehood can be used and the adverse consequences of the same, so much so that it is not possible for even an ordinary enforcer to misguide the people about the reality or to lessen its importance.

A man tends to make false statements in cutting jokes, thinking that on the occasions of entertaining people there is nothing wrong if baseless information is given or false and imaginary events are related. But Islam, which considers providing relief to hearts as permissible, has fixed only those methods proper and permissible which are within the limits of truth, because halal is much broader than haram and that truth is independent of falsehood.

Allah's Messenger has said:

> "Death for the man who indulges in story-telling in order to make some people laugh and for that he relies on falsehood. There is death for him, there is destruction for him." (*Tirmizi*)

In another *hadith* it is stated:

> "I give guarantee of a house in the middle of Paradise for the man who has given up falsehood, though he was required to indulge in humour." (*Baihaqui*)

The Prophet has said:

> "A Momin cannot have complete faith unless he gives up falsehood in his jokes and debates though in all other matters he speaks the truth." (*Ahmed*)

This is our daily observation that people give full rein to their tongues in the matter of humorous talks to make others laugh, and do not hesitate to spread the tales and stories invented by friends or foes only for the purpose of getting some pleasure or for pulling some ones's leg, when the world has absolutely prohibited such a wrong policy, and this is a fact that this kind of entertainment and amusements and false acts create enmities and rivalries.

Avoid exaggeration in praise : Some people, when they praise somebody, go to the extent of exaggerating and making false statements. For a Muslim it is necessary that when he praises somebody he should do it to the extent to which he knows about that man. He should avoid exaggeration and falsehood in showering praises of the praised one, although he may be deserving of the praises, for exaggeration is a kind of falsehood which has been forbidden.

> To a person who was praising the Prophet, he said : "Do not indulge in exaggeration while praising me, as the Christians did in the case of Ibn Maryam (Christ). I am only a slave. So only say that he is a slave of Allah and His Messenger." (*Razin*)

A group of such people is always found who lick the boots of the leaders and rulers of the country and praise them to heaven. The main purpose of their lives is to compose very lengthy panegyrical poems or to write long-drawn essays in praise of their benefactors. Thus they try to make a mountain of the molehill and place an unknown person in the palace of fame. Sometimes they do not even hesitate to call the tyrant rulers as standard bearers of justice and coward and chicken hearted soldiers as brave and lion-hearted fighters. Their only purpose in this is to earn wealth.

This is the worst kind of falsehood. Allah's Messenger has counselled us to totally reject them and expose them till they give up their wrong practices.

> Abu Huraira says that the Prophet has commanded us that we should throw dust in the face of those who indulge in exaggeration in their praises. (*Tirmizi*)

The commentators have pointed out that the persons mentioned here are those who make exaggeration as their habit and through this try to earn gifts and presents from the praised ones, but those persons who praise the performers of good acts with a view to encouraging them and to inciting others to follow their example are not meant.

The limits where a Muslim stops and which keep him distinct from the bootlickers and the exaggerators are that he praises his benefactor or a good person, but he does not let him indulge in vanity and pride. These limits have been clarified by the Prophet.

> Hazrat Abu Badr narrates that a man praised some one in the presence of Allah's Messenger and the

> Prophet told him : "Fie on you, you have separated the head of your companion." He repeated these words and then said: "If some one wants to praise his brother, then if he is aware of the facts then he should say that I think he is such and such and Allah is the real Knower, and he is the bearer of these qualities." (*Bukhari*)

Keep away from falsebood and deception in trade : Traders make false statements while showing their wares and stating their prices. The basis of trade in our midst is unlimited greed. The shopkeeper desires that there should be dearness, while the buyer wants to get the commodities free of charge. It is wealth which controls activities of buying and selling in the markets and in different fields. Islam hates this kind of deceptive affair and the senseless debate and disputation latent in it.

The Prophet has said : "The buyers and sellers are free till they do not separate and if they have acted with honesty, and have explained the defects of commodities, then Allah will bless them with prosperity. And if both of them tried to deal dishonestly and tried to hide the defects- then it is likely that they may get some profit, but the prosperity will vanish from their trade."

In another tradition it is stated:

> "The prosperity of the dealing of both the persons is terminated. The untrue and false oath will help get the commodity sold, but it reduces the earning. (*Ahmed*)

The buyers who go to the shopkeepers are mostly ignorant of the real situation, and whatever the shopkeeper says they believe it. The honest thing is not to take undue advantage of the simplicity of men for the purpose of obtaining double price or for concealing the defects.

The Messenger of Allah has said:

> "What would be a greater dishonesty than this that when you are talking with your brother, he may be thinking that you are telling the truth whereas you are deceiving him by telling lies." (*Bukhari*)

He has also said:

> "It is not lawful for a Muslim to sell such a commodity that has a defect, except that the defect is shown to the buyer." (*Bukhari*)

Ibn Abi Adna narrates that a man opened a shop in the market and swore that he would sell such a commodity as no one else would be selling, so that he may deceive some Muslims ; so the following verses were revealed:

> "Verily, those who sell the covenant with Allah and their oaths for a small price, there is no compensation for them in the Hereafter. On the Day of Judgment Allah will not speak to them, nor will He look at them, and nor will He purify them; but for them is very severe punishment." (*Baqarah*)

Disregard of truth in giving evidence is the worst type of falsehood. When a Muslim should stand up for giving evidence, he should state the truth unhesitatingly, regardless of the fact whether it is against his close friend or a favourite person. No relationship or prejudice should deviate him from the right path, nor any greed or bribe should be able to make him waver in his stand.

> "O You who believe ! Stand out firmly for justice, as witnesses to Allah, even as against yourselves, or your parents, or your kin, and whether it be (against) rich or poor; for Allah can best protect both. Follow not the lusts (of your heart), lest you swerve, and if you distort (justice) or decline to do justice, verily Allah is well-acquainted with all that you do." (*Nissa : 135*)

Hazrat Abu Bakr narrates that the Messenger of Allah has stated:

> "May I not tell you the major sins ?" Three times he repeated the same thing. We requested "Why not O Messenger of Allah?" He replied "To associate some one else with Allah, to disobey the parents and to murder some one unjustly." He was leaning. Then he

> got up and said : "And to tell lies and to give false evidence." He went on repeating it till we said to ourselves it would be better if he were silent then."
>
> (*Bukhari*)

Trickery and deception is a falsehood which has layers and layers of darknesses. It does not only involve the concealment of truth but it also tries to prove that the falsehood is truth. In some special matters it harms only a few invididuals but in public matters it becomes a severe and deadly danger against the whole nation.

For this reason the Prophet has very bluntly and emphatically counselled to keep away from it and has warned against it.

Do not break your promises : The traders and the industrialists particularly should take special care to see that they keep their promises, that they are true to their words and that they do not change their stand. It is a very sad state of affairs that among the Muslims the tendency of breaking promises and crossing the limits has become very common, when their religion has termed the false promises symbols of disruption.

The Messenger of Allah considered the words coming out from the mouth as holy and the words that fell on his ears as respectable. Before attaining prophethood, these qualities of decency and manliness were found in his character.

Abdullah bin Abi Hama says that he entered into a contract for the sale of a commodity with the Prophet before he was blessed with prophethood, and some commodities had remained to be sold. He promised to the prophet that he would hand over a certain thing to him at a certain place. Then he forget all about this. After three days he remembered his Promise and went to the appointed place. He saw that the Prophet was present at the spot. He only said this:

> "O young man ! You worried me. I am waiting here for you for the last three days." (*Ábu Daúd*)
>
> It is narrated that the Prophet had promised Jabir bin Avauuan that he would give him some gifts from the stock of articles coming from Bahrain, but before

> fulfilling this promise he died. When the stock from Bahrain arrived at the place of the First Caliph, he caused an announcement to be made in the public that any one whom the Prophet might have promised to give something from this stock or any one who had lent something to the Prophet should come to him and take away his due." (*Bukhari*)

It is worth noting how the words are appraised and they are enforced, so that they may not become worthless if left uncared for. False promises do untold harm to the interests of the society. They cause inconvenience to the people and waste time. Redeeming your pledges is a commendable quality. Allah considers fulfilling of promises as one of the attributes of prophehood

> "Also mention in the Book (the story of) Ismail; he was true to what he promised, and he was a Messenger, Prophet. He used to enjoin on his people prayer and charity and he was most acceptable in sight of the Lord." (*Maryam : 54-55*)

In these verses the order of the good qualities show what position the quality of fulfilling of promises enjoys ; and Ismail showed that he was true to his word when his father told him that he saw a dream in which he was slaughtering his son, Ismail, and asked him what he thought about it. The son, who was true to his word, replied: "God willing, you will find me patient and steadfast."

Sometimes man relies on falsehood when he commits a mistake, and he wants to save himself from the bad consequences of that mistake. This is very unwise and brings a bad name. It amounts to going from one evil to another, which is worse than the first evil. It is necessary that man should own his mistakes. It is likely that his truthfulness and his sense of sorrow over his mistake may save him from the bad consequences and he may be pardoned.

When a Muslim senses some danger or is afraid to speak the truth, it is proper that he should show courage and try to avoid getting ensnared in the net of falsehood.

Allah's Messenger has said:

> "Adopt truth, even if you see your destruction in it, for the (final) salvation is in it." (*Ibn Abi-duniya*)

In another *hadith* it is mentioned:

> "When a person tells a lie, the bad odour that emanates from it keeps the angels one mile away." (*Tirmizi*)

If a man is truthful and straight in his speech and dealings, then inevitably there will be truthfulness and sincerity in his actions and goodness and reform in his conditions. By adopting truthful and straight methods in dealing with others, this light of truth also illuminates man's heart and mind and their darkness also vanish:

> 'O you who believe Fear Allah mid (always) say a wora alrecrea to me right ; that He may matte your conduct whole and sound and forgive you your sins; He that obeys Allah and His Messenger has already attained the highest achievement." (*Ahzab : 70-71*)

Right action is the desired action, about which there is no misgiving, because it is the creation of certainty. There is no idea of defect in that, because it is the companion of sincerity. There is no curve in it, because its source is truth.

The success of the communities and nations in the matter of conveying their message depends on the fact that the bearers of the message must be performers of right action. If they have an abundant record of right and truthful action, then they can reach the zenith of success and glory, otherwise they swerve from their destination in the way, for mere idleness, senseless activities, slogan shouting and self-praise would not be of any use.

> Allah's Messenger has said : "Adopt truth, for truth shows the path of righteousness, and righteousness shows the path to Paradise. A man speaks the truth regularly and adopts truthful ways till he is recorded as a truthful person before Allah ; and keep away from falsehood, for falsehood leads to wickedness, and wickedness throws in the Hell. A person tells lies

regularly and attaches himself to falsehood till he is recorded as a liar before Allah." (*Fathul Bari*)

Evil and wickedness towards which the habit of telling lies leads is the last stage of the destruction of self and the lowness of faith.

Imam Malik has reported about the hadith narrated by Ibn Masood : "A person regularly tells lies and adopts falsehood (as his policy), till a black point is imprinted on his heart, and slowly and slowly the whole heart becomes black. At that time his name is entered in the list of liars before Allah."

Allah has stated in Quran:

"It is those who believe not in the Signs of Allah that forge falsehood; it is they who lie." (*Nahl : 105*)

Righteousness whose path is shown by truth is the highest peak of goodness to which only men of high determination can reach. In this connection the following verses of the holy Quran would suffice:

"It is no virtue that you turn yourface to the East and the West, but virtue is that one should believe in Allah, and the Last Day and the angels and the prophets ; and spend out of love for Him his wealth on relatives and orphans and the needy and the wayfarer and on those who ask and for ransom of the slaves and establish salat and pay zakat. And those who fulfil the pledges they make and steadfast in adversity and affliction and in times of struggle, such are the people as are truthful and Godfearing:" (*Baqarah : 177*)

Confidence

Islam exhorts its followers that they will be masters of live heads and wakeful conscience, which would ensure the protection of the rights of God and humanity and which would also protect their actions from the commitment of excesses. Therefore it is necessary that every Muslim should be Ameen, trustworthy.

In the eyes of the Shariah, Trust has a very broad sense. This word contains an ocean of meaning, but underneath it all is the sense of responsibility, the sense of having to appear before Allah and to account for one's actions, the details of which are given in the *hadith:*

> "Every one of you is a guardian and every one will be asked about his subjects. Imam is a guardian. He will be asked about his subjects. A man is the guardian of the persons in his household. He is answerable about them. A woman is the guardian of her husband's house. She will be asked about her responsibility. The servant is the guardian of the articles of his master. He is answerable about this responsibility of his."
>
> (*Bukhari*)

The narrator of the hadith Ibn Umar says that he heard these things from the Prophet and he thinks that the Prophet also said:' "A man is a guardian of the stock of his father and is answerable about that."

The people take trust in a very limited sense and consider it to mean the protection of others' deposits, although in Allah's religion this has a very broad and unlimited sense.

This is a duty for safeguarding which a Muslim advises another Muslim and in this conection seeks the help of Allah. When a Muslim prepares to go on a journey, his brother prays for him in this way:

> "I pray to Allah for your religion, your trust and for the happy ending of your work." (*Tirmizi*)

Hazrat Anas narrates that whenever Allah's Messenger addressed a sermon to us, he invariably repeated this sentence: "The man has no faith who cannot keep trust and the man who does not respect his promises has no religion."

Since the zenith of achievement and the highest limit of success is to be protected against the hardships of this world and the bad consequences in the Hereafter, the Prophet prays for safety from both the conditions. He has said:

> "O Allah ! I seek your shelter from the pangs of hunger, because it is a very bad companion, and I seek your shelter from dishonesty because it is the worst friend." (*Abu Daud*)

Hunger is the name of deprivation in the world and dishonesty is the name of destruction of religion, therefore the Prophet had prayed for being spared from both. Before attaining prohethood he was known among the people as Ameen (Trustworthy).

Similarly the trustworthiness of Moosa (Moses) was, observed when he fetched water for the flock of the two daughters of the good old man, had helped them, had respected their womanhood, and had treated them in a decent and gentlemanly way.

"So he watered (their flocks) for them ; then he turned back to the shade, and said : "O my Lord! truly am I in (desperate) need of any good that you do send me!" Afterwards one of the (damsels) came (back) to him, walking bashfully. 'She said: "My father invites you that he may reward you for having watered (our flocks) for us." So when he came to him and narrated the story, he said : "Do not fear ; (well) have you escaped from unjust people." Said one of the (damsels):

> "O my (dear) father ! engage him on wages; truly the best of men for you to employ is the (man) who is strong and trusty." (*Qasas : 24-26*)

This event took place when Moosa had not been made Prophet, and was not sent to Pharaoh's darbar.

And this is not at all surprising because Allah chose only those individuals for being appointed as His Messengers who were the most decent, most honest and righteous, among the people.. The self which continues to be attached to the high moral character even after undergoing the extremes or the hardship of poverty and helplessness must be belonging to a very powerful and trustworthy man; and the protection of the rights of God and His slaves demand such character only as does not change in good or bad conditions, and this is the spirit of trustworthiness.

Appointment, a Trust : There is also another sense of trust, and that is everything should be placed at its proper and deserving place. An office or a post should be offered only to the deserving person ; and responsibility should be given only to that person who is able to shoulder it and who has the capability to do justice to the trust placed in him.

Governorship, responsibilities of the party, nation or country, which are granted placing confidence in the persons concerned, are trusts, about which they are answerable. A number of proofs can be advanced in support of`this statement.

Hazrat Abuzar reports that he asked the Prophet whether he would not make him a governor somewhere. Hearing this the Prophet tapped his shoulder and said:

> "O Abuzar ! you are weak, and this responsibility is a trust. On the Day of Judgment it will be a cause of loss of honour and ignominy. However, those people will be spared who will have accepted it with all its responsibilities and would have fulfilled whatever responsibilities they had in this connection" (*Muslim*)

It is a fact that mere excellence of education or experience does not make a person most suitable for some office. It is also possible that a man may have good moral character and a righteous person, but he may not have the capabilities to fulfill the responsibilities of a certain office.

Hazrat Yusuf (Joseph) was a Prophet. He was the living example of righteousness and virtuousness, but he had not offered his services to shoulder the responsibilities of the country on the basis of his righteousness and prophethood. He had taken the reins of office in his hand on account of his learning and memory.

> "(Yusuf) Said: `Entrust to me the treasures of the country. Verily, 1 am protector and learned."
>
> (*Yusuf : 55*)

Trust demands that we should entrust such responsibilities and posts to such individuals as would be able to run them properly. If through bribery, nepotism and for some other reason we deviate from this principle and we select an unfit person for some office, then since we have ignored a fit person and have appointed an unfit and undeserving person, we have commited open misappropriation.

> Allah's Messenger has said that whoever has appointed an administrator through nepotism although there was among the people an individual who was more desirable before Allah than that person, then he has committed misappropriation against Allah, His Messenger and all the Muslims." (*Hakim*)

> Yazid bin Abi Sufyan reports that when Hazrat Abu Bakr sent him to Syria, he advised him thus : "O Yazid ! You have many relationships. It is likely that you may be influenced by them in making important appointments. I am very much afraid about you since the time the Prophet has said : "Any one who has been made responsible for some affair of the Muslims and he has entrusted some responsible job to some one, influenced by his relatives, then Allah's curse on him. No virtue or justice from him will be accepted before Allah, so much so that he will be thrown in the Hell." (*Hakim*)

The community from which the quality of keeping trust is vanished, can be recognised thus : the distribution of posts and offices in that community become a game and play of favours. The value of able men goes down and in their place unfit and undeserving men are appointed. The tradition has it that this forms part of those manifestations of corruption which will appear in the last period.

A man came to the Prophet and asked when the Doomsday would occur. The Prophet answered: "When deposits in trust would start being lost, then wait for the Doomsday." He was again asked:

> "What is the meaning of loss of trusts ?" He replied : "When responsibilities are entrusted to unfit persons, then wait for the Doomsday." (*Bukhari*)

Performance of Duty also a Trust : This sense is also included in the meaning of trust that the man to whom the responsibility has been entrusted should have the sincere inclination of satisfactorily fulfilling those responsibilities and that he should devote all his energies for doing justice to fulfil it. Undoubtedly it is a trust. Islam considers it worthy of honour that a man should be sincere in his work, should be keen on doing his job in a better way, and should be able to safeguard the right of the people that are in his charge, for however ordinary that responsibility may be, a slight negligence is likely to cause undue harm to the whole community and society ; and the germs of corruption and mischief enter the entire body politic. Dishonesty in performing official duties causes various moral diseases in the society. It causes great harm to the religion, to the Muslim public and to the country. This sin, its punishment and its evil appear in different forms.

The Messenger of Allah has said:

> "On the Day of Judgment when Allah will gather all the people, past and present, a flag will be fixed for every deceiver, by which he will be recognised. So it will be said that this is the group of such and such deceivers." (*Bukhari*)

In another tradition it is stated:

> "There will be a flag near the head of every deceiver which he will raise in proportion to his deceit. Listen, there is none worse deceiver than the Amir who deceives the public." (*Muslim*)

In other words there will be none more deceitful and deserving of bad consequences than the person who is made responsible for the affairs of men and he sleeps peacefully while the public is undergoing hardships and facing destruction.

Misuse of office betrayal of Trust : Trust demands that if a man is appointed to a certain high office he should not use it for self-aggrandisement or for the benefit of his relatives, for the use of public funds for personal purposes is a crime.

It is a common thing that the governments and the firms give fixed salaries to their employees. Then to find out extra sources of income is disrespectful, ignominious and mean. Allah's Messenger has said:

> "Whomsoever we wilt entrust with service, the provision of his needs is also our responsibility. If he takes more than this, then he is committing misappropriation." (*Abu Daud*)

It is misappropriation because he has used that property of the organisation for himself which was to be given to the weak and the needy, and it was to be spent for a greater cause and purpose.

> "If any person is so false, he shall on the Day of Judgment, restore what he misappropriated; then shall every soul receive its due, — whatever it earned — and none shall be dealt with unjustly."
>
> (*Ale Imran : 161*)

But a man who takes care of the commands of Allah in fulfilling his responsibility and he is averse to indulge in dishonest practices in performing his duties, then he is considered by Allah one among the fighters for the supremacy of the religion. The Prophet has said :

> "When the Administrator is given a job, he should receive his due and should pay the dues of others, then he is like a fighter in the cause of Allah till he returns home." (*Tibrani*)

Islam has forbidden the exploitation of one's office and taking undue advantage from it. It has been very severe in closing all the avenues of earning illegal wealth.

Adi bin 'Umaira narrates that he has heard the Prophet as saying: "Whomsoever we have given some post and he has concealed a needle or a thing smaller than that, then it will be a misappropriated thing with which he will have to appear on the Day of Judgment." Thereupon a dark-skinned Ansari got up and said : "O Messenger of Allah ! take away my governorship." The Prophet inquired what was the matter. He replied "I have heard all your talk just now." The Prophet said :

> "I still say that whomsoever we may make a governor, he should place everything before us. He should take whatever is given to him, and should keep away from whatever he is asked to desist." (*Muslim*)

It is said that a man from the tribe of Uzd, called Ibn Labtih, was sent as an administrator by the Prophet to collect charity and donations. When he returned with the collection he said : "These are your things and these have been gifted to me." The narrator of the *hadith* says that hearing this the Prophet stood up and after the praise of God said:

> "... I appoint, from amongst you, an administrator for these affairs for which Allah has made me responsible. When that man comes back, he says this is for us and this has been gifted to him. If he tells the truth, then why does he not sit in his parents' house. Let us then see from where the gifts come to him ? By God, if any one of you receives even an ordinary thing without it being due, he will have to appear before Allah carrying that thing. I do not want to see any one of you meeting Allah in this condition that he is carrying a camel on his head or a cow which is bellowing or a goat that is bleating." Then he raised his two hands till the whiteness of the armpits was visible and said : "O Allah ! I have conveyed your message." (*Muslim*)

Wealth and ability given by Allah also a Trust : Trust also means that you should take a survey of your powers of perception with which God has blessed you. You should have a look at those special abilities which God has given you. If you look at your property and your children, who are very dear to you, you will feel that all these are God's trust which has been deposited with you. Therefore it is necessary that they should be sacrificed in His cause, and they should be utilised for seeking His pleasure. If you suffer a loss in them, you should not start crying and wailing and you should not consider that it was your personal property that has been taken away from you, because compared to you Allah is the more rightful owner and He has the right to use it in any way He likes. If you are tested by an increase in them, then you should not hesitate to undertake jihad when called upon to do so, and you should not turn away from obedience to Allah on account of them. Or you should not feel conceited on their strength.

> "O you who believe I betary not the trust of Allah and the Messenger, nor misappropriate knowingly things entrusted to you. And know that your possessions and your progeny are but a trial; and that it is Allah with whom lies your highest reward."
>
> (*Anfal: 27-28*)

Others' secrets a Trust : Trust also means that you should protect the rights of the gatherings which you attend. You should not disclose their information and their secrets to others.

A number of relationships are severed, rifts are created in friendships and interests are endangered when the information about or the secrets of the gatherings are disclosed by someone by correctly or incorrectly quoting the source, thus jeopardising all the plans.

Allah's Messenger has said : "When a man says something to someone and then turns to you, then it is a trust."

The confidential talk of the meetings should be guarded, provided it conform to the moral laws and the principles of religion, otherwise its sanctity vanishes. If a Muslim is present to such a meeting where criminals, are conspiring among themselves, so that they may inflict some loss on others, then it is his responsibility that he should try to prevent this evil to the best of his ability.

> Allah's Messenger has said : "The secrets of the gatherings are a trust, but three kinds of gatherings are exceptions : one in which haram (illegal) blood is being shed, one in which haram (illegal) sex is being indulged into, or in which property is being illegally usurped. " (*Abu Daud*)

The conjugal relations are sacred in the eyes of Islam. The domestic relationship between a husband and wife and their mutual affairs should be fully protected. The closest man should also not be informed about them.

But foolish people relate their private matters and domestic affairs here and there to outsiders. This is a very bad habit and Allah has declared it haram.

Asma binte Yazid reports that she was with the Prophet and a husband and a wife were sitting there. The Prophet said:

> "Is there a man who narrates the acts performed with the wife? And is there a wife who relates her relation with her husband to others ?" People did not say anything from fear. I said : "O Messenger of Allah ! By God, husbands also do this and wives also do likewise." He said : "Do not say like this. Its example is like a devil-man meeting a devil-woman, and he covers her and performs the sexual act and people are watching." (*Ahmed*)
>
> The Prophet said : "On the Day of Judgment before Allah the greatest act of misappropriation will be that a man may love his wife and the wife may also be inclined towards her husband and then he may disclose his wife's secrets to others." (*Muslim*)

The deposits which are given to us in trust are for keeping protected for a fixed period, and then to be turned on demand. We are answerable for these acts.

While migrating to Medina, the Prophet left behind his cousin so that he may return to the polytheists the deposits kept with him in trust, although these polytheists were the members of the same community which was driving him out of his native place. He was being compelled to leave his home in the cause of his belief, but how can a decent man behave indecently even with indecent and infamous people?

Maimoon bin Mehran says that three kinds of treatment be always meted out to good and bad man alike keeping trust, fulfilling promise and kindness.

To consider trust as personal property is a wicked act, theft.

Abdullah Ibn Masood says that fighting in the cause of Allah vanishes all the sins except the misappropriation in trust. He says that on the Day of Judgment a person will be brought who had fought in the cause of Allah, but he would be asked to pay up amounts in trust. He would reply: "O Our Lord! how is it possible when the world has ended." Then it would be said : "Take him to Hell." And in his presence the amounts of trust will be presented in the same form in which they were handed over to him in the world. He would see them and recognise them. He would go after them and seize them and carry them on his shoulders, till he would be under the impression that he has come out, when the trusts would slip from his shoulders. He would again run after them. This act would continue with him for ever. Then he said that Salat (prayer) is a trust, Wuzu (ablutions) is a trust, to weigh a thing is a trust, to measure a thing is a trust, and he listed many things and said the greatest trust is that wealth or articles which are deposited or handed over.

The narrator of the *hadith* says that he went to Bara bin A'azib and asked him what he thought about what Ibn Masood said. Bara bin A'azib replied : "He spoke the truth. Did you not hear this command of Allah:

> "Allah commands you to render back your trusts to those to whom they are due ; and when you judge between man and man that you judge with justice."
>
> (*An-Nissa : 58*)

Keeping trust protects the rights of Allah and those of His slaves. It keeps away men from lowliness and meanness. It reaches the desired heights only when this quality is absorbed by men in their natures and consciousness, when it reaches the depths of their hearts and when it is guarded against the influences of close and distant relationships.

This is the meaning of the hadith narrated by Huzaifa bin Yaman:

> "Keeping trust has been naturally ingrained in the depths of men's hearts. Then Quran came and people learned it from Quran and Sunnah." (*Muslim*)

The knowledge of Shariah cannot be indifferent to the righteous conduct, and keeping trust signifies the correct knowledge of Quran and Sunnah as well as a wakeful conscience. If the conscience dies, then the quality of keeping trust is taken away. At such a time the recitation of the Quranic verses and the study of hadith cannot be profitable, but the claimants of Islam think about others and also about themselves that they are the bearers of this quality, but one may ask how can the heart that rejects the truth be expected to keep trust?

For this reason Hazrat Huzaifa has stated that the heart that has no belief loses the quality of keeping trusts. Accordingly he reports : "Then we started talking about vanishing the quality of keeping trust, and the Prophet said : 'When a man goes to one kind of sleep, the trust is squeezed from his heart till its effect remains equal to a point. Then he goes to another kind of sleep, then the trust shrinks from his heart in such a way as if it were merely a scar: Then the Prophet said: "Then people indulge in buying and selling, but no one can give a thing in trust, so much so that it is said that in a certain family there is a trustworthy man, and about him it is said how tolerant, well-behaved and wise he is although there is not an iota of faith in his heart."

This *hadith* draws a horrible picture of vanishing the quality of keeping trust from the hearts of dishonest people. It is like finding sparks of goodness in the nature of some mischievous people sometimes, although they have no influence on their lives. And sometimes the good acts overshadow their evil deeds, but it is clear that these acts cannot revive the dead heart. This conscienceless person appraises men on the basis of his desires and preferences. He does not distinguish between faith and infidelity in them.

Keeping trust is a very important quality. Men with weak faith cannot bear it. Allah has given an example of how its burden bears down man's whole existence. Therefore, it should not be considered an ordinary thing and no laxity should be shown in fulfilling its demands:

"We did indeed offer the Trust to the Heavens and the Earth and the mountains ; but they refused to undertake it, being afraid thereof ; but man undertook it ; he was indeed unjust and foolish." (*Ahzab : 72*)

Injustice and ignorance are two evils which beset man's nature, and man has to face the problem of fighting a jihad against them. His faith cannot be complete without cleaning and purifying it from injustice.

"It is those who believe and confuse not their beliefs with wrong-that are (truly) in security, for they are on (right) guidance." (*Ana'am : 82*)

"Verily, from among the slaves of Allah those who are learned fear Allah." (*Fatir : 28*)

This is the reason why after mentioning man's bearing trust in the foregoing verses of Surah Ahzab, it is said that those who are unjust and ignorant indulge in misappropriation, they are hypocrites and are the deserving recipients of Allah's punishment; and security is granted to men of faith and keepers of trust:

"(With the result) that Allah has to punish the hypocrites, men and women, and the unbelievers, men and women, and Allah turns in mercy to believers, men and women, for Allah is Oft-Forgiving, Most merciful." (*Ahzab:73*)

Word of Honour

When a Muslim undertakes a thing, he should respect the undertaking. When he enters into any contract he should honour it till the last. This is the demand of the faith that when a man talks of any enterprise, he should have the intention of taking it to completion, like the water which does not rest till it flows down to the lower level. He should be known among the people as a man of reliable promises, and there should be no fear of any breach of promises or of any dubious dealings from him.

Fulfilment of the promise is necessary. Similarly when an oath is taken, it should be redeemed. But this fulfilment of promise or the redeeming of the oath and pledges is necessary when the dealing is legitimate and concerns truth, otherwise honouring the promise in connection with something sinful and disobedience to Allah has no value, and there is no importance of oath in sin.

> Allah's Messenger has said : "If someone has taken an oath, but saw an aspect of goodness in another thing, he may break his oath and pay compensation (atonement), and should perform the act which is better and has goodness." (*Muslim*)

It is not proper for a man to insist on redeeming the oath. On such occasions it is better to break the oath. In a hadith it is stated:

> "It is sinful for a man among you to go to his wife with his oath (unredeemed) compared to his paying the compensation (atoning) which He has fixed for breaking the oath." (*Bukhari*)

For this mason no promise and covenant is proper and correct except in rightful matters. When a man has promised to do a certain good thing, then he should try his best to fulfil it, as long as it appears good to him. He should very well know that he should stick to manly talk, faith and belief. There is no room in this for breach of promises or doubts and hesitation.

Anas bin Malik says that his uncle Anas bin Nadar could not take part in the battle of Badr, and he said to the Prophet : "O Messenger of Allah ! In the first battle that you fought with the polytheists I could not take part. If Allah kept me with the Prophet then they will definitely see my achievements in the second battle against the polytheists."

When in the battle of Uhad, there was fierce fighting and the Muslims were retreating. He prayed to Allah "O Allah ! I ask your pardon for the mistake that they have committed, and I declare myself innocent of the transgression of the polytheists". Saying this he rushed into the battle. In the way he met Sa'ad bin Ma'az whom he said : "O Sa'ad bin Ma'az! By the God of Nadir, Proceed towards Paradise. I smell its fragrance in the valley of Uhad."

Sa'ad said: "O Messenger of Allah! The love for martyrdom which he showed cannot be expressed. Then he advanced:"

Anas says that we found more than eighty wounds on his body, which were caused by swords, the points of lances and the shower of arrows. The polytheists had disfigured his body and it was difficult to identify him. With great difficulty his sister identified him with the help of a mole on his fingers.

Anas says that he thinks that the following verses were revealed about him or about persons like him:

> "Among the believers are men who have been true to their covenant with Allah ; of them some have completed their vow to (the extreme), and some (still) wait; but they have never changed (their determination) in the least." (*Ahzab: 23*)

Memory and determination—essential : Fulfilment of promises depends on two factors. With these two things, fulfilling one's promises would be easy. Allah had taken a promise from Adam that he would not go near the forbidden tree, but Adam forgot the promise within a few days. He became a prey to weakness and broke his promise:

> "We had already beforehand taken the covenant of Adam, bus he forgot ; and We found on his part no firm resolve." (*Taha : 115*)

It shows that deficiency in memory and weakness of determination are two obstructions which come in the way of performance of duty. And this is a strange thing that man, being overwhelmed by the hardships of the times, various difficulties and different pressing problems forgets the open and clear realities. To him the clear figures appear blurred, and the realities which are as striking as the light of the sun disappear from his sight.

There the necessity of a reminder becomes very pressing to overcome the negligence and forgetfulness, and to keep this important thing before men's eyes. There are a number of verses of the Quran which were revealed for safeguarding the memory:

> "Follow the revelation given to you from your Lord, and follow not, as friends or protectors, other than Him. Little it is you remember of admonition."
>
> (*A'araf : 3*)

> "This is the way of your Lord, leading straight ; 'We have detailed the signs for those who receive admonition." (*Ana'am : 126*)

Alive and wakeful memory and remembrance is essential for fulfilling promises. A man who forgets his promises and covenants, how can he fulfil them ? That is why the following verse has been ended on a note of admonition after giving command of fulfilling them:

> "And fulfil the Covenant of Allah; thus does He command you, that you may remember."
>
> (*Ana'am : 152*)

If a man has a strong memory in respect of fulfilling his promise, it is also necessary that he should have a determination to do so — a determination which should not have any laxity or slackness in this matter — a determination which should be able to overcome all the rebellious desires, and which should lighten the coming burden of difficulties. It should be a determination which should be able to cross all the difficult valleys and blocks and should be able to set an example of selfless sacrifice for others.

The measures for weighing and appraising people are different with different people. The price one has to pay for remaining faithful sometimes is very high. At times one requires to sacrifice all the wealth, property and the most desired thing in this respect.

But these difficulties, sacrifices and trials of determination prove in the end to be the steps for achieving greatness and honour, as the poet says:

"Why he, who considers his life and heart dear, should go to (seek) the beloved in her street."

The holy Quran has severely criticised those who seek to achieve heights of success and glory in the shadow of comfortable living

> "Do you think that you will enter paradise without such trials as came to those who passed away before you ? They experienced suffering and adversity and were so shaken in spirit that even the prophet and the faithful who were with him cried: 'When will Allah's help come ?' Ah I Verily, Allah's help is near."
>
> (*Baqarah : 214*)

When a man develops in himself the combined forces of a conscious and wakeful mind and a heart full of determination, then he can be considered to have been qualified to enter the group of the faithful people.

Moral Binding

For a Muslim the most honourable and the holiest covenant is the one which he has made with his Lord, for Allah has created him with His Power. He has nourished him under the shadow of his favours and blessings, and has demanded of him that he should recognise what is the reality and admit it. No misguiding factors should cause him to deviate from the right path lest he may deny these realities or he may lose sight of them:

> "Did I not enjoin on you, O you children of Adam! that you should not worship Satan ; for that he was to you an enemy avowed? And that you should worship Me, (for that) this was the straight way ?"
>
> (*Yasin : 60-61*)

Those who do not listen to the prophets and do not follow their teachings, in their nature also there is a motivator which pricks them, shows them the path of their Lord, and tries to make them realize the greatness of the Creator, however corrupt and polluted the environment may be.

This is the meaning of this covenant which Allah has taken from all the humans:

> "When your Lord drew forth from the children of Adam from their loins-their descendants, and made them testify concerning themselves, (saying); `Am 1 not your Lord( Who cherishes and sustains you ) ?' They said: `Yes, we do testify.' (This), lest you should say on the Day of Judgment: `Of this we were never mindful.' Or lest you should say:"Our fathers before us may have taken false gods but we are (their) descendants after them ; will you then destroy us because of the deeds of men who were futile ?' Thus do We explain the signs in detail in order that they may turn (to Us)." (*A'araf: 172-174*)

Here no regular dialogues had taken place as is clear from the apparent sense of these verses, but this is a picture of the right-natured people showing how they are mindful of Allah, how they recognise Him, how they discover His Oneness and Greatness from the proofs scattered in the universe, and shun from all the conventional customs and habits which keep men away from this Lord, and which associate some one with Allah. This style of speech and writing is common in the Arabic language.

With honouring this Covenant, a man's faithfulness is the foundation of his respect and honour in this world and of success and glory in the next world.

It is an undue misgiving and fear from Allah that we should fulfil the covenant made with Him and still be apprehensive that some disaster would befall us

"Recall the favour which I bestowed on you, and fulfil your Covenant with Me; I will fulfil My Covenant with you, and fear none but Me."

The Prophet used to give these instructions to the tribes which came to him, while conveying the Message of Islam, and used to place before them only a few aspects in the beginning according to the intellectual and physical capacities of the people instead of giving them the complete teachings.

Auf bin Malik says that he was with the Prophet when there were about seven, or eight or nine persons present. He asked us:

"Will you not take a pledge on the hand of the Messenger of Allah ?" We stretched our hands and said : "We take a pledge on your hand, O Messenger of Allah!"

He said : "(Your pledge is) That you should worship Allah. Do not associate anybody with Him, and offer salat for five times and listen and obey." And he said in a low voice : "And do not ask for anything from the people."

> Auf bin Malik says : "I saw some of these persons who had taken pledge that when their hunter fell on the ground, they did not ask anybody to pick it up and give it to them." (*Muslim*)

How scrupulously the pledge is being observed and how severely and strictly it is being enforced ! There was no special significance of this pledge. Every group used to be instructed according to its nature and circumstances. The ruler used to be advised not to be cruel. The trader used to be instructed not to indulge in adulteration and deceit, and the employees were admonished against accepting bribes. Otherwise every Muslim is bound to follow the entire religion, all its tenets and principles, and he will be asked on the Day of Judgment about the entire Shariah. However, in the Islamic world there have appeared a few sects which take a pledge of a special kind. They should not be entertained. They are like quacks who pose as physicians. They administer spurious drugs and complicate the disease and endanger the life of their patient.

Islamic teachings cannot be divided and distributed. All of them must be followed, and their enforcement is necessary in every place at every time.

The ideal pledge : Allah's Messenger took a pledge from the Ansar that they will support this Message with their lives and properties, and try their utmost in protecting the Prophethood, till the time the Message is conveyed to the Arabs and the non-Arabs.

The Covenant entered into by the Ansar is considered as the most glorious pact in the annals of belief. In sincerity, selfless devotion and total submission to Truth, no other parallel can be found.

This covenant was completed in a glorious night of the season of Hajj. After this, people went their way and busied themselves in their affairs. But the people who had pledged their words busied themselves in fulfilling this historical covenant, and they accepted willingly all its demands and challenges.

In the Battle of Badr and in other battles of Islam against idolatry they shed their blood like water. The Prophet had great confidence in this covenant for the supremacy of the religion in times of difficulty and for raising the world of Allah. Accordingly when in the first assault in the Battle of Hunain Muslims were falling back, the Prophet did not look at the armies of the newcomer Muslims, but called his old faithfuls who had taken a pledge in the valley in the night of the season of Hajj, so that they may take the control of the situation.

Anas narrates that when the Battle of Hunain was fought, the tribes of Hawazan and Ghatfan participated in the fighting with their wealth, equipment and sons. The Prophet had an army of ten thousand men, which also included the indebted men at the time of victory of Mecca, but all left him. He was all alone.

At that time he gave a second call. He turned towards his right and called : "O People of Ansar !" They said : "We are present, O Messenger of Allah ! We are with you, rest assured." The Prophet was riding a grey mule. He got down from it and said "I am a slave of Allah and His Messenger."

The polytheists were defeated and much booty was collected by the Islamic army. The prophet distributed the booty among the newcomers who accepted Islam on the day Mecca was conquered and among the Muhajereen (refugees). He did not distribute anything among the Ansars. The Ansar were a little perturbed. They talked among themselves : when the situation was .critical we were called and when the booty came to hand it is distributed among others. When the Prophet came to know about this he gathered them and asked:

> "O People of Ansar! What news am I hearing from your side?" They remained silent. Then he said : "O People of Ansar! Do you not like that others should take away the worldly goods with them, and you

> should return with Muhammed (Pbuh) to your house."
> They answered : "Why not O Messenger of Allah ! We are pleased." The Prophet said : "If people walk in one valley and the Ansar in another valley, then I will walk in the valley of Ansar." (*Bukhari*)

The fact of the matter is that this great Message needed the sharpness of the swords of Ansar. They fulfilled their promise by sacrificing their lives and everything that they had. They did not have before them the ephemeral profits of this world, nor any temporary pleasures and advantages.

The policy of the Prophet in distributing the booty of the battle was based on the levels of their sincerity and faith. The Bedouin who became Muslims at a later stage were in need of financial help so that they might not be disheartened by the difficulties coming in their way as a consequence of embracing Islam. Therefore,the Prophet wanted to give them re-assurance and comfort, and because the Ansar were endowed with full faith and unshaking belief, the Prophet left them to their condition.

In such conditions the Prophet has said

> "I give some things to a man so that he may not (on account of his bad deeds) be thrown into hell by Allah, although there are other persons more dear to me."
> (*Bukhari*)

Forgetting breach of promise : The praiseworthy quality of the fulfilling of promise also demands that a man should always remember his past, so that he may take a lesson from it for his present and future. If he was a poor man and Allah has made him rich, or he was a sick man and now Allah has made him healthy, then it is not proper for him to erect a strong wall between his past and present and should not think that he was never poor nor was he ever healthy, and should not build up his present on the basis of this pride. Such a behaviour is open ingratitude and immoral.

This is a breach of promise which leads man to disruption. Many times such a man gets away from the blessings of Allah, and after this he does not get the guidance and inclination to come under the shadow of this blessing.

It is said that in Medina a man, known as Sa'alba, went to the locality of Ansar, and keeping them as witness declared that if Allah blessed him with favour, he would pay the dues of every rightful claimant, would give money do charity and would show kindness to his relatives. Incidlentally his cousin died and he inherited all his property. He however did not fulfil his promise nor did he care for 'what he had declared. Thereupon Allah revealed the following verses:

> "Amongst them are men who made a Covenant with Allah, that if he bestowed on them of His bounty they would give (largely) in charity, and be truly-amongst those who are righteous. But when He did bestow of His botany, they became covetous, and turned back (from their covenant), averse (from its fulfilment). He has put as a consequence hypocrisy into their hearts, (to last) till the day whereon they shall meet Him ; because they broke their Covenant with Allah, and because they lied (again and again). Do they not know that Allah does know their secret (thoughts) and their secret counsels, and that Allah knows well all things unseen ?" (*Tauba : 75-78*)

The worst example of breach of promise, ingrartitude and disloyalty is that tale of Bani Israel which Hazrat Abu Huraira has quoted from the sayings of the Propyet. The Prophet has said:

There were three persons in Bani Israel, a leper, a bald man and a blind man. Allah wanted to test them. He sent an angel to every one of them. The angel who went to the leper asked him what he coveted most. He replied : "Fair complexion, beautiful skin and a cure for my disease, for which I am hated by the people." The angel touched his body with his hand and his leprosy was removed and he became the owner of a fair complexion and a beautiful skin. The angel again asked him : "What thing you like most?" He said: "Camel." The angel gave him a pregnant she-camel and prayed: "May Allah increase this property of yours."

Then he went to the blind man and asked him what he coveted most. He replied : "May Allah give me back my sight." The angel touched his eyes and his sight was restored. He asked for the second time as to what thing he liked most. He replied : "A goat." The angel gave him a pregnant goat.

Then he went to the bald man and asked him what thing he liked most. The bald man replied : "Beautiful hair, and my ugliness be removed as people run away from me." The angel touched him and his disease was cured and he had a tuft of beautiful hair. Then he asked him what thing he liked most. He answered "A cow." The angel gave him a pregnant cow and prayed to Allah to give him prosperity.

All the three animals gave birth to their offshoots. Their numbers increased. One had a flock of camels, the second one had a large number of cows and the third one became the owner of many goats.

Then the angel appeared before the leper in the form of a man and said : "I am a poor man. All my relatives have been separated from me in the journeys and now my only support is Allah and through Him you. I request you in the name of the Being who gave you fair complexion and a beautiful skin, to give me a camel. Will yon help me in this journey of mine ?" He replied that there is an abundance of rights. The angel said: "I recognise you. Were you not suffering from leprosy and people were hating you ? Were you not needy and Allah gave you lot of property?"

He replied : "No. This property I received from my father and grandfather in inheritance." The angel said: "If you are a liar, then may Allah return you to your old condition."

In the same form he went to the bald man and talked to him in the same manner. He also gave the same reply which the first one had given. The angel then gave a curse and said that if he was a liar then may Allah return him to his old condition.

Then he went to the blind man and talked to him in the same manner, and begged for a goat to be given to him. The blind man said : "I was really a blind

> man, but Allah restored my sight. You may take away whatever you like and leave whatever you want to leave. By God, I cannot enter into any dispute with you about a thing which I have taken by Allah's pleasure." The angel told him to keep his things with him. The purpose was merely to test them. Allah was pleased with him and his two companions became the victims of His wrath. (*Bukhari*)

In trade, business, and other financial and economic matters an atmosphere of confidence can be created only when the fulfilment of promise is considered a duty.

It is necessary that the written conditions should conform to the limits of the Shariah, otherwise there would be no sanctity in them, and a Muslim will not be bound to honour them.

Islam has given extra consideration to the marriage contract. Allah's Messenger has said: "Among the conditions which you mutually agree upon, the most deserving of fulfilment is the contract by which you make the private parts halal (permissible) for yourselves."

For this reason it is not lawful for a husband to manipulate a single dirham that rightfully belongs to his wife, or to consider the bond with which he is tied as unimportant.

> It is mentioned in the hadith : "If a man has married a woman for a small or a big dower (mehr) and in his heart he has the intention of not paying that dower, then he has deceived her. If he dies and he has not paid her right, they on the Day of Judgment he will be presented before Allah as a rapist. And a man who has borrowed money from another man while he did not have the intention of repaying the debt, then he has deceived him, and consequently he defrauded him. If he dies in this condition, without paying back his debt, then he will meet Allah as a thief." (*Tibrani*)

There is nothing surprising about this, as there are a number of Quranic verses which insist on fulfilling the promises and warn against indulging in disloyalty and breach of promises:

And fulfil your promise. Verily, you will be answerable for your promises." (*Isra : 34*)

"And fulfil the covenant of Allah when you have entered into it, and break not your oaths after you have confirmed them; Indeed you have made Allah your surety; for Allah knows all that you do." (*Nahl: 91*)

Allah clarifies that breach of promises and disloyalty destroy confidence, create disorder and disruption, cut relationships, reduce power and make individuals weak and low:

"And be not like a woman who breaks Into untwisted strands the yarn which she has spun, after it has become strong. Nor take your oaths to practise deception between yourselves, lest one party should be more numerous than another : for Allah will test you by this; and on the Day of Judgment He will certainly make clear to you (the truth of) that wherein you disagree." (*Nahl: 91*)

Many times a man enters into a contract, but breaks it in the greed of more profit elsewhere. Or one nation makes an agreement with another nation, but the greed of better advantages and other considerations compel her to break the agreement. The religion considers it highly objectionable that for the sake of a temporary benefit virtuousness be trampled, and deception and trickery should enter in the dealings among men. Islam makes it compulsory for an individual as well as a group to be honest, decent and sincere, so that in all the conditions of poverty and richness, and victory and defeat the covenants be safeguarded.

That is why after giving a command to honour the covenanta, Quran says

"And take root your oaths to practise deception between yourselves, with the result that someone's foot may slip after it was firmly planted; and you may have to taste the evil (consequences) of having hindered (men) from the path of Allah, and a mighty wrath descend on you. Nor sell the Covenant of Allah

> for a miserable price ; for with Allah is (a prize) far better for you, if you only knew." (*Nahl: 94-95*)

The entire humanity deserves : The promise given to everybody should be fulfilled, whether the other party is a Muslim or an infidel, for morality, greatness and righteousness cannot be cut into pieces, that some people are treated with meanness and others are treated decently.

The fulfilment of promise and covenant depends on truth and straight dealing. As long as it is bound on righteousness, it should be fulfilled in relation to every individual and at every time.

In connection with the covenants with non-Muslims the Prophet is reported to have said that if in the time of Islam he were invited to enter into such a contract, he would gladly accept the offer.

A'mar bin Al-Hamaq says that he has heard theMesaenger of Allah as saying : "If a man gave shelter to a man for life, and subsequently killed him, then I have no connection with the killer, even if the murdered person be an infidel."(Ibn Habban)

This statement of the Prophet shows how Islam treats even those who have not accepted it as their religion. On the other hand the behaviour of the Jews is worth noting. They do not like to fulfil their promises with others. They do not consider it a good thing to treat others justly and decently. They consider themselves 'Allah's son and His favourite'. Their belief is that Allah has reserved his blessing and shelter for the Jewish race only. As against this, have a look at the Islamic teachings. It makes complete arrangements for safeguarding all those whose responsibility it has assumed, and with whom it has entered into a covenant. Quran addresses the Mulims and speaks about the infidels thus:

> "O you who believe ! violate not the sanctity of the symbols of Allah, nor of the sacred month, nor of the animals brought for sacrifice, nor the garlands that mark out such animals, nor the people resorting to the sacred house, seeking of the bounty and good

> pleasure of their Lord. But when you are clear of the sacred precincts and of pilgrim garb, you may hunt, and let not the hatred of some people in (once) shutting you out of the sacred mosque lead you to transgression (and hostility on your part). Help one another in righteousness and piety and do not help one another in sin and rancour." (*Maida : 3*)

It is remarkable now beautifully the viewpoint of the non-believers and their beliefs have been stated. Although they are idolaters, yet they have been mentioned as seekers of Allah's pleasure and blessings, and Muslims, however powerful they may become, they have been asked to cooperate with one another in the acts of righteousness and piety and not to help one another in the acts of sin and rancour.

At another place we have taken a survey of the covenants between Muslims and Non-Muslims and the revealed teachings of Allah in this connection. (Refers to a book in Arabic by the author)

Re-payment of debt necessary : One of the things on which Islam has insisted most and has considered it very important is the re-payment of loan. With Allah, right behaviour in this respect is more important than attending to other rights. Islam has ended all the misgivings and avarice and greed which make the debtor their victim, as a result of which he tries to find excuses to avoid re-payment or finally does not re-pay.

In this connection Islam has advised that a loan should be taken only in inevitable circumstances. To try to borrow money in a matter where it is avoidable is a very dangerous thing, and it should be avoided. In one hadith it is mentioned that it is one of those sins for which retribution is necessary.

> "When a borrower dies, he will be subjected to retribution on the Day of Judgment. However, in three cases it is permitted : first when a man loses his strength fighting in the cause of Allah and borrows in order to prepare to fight against his and Allah's enemies, secondly when a man near whom a Muslim

> has died and he borrows to meet the expenses of his funeral, and third the man who is afraid that he would remain unmarried and to safe guard his religion he borrows to meet the expenses of marriage. Allah will pardon them on the Day of Judgment." (*Ibne Maja*)

In another tradition it is stated that Allah's Messenger has said:

"On the Day of Judgment Allah will call the borrower and he will be made to stand before Him. Then he will be asked: "O son of Adam ! For what purpose did you take the loan? And why did you waste the rights of others ?" He will reply : "O our Lord ! You know that I had borrowed, but I did not eat it, nor drank, nor wasted it, but sometimes an accident of" fire occurred, sometimes there was a theft or it was lost, or a loss was incurred." Allah will say :

> "O My slave! I You have told the truth. I have more right to re-pay it." Allah will call for some acts of virtue and will weigh them in a balance, and his acts of virtue will be heavier than his evil acts, and he will enter the Paradise with the favour of his Lord."
>
> (*Ahmed*)

This shows that Allah will accept the excuses of those who were compelled to borrow being forced by the circumstances, and were unable to repay it on account of various genuine difficulties.

But there are men who are the slaves of their carnal desires and pleasures, and whose own wealth is not sufficient to meet the demands of their desires ; they at once rush to borrow money, regardless of the consequences. They do not care to be free of the burden of loan. Such a person according to the hadith is a shameless thief.

> Allah's Messenger has said: "He who takes others' property (as a loan) with intention of repaying it, (then is unable to re-pay) then Allah repays his loan. And he who takes a loan with the intention of not re-paying it, then Allah wilt destroy and ruin him." (*Bukhari*)

Islam wants that the loans should be given different kinds of guarantees, so that they may be considered live properties, and their re-payment should become definite and essential, and nobody should be able to escape re-paying this due, committed to writing, although performance of other acts of worship earns great rewards.

Abu Qatada says that one person asked:

> "O Messenger of Allah ! If I am killed in the cause of Allah, will all my sins be pardoned ?" He replied : "Yes, if you are killed, and if you are patient, thankful and seeker of Allah's pleasure, if you remain in the front ranks and attack the enemy and do not retreat." Then the Prophet asked him what did he say. The person repeated his question and the Prophet replied : "Your sins will be pardoned, but your loan will not be pardoned. Just now Jibrail has informed me about this." (*Muslim*)

Since the wise people knew how the debt falls as a lightning on a Muslim's honour and his earnings for the Hereafter, they used to advise people to get themselves free from all debts before putting their lives in danger.

> It is narrated through Abu Darda that while proceeding for a jihad, the Prophet used to stop at a junction of the streets and shout to the soldiers "O people ! If anybody has to re-pay a debt. and if he feels that he would die in the battle and the debt would not be re-paid, then he should return. He need not come after me, because this thing will not be enough to save him from hell." (*Razin*)

Today the Muslims have made borrowing and lending an amusement. To satisfy their hunger and the sexual desires they take loan, and they indulge into paying interests to the Jews and the Christians, which Allah has totally prohibited as haram. As a result of this they have become aliens in their own land, and they are deprived of their properties and are wandering helplessly.

Re-payment of loan is very difficult.

How many rights would have been trampled, if there were no fear of the law enforcement !

Allah likes those of His slaves who fulfil their convenats, and after destroying a number of townships has stated about them:

> "We did not find most of them true to their covenant' and most of them We found rebellious and disobedient. (*A'araf:102*)

How many rights would have been trampled, if there were no fear of the law enforcement!

Allah likes those of His slaves who fulfil their covenants, and after destroying a number of townships has stated about them:

> "We did not find most of them true to their covenant and most of them We found rebellious and disobedient. (A'raf:102)

SIX

Tolerance

"Patience is a light." (*Muslim*)

In the intricate paths of life when difficulties and hardships confront a man, and the darkness of adversities and suffering becomes long, it is patience only that acts like a light for a Muslim, that keeps him safe from wandering here and there, and saves him from the muddy mire of disappointment, desperation and frustration. Patience is such a basic quality that a Muslim needs it to shape his life in this world and in the next. On this basis only he should attend to all his work. He should make it a torchlight for guiding his way, else be will be defeated in the field of life. He should prepare his self to tolerate the hardships and difficulties, and should not holler or raise hell. He should not sit waiting for the results, however late that may take. He should not run away from responsibilities, whatever they may be. No doubts and misgivings, no hardship of trouble should prompt his intellect to indulge in violence. He should have plenty of self-confidence. He should not be frightened by the dark clouds appearing on the horizon of life, even if they may be appearing continually, nay, he should be fully sure that these clouds of adversities and hardships will disappear, and the clear and bright atmosphere of success and glory wilt appear again. Therefore, the demand of wisdom and far-sightedness is that its coming should be awaited with patience, peace and conviction.

The Almighty God has stressed this point sufficiently that no man can escape tests and trials, so that man may be alert and ready at the time when these hardships and difficulties descend on him, and he should not be frightened by these heavenly and earthly tribulations, and need not be disappointed and disheartened.

"And verily We shall try you till We know those of you who strive hard (in the cause of Allah) and the steadfast, and will We test your record."

(Muhammed: 31)

The poet has expressed the same idea in these words .

"We had anticipated the hardships of the night before their coming. So when they descended, there was no addition to our knowledge."

Undoubtedly if accidents and debacles are faced with a clear sight and full preparations, it will prove advantageous for man and this will help in stabilising and consolidating his position.

Patience Realities

Patience relies on two important realities.

The first reality is concerned with the nature of this worldly life. Its details are : Allah has not made this world a house of peace and satisfaction or of rewards and recompense, but He has made it a house of trials. The time that a man spends in this world is really a time for unending experiences. He comes out of one trial in order to undergo another trial which is harder and different from the one through which he has already passed, that is man is tested once by one thing and again by its opposite, as iron is first heated in the fire and then it is put in the water. Similarly man is tested by favourable as well as opposing means.

When Allah blessed Hazrat Sulaiman with a grand and magnificent empire, he knew about these natural laws of the world. He had said:

"This is of the bounty of my Lord, that He may try me whether I give thanks or am ungrateful. Whoever gives thanks, he only gives thanks for (the good of) his own soul; and whoever is ungrateful (is ungrateful only to his own soul's hurt). For surely, my Lord is Absolute in independence, Bountiful." (*Nahl: 40*)

The causes of trial through sadness and hardships are vague and unfixed. However, we can understand them properly by the example of the soldiers fighting in the battle-field. In the battlefield some groups are made to fight till they have to lose their valuable lives, so that the lives of other groups may be saved. The security of other sections is dependent on the remaining groups being made to fight in new battles. This strategy is followed in the wider interest of the country and for greater advantages, by the great leadership of the army. In this fighting the life of a man has no importance, because the problem is much wider.

Same is the position of luck or fate. A certain man is put to different kinds of trials, till he falls down defeated, as there is no other way for him, except that he should greet the hardship that has arrived with patience and submission. Since this life is a testing ground, we should strive hard for success in it.

What is the trial or examination of life ? It is not words that they can be written, or talks to which attention may be paid. The questions of the examination are these hardships and difficulties which confront a man, and which open before him the path of fright, terror, and frustration. Examination is the name of the anti-reality defects which prompt a man to be jealous and nourisher of rancour against his sincere friend ; examination is the name of the tyrannies for which a nation occupies the place of god and the other people offer their blood as sacrifice for retrieving their usurped rights.

The history of life on this earth from the first day till today is very sorrowful. The right thing is that man should himself make his own way in this life, and he should be sure that the way to his destination is full of thorns and filth.

The second reality is concerned with the nature and temperament of faith.

Faith is the name of the relationship between man and his Lord.

As in the relationship of men, the true friendship and sincerity can only be judged when it is confronted with unfavourable and bitter conditions, when they have to deal with the hardships brought about by the vagaries of time, and when they are surrounded by various kinds of problems. At such a time a man's real worth and sincerity is known. Exactly similar is the case of faith. To find out the truth and sincerity about faith it is necessary that a Muslim be tried, he should be put in the crucible of fire to see whether he comes out glowing like the gold or whether he will he burnt away with the impurities.

Undoubtedly, Allah's knowledge covers all manifest and concealed matters, and from this examination there will be no addition to His knowledge, because He knows all the conditions from the beginning till the end. The Divine knowledge cannot be made a basis for man's reckoning. His reckoning will be on the basis of his own personal deeds. If some criminals deny their crimes, then on the Day of Judgment in what way proof can be brought against them except by putting them to trial in this world and man's own parts of the body may give evidence against him?

About such people Quran has to say this :

> "And on the Day We gather them together: We shall say to (hose who ascribed partners (to Allah). Where are (now) those partners of your makebelieve ? Then they will have no contention except that they will say : By Allah, our Lord, we never were idolaters. See how they lie against themselves, and (how) the thing which they devised has failed them !"
>
> *(Al-An'am : 22-24)*

How can the reckoning of such criminals be taken in the light of the Divine knowledge ? Their justifiable retribution will be proper only when all their misdeeds are placed before them. Their efforts and striving to create corruption and mischief among others and all their misdeeds will be repeated before them.

On these two bases the foundation of patience has been kept. And for this reason religion demands it, but he who shuts his eyes from realities by force of his nature is dumbfounded when he has to face hardships and his hands and feet become inactive when he has to fight difficulties. His rashness dislikes waiting and patience and he is unable to tolerate it. Therefore, when anything untoward happens, or he has to suffer some kind of failure, or when he meets with an accident, the earth with all its great vastness becomes narrow for him, and the conditions become exasperating for him. He wants to come out of these conditions in the twinkling of an eye, but it is obvious that in this effort he will not be successful for it is against the temperament of the world and the religion. It is proper for a Muslim to earn to be patient and to wait and to wait for long.

> "Man is made of haste. I shall show you my aim, but ask Me not to hasten." (*Al-Ambiya.* 37)

It is written in a *hadith:*

> "He who will adopt the policy of patience, Allah will give him patience, and no man has been given a greater and better gift than patience." (*Bukhari*)

Patience is the sign of manliness : Patience is a symbol of greatness, glory and perfection. It is a means of security against the environmental conditions and losses. That is why 'Sabur' is one of the beautiful names of Allah, because He gives respite to His sinning slaves and does not hasten to punish them. If they are quick in committing crimes, he enforces his destined decisions and verdicts in centuries. He gives respite to people for a longtime. He does not catch them immediately on their wrong action:

> "And they will bid you hasten on the doom, and Allah fails not His promise, and surely, a day with Allah is as a thousand years of what you reckon." (*Hajj: 47*)

Patience is included in the factors of manliness, heroism, bravery and courage, because the burden of life cannot be borne by the owners of weak and puny bodies. When a man has a heavy load, and he wants it to be carried from one place to another, he does not employ for the purpose of infants, sick persons or cowards, but he engages such persons as have strong shoulders and powerful arms. Same is the case of life. The burden of this great responsibility can be lifted and it can be shifted from one place to another place by only that person who is lion-hearted and is a mountain of patience and determination.

For this reason the leaders, rulers and the great men of the nation have to face hardships and troubles in accordance with their capabilities and qualities.

Allah's Messenger was asked: Which people have to face the hardest trial. He replied:

> "The Prophets, and then the people of the lower rank, and then lower and still lower. People are tested in accordance with their religiousness. The man whose relationship with the religion will be strong and firm, his trial will be hard. And the man whose religiousness will be weak, his trial will also be lenient. A man's test goes on till he is successful in his tests and then he walks on the ground and there is then no sin on him." (*Ibn Habban*)

The fall in the achievements of the people on account of tiredness, hard labour, harassment and hardship is really in proportion to their power of endurance, patience and forbearance.

The knowledge of this secret of greatness and success compelled an American leader to remark : "Do not pray to God to make your burden light, but pray to Him to make your back strong." If the burden is light, and the hands are empty and there is no fear of any danger, then infants also can do a lot of things. But the busy schedule of life, sorrow and harassment in connection with duties, bitterness of the fighting, the hardship and tiredness of striving are the conduct of the fighters and builders of life. The man who sits in his house, how can he be affected by the dirt and dust of the road ? How can the soldier running away from the battle-field taste the difficulties of carrying heavy weapons and the pangs of fighting ? But those who are participating in the battle of life, and are bearing its hardships, they will have to face difficulties, they will receive wounds, and they will have to experience extreme fatigue and hard labour.

Because of this Islam has honoured those who have been involved in the trials and tribulations of the worldly problems, and it has comforted the tired and fatigued people, in order that they may get relief in their sorrow and their burden of adversities may be lightened.

> "A Momin is like a soft and delicate plant, which is moved by the wind. Sometimes it bends it and

> sometimes it raises it up, till he completes his span of life. But the example of an infidel is like that of a hard plant, whose roots are not deep. One blow of the wind uproots it." (*Muslim*)

A Momin who is striving in the field of life is subjected to various difficulties and hardships, but he who is helpless and weak, and who has run away from the battle-field, how can he suffer? This is the meaning of the following sayings of the Prophet:

> "Whom Allah wants to bless with virtue, He inflicts on him wound." (*Bukhari*)

> "If Allah likes a nation, He puts them to trial.
>
> With whom He is pleased, for that (nation) His pleasure is sufficient, and with whom He is displeased, for that His displeasure becomes a cause of suffering." (*Tirmizi*)

A man who fights with the hardships of life, some times he defeats them and many times he is defeated by them. The value of such a man before Allah is much higher than the man who sees the fun from a distance, neither he has to fear any danger nor is any other thing afraid of him.

The reward that the patient and hard-working fighters in the field of life will get on the Day of Judgment, the prizes and the honours that they will receive, will be much more than what the other persons who were performing other compulsory duties (worships) will be getting.

> "People who were in comfort and ease will wish on the Day of Judgment, when they would see the reward and honours received by those who were successful in the trials, that would it that there skins were cut by the scissors and they would also have got the same reward that day." (*Tirmizi*)

To invite adversities is against the faith : It is a strange thing that some people have, from these Islamic teachings, misunderstood that Islam honours adversities and hardships, invites difficulties and sorrows and wishes for them, because these things become the cause of giving honour and mutual brotherhood.

This is a great misunderstanding. Anas bin Malik narrates

> "The Prophet saw an old man walking with the support of his two daughters. He asked him 'What is the matter?' The people informed him that that man has taken a pledge that he would walk on foot. The Prophet said : 'Allah is unconcerned with the act of subjecting oneself to hardships.' He ordered him to take a mount." (*Bukhari*)

Ibn Abbas says that the sister of Uqba took a pledge to go for Hajj on foot, and Uqba related this to the Prophet and complained that she is not fit to walk on foot. The Prophet said:

> 'Allah is unconcerned with your sister's walking on foot, she should take a mount, and for kaffara (atonement) she should give the sacrifice of an animal." (*Abu Daud*)

Allah has said:

> "What concern has Allah for your punishment if you are thankful (for His mercies) and believe (in Him) ? Allah was ever Responsive. Aware." (*An-Nisa : 147*)

Islam praises people who are in difficulties and who are subjected to trials, so that they may get encouragement, and their faith and belief may be increased. When it talks of difficulties and diseases, it means that these are the question papers of the examination and they should be solved with strength, patience and equanimity, and one should not fall a prey to laziness, and weakness and should not complain of the fate fixed by Allah, as beautifully put by an Urdu poet:

> "Why is there no storm in your waves?
>
> Why is your self not Muslim?
>
> Your complaint of the fate fixed by Yazdan is useless,

Why you yourself are not the fate fixed by Yazdan?" 1t is mentioned in a tradition that the Prophet went to see a sick woman, and found her cursing her sickness and reproaching her fever. He dissapproved of this act of hers and spoke to her in a sympathetic way:

> "This fever removes the faults of the sons of Adam, as the oven removes the dirt and impurities of the iron."
>
> (*Muslim*)

Then, does it mean that we should rear germs of the diseases and give them as gifts to our relatives and friends ? There are some people who think like this and went to explain like this ! This is sheer madness and senselessness!

During war time man gets dirtied with dust and mud, and sometimes he is confronted with distressing troubles, but every hardship that befalls a man in the battle of life raises his rank and takes him nearer to God, if his faith is strong and not wavering.

It is extreme foolishness if one thinks that when a man is troubled by an unending series of sufferings then he is forgotten by Allah and he has been deprived of Allah's blessings. It is a pity in the time of our decline and disruption this idea has spread far and wide, although we have shown earlier that adversities and hardships come in proportion to man's determination and will to fight.

Allah's Messenger has said

> "Undoubtedly, that decent man whose father, grandfather and great grandfather are decent, is Yusuf bin Yaqoob bin Ishaque bin Ibrahim (B.P.U.T.)."
>
> (*Bukhari*)

Yusuf is such a Prophet as was brought up in the lap of Prophets, and he belonged to a noble and decent family. By selecting him for Prophethood, Allah has put a seal of confirmation on his chastity and decency. Have a glance at this noble man, how he passed through the early stages of his life. He is brought out from one difficulty to be put in another difficulty. His mother passes away during his childhood. Then his brothers conspire against him, and throw him into a well to deprive him of the love of his father. A passing caravan takes him out from the well and makes him a slave. Then he is sold for a paltry sum in the market of slaves. He is bought by the King of Egypt. Only after a few days since his coming to the palace, he is made a victim of trickery, deception and waywardness. He comes out chaste and innocent out of this trial. But inspite of his being innocent he is sent to jail with some unlucky persons. Not for a few days, nor for a few months, but for years he has to remain in the prison.

Any other man would have found these hardships unbearable and a sufficient cause to curse his fate, but no, the true believer remained firm like a tower of light, and carried on his task of inviting people to believe in the unity of Allah and conveying the ignorant and illiterate people His message.

> "O my two fellow-prisoners! Are diverse lords better or Allah, the One, the Almighty ? Those whom you worship beside Him are but names which you have named, you and your fathers. Allah has revealed no sanction for them. The decision rests with Allah only, Who has commanded you to worship none save Him. This is the right religion, but most men know not."
>
> *(Joseph, 39-40)*

Really great and talented people have such character. If the charms of the world are taken away from them, they do not care and their sincerity in their belief does not suffer. If any adversity befalls them or they suffer an accident, they do not feel disgraced in their own eyes. A poet who strives for greatness and honour of the world also invites the difficulties and hardships and says very proudly:

"Decent and purified selves have to become a target of the world's dust and dirt. If they keep away from sorrows, then how can they achieve nobility and glory."

From the lives of the Prophets, Siddiqueen, martyrs, and our righteous forefathers we learn that honoured people and persons of high reputation can only be those men who can bear the hardships and carry the burden.

Allah's Messenger has said:

> "For the slave high position is written from Allah, but through his deeds he cannot reach there when Allah

> puts him to test in respect of his body, wealth and children. Then he is successful in that trial and he reaches that high position, which was written for him by the sanction of Allah." (*Ahmed*)

In other words the series of difficulties and adversities that confront a man is the proof that the paths of goodness and prosperity are being made ready for him, and his position is being raised. Sometimes the difficulties come so that a faithful man should get himself totally entangled in the material world, should not feel proud over abundance and may not be under the influence of the deception of the world for a long time. A number of disadvantageous things become advantageous and a number of stages of the trial prove to be the gates of blessings.

A Natural Habit

Patience, steadfastness, waiting and consistency is the law of nature. On sowing seeds sprouts do not appear immediately, and when they come they are not immediately ripe for cutting. It requires a waiting of months. In the mother's womb the embryo remains for months and then it takes proper shape. Allah has informed us that He created this universe in six days, although He could have accomplished this task in the twinkling of an eye. The passage of morning and evening and the rotation of day and night mark man's growth, their development and bring maturity in their conciousness. And they return to their Lord:

> "As He brought you into being, so return you (to Him). He has guided a group aright, and waywardness has taken hold of another group." (*Al-A'araj: 29-30*)

Time is the raiment of every kind of action and inaction of life. If we do not display patience and steadfastness, it can blast us in the fire of our impetuosity. We cannot also change the temperament — inherent attributes — of things, that are moving according to the pre-determined destiny.

There is a necessity for every type of patience : There are many varieties of patience. One is that patience which manifests itself as steadfastness in obedience. Another variety is the name of keeping away from trouble, and to stand firmly in adversities and display courage in difficulties is also a kind of patience.

The basis of the first kind of patience, that is to be steadfast in obedience is the performance of the basic items of Islamic worship correctly, and for remaining constant on it requires patience and perseverence.

For example, salat (prayer) is a worship and compulsory duty of life which is required to be performed repeatedly. About this Allah says:

> "And enjoin upon your people prayers, and be constant therein." (*Taha : 132*)

In the holy Quran the mention of exhorting one another to patience is made with the mention of exhorting one another to truth. The Almighty Allah has sworn that the human welfare is equally dependent on both these:

> "By the Time. Indeed, man is in the state of loss, except those who believe and do good deeds, and exhort one another to truth and exhort one another to patience." (*Al-Asr : 1-3*)

Opposed to the sins, it is only patience and steadfastness which counter the pleasures and temptations which glamorize the crimes.

Allah's Messenger has said:

> "Paradise has been surrounded by the unliked things, while the hell is surrounded by carnal desires." (*Muslim*)

To invite undesirable and unliked things and to keep away from carnal desires is a quality which can be found in an epitome of patience only. Here patience is generated as the outcome of an unshaken belief and the desire for seeking the pleasure of Allah. And this is the soul of purity and chastity which saves a true believer from the tricks of the evil and snares of the mean things.

> "O our Lord! Vouchsafe to steadfastness and make us die as men who have surrendered (to You)." (*Al-A'raf : 126*)

Here a true believer has to show patience when his life, property, family and position receive any harm, and if he is hurt, he has to be patient. It is inevitable that a man should pass through one of these stages. Pitiable is that life which does not get a taste of these waves of storm. If he is not subjected to these storms, he cannot be prepared to face dangers squarely.

But when a Muslim goes under the shelter of Allah and seeks His help, then the weapons of accidents and calamities become blunt and useless, and they do not leave any effect on his body. Many times their irrevocable faith and unshaken belief make the assault of calamaties futile, as the anaesthesia at the time of surgery makes the patient unaware of the pain. A Muslim cannot be separated from the favours and blessings of Allah until his belief is shaken on account of the onslaught of the calamities, and his faith is weakened in adversity:

> "And surely We will test you with something of fear and hunger and loss of wealth and lives and fruits ; but give glad tidings to those who persevere patiently ; who say when a misfortune strikes them 'Surely to Allah we belong and to Him: shall we return.' These are the persons on whom are the blessings and mercy from their Lord and they are the people who are rightly guided." (*Al-Baqarah : 155-157*)

Ummul-u'la narrates that she was called by the Prophet when she was sick, and said

> "O Ummul U'la ! Be happy that a Muslim's sickness removes his faults, as fire cleans the dirt of iron and silver." (*Abu Daud*)

It is written in a hadith:

> "When a faithful slave's dearest person in this world is snatched away from him, and he displays patience and seeks Allah's pleasure, then Allah does not agree to give him anything less than paradise in compensation.' (*Nisai*)

We should not forget the fact that the things with which we establish our relations, and on which we claim our rights, are things which have a stronger relationship with Allah and He has prior and greater rights on them. What can be a dearer thing for a man than his son ? The son is the dearest of all his relations. He is part of his blood and flesh. He grows in his lap and is cared for by him. And when death snatches him away from the father, the world becomes dark for him and he cannot help weeping.

But in spite of all this sorrow and sadness, truth compels us to say that while the father has been separated from the son, the real king has called back his slave. The Being who had given sight to the eyes has taken away the sight.

When the father says : "My son," the real Creator says : "No, this is my slave and My right is first on him prior to that of others."

Qasim bin Muhammed says that when one of his wives died, Muhammed bin Ka'ab al-Qarzi came to give him condolences. He narrated an incident. There was in Bani Israil a learned and a pious man. He had a wife whom he loved very much. She suddenly died. This accident so much affected him that he closed the doors of his house and went on mourning her death inside his house. Nobody could go to him. A woman of Bani Israil came to know of this and she said that she wanted to ask him something, which is not possible without meeting him, and she stationed herself at his door. At last the learned man was informed of this and gave her permission to see him. "I have come to ask your opinion about a problem. " He inquired what was the problem. She said : "I have borrowed some ornaments from a neighbouring woman, and I have been using them for a long period. After a long period she has demanded her ornaments. Should I return them to her ?" The learned man said : "Undoubtedly, by God there is no other way than this."

> The woman said: "But they had been with me for a very long time." The learned man said : "Even then it is more proper to return them." Then the woman stated : "May Allah have mercy on you. Are you sorry for a thing which Allah had given you as a loan, and then He has taken it away, though He had greater claim on it ?" The learned man understood the point and this wisdom of the woman benefited him. (*Malik*)

SEVEN

Brotherhood

There are no reasonable causes which induce men to be divided into different groups and sects. Truth, Rightness and Nature demand that all humans should be kind towards each other and should live in the society formed on the basis of love and brotherhood, to let the roses of love and peace bloom on this earth. Allah has connected all the racial relations to Adam and Eve in order that these teachings may become more strong and firm:

> O Mankind! Verily, We have created you from man and woman, and have made you nations and tribes that you may know one another. Surely, the noblest of you, in the sight of Allah, is the best in conduct. Verily, Allah is Knower, Aware. (*Hujurat : 13*)

Mutual introduction — not hatred and repulsion — is the only foundation of human relationship. But such obstructions come which do not allow mere introduction to do its work. The explosion of human populatior in search of work, crowding, clashes, differences in understanding the truth and deciding on what is good, create mutual fractions and this leads to quarrels and wars. But on account of these bad conditions the main purpose of man's creation and the original objective of populating this earth should not be lost sight of.

Every method and co-ordination which make this introduction strong and firm should be supported. It should be strengthened. Its characteristics should be utilised. Islam is not only a co-ordination that brings together a lot of people, but it is also based on those realities which create the best relationship between humans and their Lord and among the humans themselves.

Therefore, it is necessary that the believers in Islam and the bearers of this Message should be fully aware of its importance and greatness, by means of which Allah has expanded their bosom. They should adopt on its basis the mutual introduction, the love and the brotherhood with the respect which is their sue. This mutual introduction revives the common relationship of the human individuals which had been dead, and it makes it strong. In this way this pure religion provides the foundation for a strong brotherhood, by which all the followers of Islam; in the East and West get united, and inspite of the differences of the time and space such unity and oneness is created among them that even the strongest storms cannot remove it.

This brotherhood is the soul of the living faith and the essence of the delicate feelings which a Muslim has in his heart for his other brethren, and it reaches such a stage that his life is reserved for others and the lives of others are sacrificed for him, as if they are the different branches of the same tree, or the same soul that is running in different bodies.

Cooperation

When selfishness rules over a man then it devours all its goodness and nourishes wickedness in him. It confines him to a very limited circle, where he does not see anybody else except his own self. He is happy or sad only when his own interest is involved. He has concern with the surrounding environment or the world where lakhs of people like him are residing only if he has any expectation of receiving profit from them or if he is afraid of receiving any harm or losses.

Islam has remedied this tyrannical selfishness by the justice-bearing brotherhood. It has taught men that the life is not his own alone, and merely his own welfare and benefit is meaningless. He should know that like him many other men also reside there. If he remembers his rights and privileges on others, then he should also remember what are others' rights and privileges on him. Therefore, man should keep away from selfishness and profit-making. If he is conscious of his presence or existence then he should also be conscious of the existence of others. Instead of indulging in excess and intemperance he should try to be balanced and moderate.

The right of another Muslim brother on you is that you should dislike his losses and try to remove their cause. If he is in difficulty then you should try to share it in equal measure. You should feel his difficulty and trouble. But if your feelings are not stirred, if you do the circumstances, you think that your being anxious for him is useless, then this is meanness. And this kind of thinking has no concern with that love and brotherhood, which becomes a part of Muslims' temperament and nature, and which make them moan with pain on every adversity that falls on their other brethren. Allah's Messenger has said:

> The mutual love, kindness and graciousness of the Muslims is like a body, when some of its part is in pain then all the other parts of the body become a victim of fever and sleeplessness. (*Bukhari*)

True sympathy will spur you to find out what are the difficulties and the needs of your brethren ; and do not rest till you remove those difficulties and needs. If you are successful in this then your face glows and your conscience is satisfied.

The Prophet has said:

> "A Muslim is a brother of another Muslim. He should neither oppress him nor should he usurp his right. He who provides for the needs of his brother, Allah will help him. And he who removes one difficulty of a Muslim brother, Allah will remove his one difficulty on the Day of Judgment, and he who covers the defect of a Muslim brother, then on the Day of Judgment Allah will cover his defect." (*Muslim*)

The sign of true brotherhood is that you should desire the benefit of your brother and you should be glad to see him benefited as you would have been glad to be benefited yourself. If such a quality has been developed in you, then with the best obedience you will be near to Allah and you will be deserving of the best reward from Him.

Hazrat Ibn Abbas (S.A.W.) says that he was confined within the four corners of the mosque in E'tikaf (meditation), when a man came to him. He saluted him and sat down. Ibn Abbas said to him that he looked worried and inquired what was the matter. The man replied "Yes, O cousin of Allah's Prophet ! 1 have to pay the right of a certain man's friendship, by the Owner of this grave, I have no means to pay it."

Ibn Abbas (S.A.W.) said:

> "May I talk to you in this connection ?" He replied that if he wished to be mighty. The narrator says that Hazrat Ibn Abbas put on his shoes and came out of the mosque. The man reminded that he was sitting in E'tikaf. Ibn Abbas (S.A.W.) replied : "No, (I have not forgotten). But I have heard from the owner of this grave, and many days have not passed — tears came to Ibn Abbas's eyes — he says: 'he who walked for the need of his brother and satisfied his need, then this act is better for him than ten years' E'tikaf, and he who performed one day's E'tikaf for Allah's pleasure then Allah will place three trenches between him and the hell, and whose distance will be more than the distance between the East and West'."
>
> (*Baihaqi*)

This *hadith* shows what importance Islam has given to the relationship of love and brotherhood, and how important it has considered the welfare and public service, which every society needs for safeguarding its foundations.

Hazrat Ibn Abbas (R.A.A.) left *E'tikaf,* although it is a special kind of worship, for which there is a great reward from Allah, because E'tikaf is the name of being totally immersed in prayers, fasting, recitation and meditation, and then he was in the Masjid-i-Nabavi (Mosque of the Prophet) where the reward is much more than in the other mosques, and inspite of all this Hazrat Ibn Abbas (R.A.A.) left E'tikaf for a Muslim. This was the teaching that he received from the holy Prophet (S.A.W.)

Be helpful : The Problems of the world are very complicated and intricate. Adversities confront all men, as the rains, when they fall, make all the dry and moist regions wet. A man cannot fight these adversities for a long time single-handed, if he does not know that his brothers and friends will rush to his help and will relieve him of the present difficulties. For this reason it is said that if man is alone he is without any position, and if he has supporters and friends then none has a position better than his.

Brotherhood demands that every Muslim should keep alive the feeling that his brethren, friends and associates will be with him in his good and bad conditions, in the field of life only his strength is not in operation, but that the strength of all the Muslims is with him.

Allah's Messenger (S.A.W.) has said:

> A Momin has the position of a structure for another Momin, whose one part supplies strength to the other part. (*Bukhari*)

From here pure brotherhood becomes a double-edged blessing. Not only the unity of spirit and faith is available, but material benefits also follow for the Muslims.

Allah has repeatedly mentioned of this blessing in a single verse:

> And remember Allah's favour to you; how you were enemies and He made friendship between your hearts so that you became as brothers by His grace.
> (*Al-i-Imran : 103*)

This brotherhood of religion makes it a duty for every Muslim to co-operate with other Muslims. It is not a cooperation of blind prejudices but a co-operation among the virtuous faithfuls to prove that truth is truth, and to destroy falsehood, to stop the hand of the tryant and to help the oppressed. It is not proper and permissible to leave a Muslim alone, if he has entered a campaign. He should be helped in every way. If he is on the wrong path, then it is necessary to bring him to the right path. If he is conceited and proud, then his false pride is to be broken. If he is being attacked, he is to be defended. If his life and property have been placed in danger by his enemies, then he is to be helped in his fight. This is the meaning of the assistance and co-operation which Islam has declared as compulsory (Farz).

> The Prophet (S.A.W.) has said : Help your brother, whether he is an oppressor or the oppressed." Some one said that if he is an oppressed person the help to be given to him can be understood, but how can an oppresor be helped ? He replied : "Prevent him from oppressing, this is his assistance." (*Bukhari*)

To leave a Muslim helpless and isolated is a very mean act. If this happens it amounts to leaving all the Muslims helpless, because from such an act the courage and the sense of shame receive a great setback, and the oppressed person submits to the oppression willingly or unwillingly. Then the brotherhood among those who left him helpless vanishes.

The Muslims were disgraced individually and also entire nations were subjected to such an unfortunate fate, when their relationship of the Islamic brotherhood weakened. They began looking at each other as strangers and they disliked each other, and when they heard about the misfortunes of their brethren they merely raised their shoulders and did not care, as if it were none of their concern.

This despised habit of the Muslims threw them into the pit of disgrace and dishonour, although Islam has very strongly opposed this wicked habit, and it has cursed and reproached those persons who sacrifice their community for their personal benefits.

Allah's Messenger (S.A.W.) has said:

> None of you should ever stand quiet when before him an oppressed person is being beaten. That man receives Allah's curses who is present when the act of oppression is being performed and does not defend the oppressed. (*Tibrani*)

When you see a brother of yours being badly treated or being subjected to disgrace or dishonour, prepare yourself for his help, and assist him till you achieve what is right and the oppression is terminated.

> In a *hadith* it is stated : "He who accompanied the oppressed till he got him his right, then Allah will make his steps firm on the 'Pul Sirat' when all steps will be slipping." (*Asbahani*)

This responsibility increases when you hold some important position in the society or when people look at your office with love and fear. As zakat is taken out of wealth and property, similarly it is taken out of the position and office also. If Allah has blessed you with leadership in the land or you have some power or influence, it is not for your getting puffed up with pride, but this position has been granted to you by Allah so that through you all those needs may be met which cannot be met through other sources. If you helped in meeting the needs of the individuals then you have fulfilled your duty and you have earned sawab (reward), otherwise you have rejected this favour of Allah and caused it to be wasted.

Allah's Messenger (S.A.W.) has said:

> "Allah has blessed certain persons with his favours (high office), which are connected with the needs of the Muslims. He keeps them with those favours until the general public feel harassed by them. But when the persons of high position become unbearable for the people, then Allah transfers these favours to others." (*Tibrani*)

The use of power and influence to give benefit to the people and to save them from harm should be within the circle of sincerity and purity. But if he does this virtuous act in the hope of receiving some present or compensation, then he loses his reward from Allah, and this forbidden earning destroys all his deeds.

Allah's Messenger has said:

> "Whoever recommended the case of persons and in compensation he is given a gift and he accepted it then he entered a big gate of the major sins." (*Abu Daud*)

Conditions of brotherhood : There are many evils which Islam has vehemently opposed because they were against the etiquette and conditions of brotherhood.

Those principles, which bring back the persons who cross their limits to their original place and push forward those who remain behind and make them stand in the same line, are really in the true spirit of brotherhood. If there arises some difference and it becomes a dispute and a quarrel, then the rules of brotherhood should be made the deciding factor and they should be enforced:

> "The believers are nothing else than brothers. Therefore, take peace between your brethren and observe your duty to Allah that you may obtain mercy." (*Hujurat : 10*)

The dear Prophet of Allah (S.A.W.) has, in a very lengthy *hadith* warned about all the evils, though apparently appearing ordinary, that corrode the hearts and dries the spring of love and compassion:

> "Keep away from undue misgiving, because misgiving is the biggest lie. And do not be inquisitive, and do not be over-curious and prying. Do not indulge in competitions. Do not be jealous of one another. Do not hate each other. Do not be enemies of one another, become slaves of Allah, brethren, as He has commanded you. A Muslim is the brother of another Muslim. He should not oppress him (his brother), should not leave him isolated, should not think him mean, it is enough to be wicked if he considers another Muslim mean. The property, blood and honour of a Muslim is haram for another Muslim. Allah will not see your faces, and your bodies, but He will see your deeds. (Pointing towards breast), Allah's fear is here, Allah's fear is here. Beware, none of you should purchase a thing over the purchase of the other, resulting in the other person's loss. And be Allah's slaves, brethren among yourselves, and it is not permissible for any Muslim that he should keep his

> relationship with another Muslim severed for more than three days." (*Muslim*)

That society where the seeds of love and brotherhood among men are sown on the basis of the love of God, where the symbols of Islam are safeguarded and are watched, in such a society the spiritual brotherhood takes the place of racial brotherhood, and many times this relationship of faith proves to be more strong and firm than the relationship of blood.

The fact is that sincere brotherhood was that foundation oil which for the first time the Muslim society was formed, under whose shadow the Islamic government was brought into existence, and it raised the banner of Islam's supremacy ; and keeping this basic quality before him the Messenger of Allah founded an Ummah that resisted the onslaught of the hostile idolworshippers and all the cryptic enemies simultaneously, and became successful after a protracted conflict, when its enemies were vanquished and destroyed.

Things are recognised by their opposites. In the present time we are seeing how the Jews have gathered around their false purpose and tried to establish their government. They ran away from the East and the West and gathered in the holy land. They left their native places. They kicked at their wealth and property and leaving behind all the remembrances came and settled in Palestine. This awakening under a wrong belief and false ideal reminds us of that magnificent awakening which had taken place fourteen centuries ago, when Muslims were collecting in Yathrib from all corners of the country. They had left their native places and homes so that the first Muslim Government might be established in Medina.

The Muslim citizens of Medina embraced these refugees. They established mutual brotherly relations on the basis of sincere love, sacrifice, equality of race and birth, exchange of love and respect, propagation of truth, holiness and virtue, liking and adopting of the righteous ideal and its propagation. Allah has praised them thus:

> But those who, before them, had homes (in Medina) and had adopted the faith, show their affection to

> such as came to them for refuge, and entertain no desire in their hearts for things given to the (latter), but give them preference over themselves even though poverty was their (own lot). *(Al Hashr : 9)*

Allah's Prophet (S.A.W.) has said:

> "It is not permissible for a Muslim that he should frighten any Muslim." *(Abu Daud)*

Another *hadith* has it:

> "Whoever looked at a Muslim in such a way that it frightened him, then Allah will frighten him on the Doomsday." *(Tibrani)*

The thing, from which there is a fear of any Muslim receiving some harm, or any act, which is likely to be an aggression on a Muslim, is the worst crime, then what will be the consequences of directly harming the Muslims and subjecting them to aggression and oppression ?

Allah's Messenger (S.A.W.) has said:

> "Whoever points towards his brother with iron, the angels send their curses on him till he stops it, even if he is his real brother." *(Muslim)*

On account of these commands and orders, the spirit of brotherhood has spread the scent and fragrance of peace and security, comfort and satisfaction in the Islamic society.

To make this brotherhood lasting, Islam has declared pride as haram, because the people who have a feeling in their hearts that they are the children of the same father and the followers of the same religion cannot be hostile towards each other in their worldly dealings, and those who know that greatness and honour is obtained by fearing Allah and truly worshipping Him, and that this fear of Allah is found in the hearts, and the secrets of hearts are known to Allah only such persons cannot indulge in false pride and conceit.

The Prophet (S.A.W.) has said:

"Allah has sent down revelation to me that you should adopt humbleness to such an extent that none should oppress anybody and should not indulge in undue pride. (*Abu Daud*)

Islam has warned those persons who follow the path of Satan, and for Supremacy they behave coneceitedly. It has been explained that on the Doomsday the proud people will be squeezed, and they will be made small in the proportion in which they showed their greatness, so much so that they will be reduced to dust that will stick to the shoes.

In the *hadith* it is written:

On the Doomsday these proud people will be raised like the particles of dust in the form of men, everywhere they will be treated with disrespect." (*Tirmizi*)

Insulting and making fun of others damages the relationship of brotherhood. To consider others inferior and to make fun of them is immoral, pure ignorance and the product of worst negligence, for the right of the weak is that his difficulties should be shared, and the weak and bewildered man, should be guided and not made fun of. When any person is confronted with some adversity or he has some defect then it is far from a Muslim that he should make him a target of his objections and criticism.

O you who believe ! Let not a folk deride a folk who may be better than they are, nor let women (deride) women, who may be better than they are. (*Hujurat : 11*)

Hasan says : "For deriders in the Hereafter one gate of the Paradise will be opened, and he will be asked to come. He will go with his difficulty and sadness, and when he will reach the gate, it will be closed. Then the second gate will be opened and he will be called. When he will reach the gate with his difficulty and sorrow, it will also be closed. This will continue till one of them before whom one gate of the Paradise will be opened and he will not come near it on account of disappointment." (*Baihaqi*)

This is the recompense of the deriders and funmakers, as if on the basis of tit for tat they will be reproached and cursed, they will be disdained, and they will be derided and made fun of on account of their past deeds.

Avoid pride : In order to demolish the artificial wall of the security and distinction of the common brotherhood, Islam has declared the blood of all people equally honourable. It has given them equal rights and privileges, and convinced the masses and the classes that to be proud of one's race and birth is wrong, for all are sons of Adam, and Adam was created from dust. Here a person can achieve greater importance compared to his fellow-being only if he has put in more labour and strived more. One who has not done a great deed cannot be made great by the greatness of his forefathers, even if they were the kings of their time.

> Hazrat Abu Huraira (S.A.W.) narrates that Allah's Messenger (S.A.W.) has said: "On the Doomsday a caller will announce by the command of Allah : Listen, I had created only one lineage and you formed other lineages ; I had made those of you who were righteous the most noble, but you went on saying that this is the son of that person, but today I will make high my lineage and the lineages formed by you will be lowered." (*Baihaqi*)

The command of Allah is:

> Then when the trumpet is blown, there will be no more relationships between them that day, nor will one ask after another. Then those whose balance (of good deeds) is heavy,they will attain salvation ; but those whose balance is light, will be those who have lost their souls ; in Hell will they abide.
>
> (*Muminoon : 101-103*)

It is very strange that among the Arabs the disease of feeling superiority on account of birth, lineage and family and national pride increased to such an extent that the Islamic teachings were left behind. In the past and the present the causes of the majority of our defeats are these family and national demarcations.

Similarly Islam demolished all the idols of country, nation, and family to strengthen the relationship of love and brotherhood, and attacked the family conflict and alien prejudices.

It is quite natural that a man should love his country and his nation, but how can this thing be the cause of negligence towards God and indifference towards His creatures ?

Allah's Messenger (S.A.W.) has said:

> "The person who defends his family is the best among you, provided he does not commit sin." (*Abu Daud*)
>
> The Prophet (S.A.W.) was asked what was prejudice. He replied : "That you should help your nation in her aggression." (*Abu Daud*)

The meaning of Islamic Brotherhood is that there should be sincerity and unselfishness for Islam. There should be an urge to follow its path. There should be a determination and strength to work on its command, and that its spirit should rule over all the relationships, general and particular. In every difficulty that confronts one its principles should be consulted, and no attention should be paid to its opposition, other assistance and co-operation.

Unity in Diversity

It is incumbent upon a Muslim to observe the commands and rules of Islam because he is an indivisible part of the existence of the Ummah. He is a part that is attached to the whole body. Separated from the body, it has no existence. He, willingly or unwillingly, takes his share,from the food that is supplied to the body, from its development and nourishment and its consciousness and awareness.

The Divine revelation has admitted this position of the individual. It has not given the command of ordering the performance of the righteous act and preventing the commitment of the forbidden act to an individual, but it has entrusted this duty of guidance to the whole group, of which the individual is a part. He is to perform this duty being the part of the Ummah. The meaning of the commands of the holy Quran and the Sunnah, with reference to the context, appears to be only this:

> O you who believe ! Bow down and prostrate yourselves, and worship your Lord. and do good, that you may prosper, and strive for Allah with the endeavour which is His right. (*Hajj: 77*)

When a Muslim stands before Allah, meekly and submissively prays, cries and pleads, this worship of his is not performed in seclusion, away from his brethren, but that he prays on behalf of the whole society in this way:

> We worship only You and ask for help only from You. (*Fatiha* : 4)

It should be noted that here the pronoun we is used and not I. Here it is not said that I worship only You and I ask for help only from You.

Then the slave prays to his Lord for giving him guidance and favours ; it is not for himself alone, but he asks for all the people:

> Show us the straight path, the path of those whom You have favoured. (*Fatiha* : 6, 7)

The Almighty God has not created humans so that they may be divided among themselves and should create differences. He has sent down one religion for all the people. All the Prophets that came to this earth, in the different parts of the world, invited the people to only one religion. From the very first day, Allah has forbidden that people should cut the religion into pieces and should divide themselves in various sects.

But having been misled by the satanic tricks, humans forgot this warning, and expressed their disregard for the divine heritage. They divided into various sects and each sect fought the other.

The fact of the matter is that when learning is from morality, and when it has no relation also, then such a learning becomes a matter for the man of learning himself and also for all people. Before Islam, ignorance caused men to different valleys, but when Islam came and of hypocrites and cryptic believers made Islam a means of their trade for their benefits and profits, this Ummah went to the and.

Allah's Messenger (S.A.W.) said:

> "For you I fear the excesses of that hypocrite who will be a glib talker." (*Bazzar*)

It is true, the wayward heart makes knowledge the corruption and mischief. In the olden and modern times humanity has suffered considerably from dangerous learning. Allah has mentioned this reality that those learned men whose knowledge does not descent lower than the tongue and does not find a place in the heart have caused considerable harm to humanity:

> The same religion has Ile established for you as that which He enjoined on Noah-the which We have sent by inspiration to you-and that which We enjoined on Abraham, Moses and Jesus; namely that you should remain steadfast in religion, and make no divisions therein. To those who worship other things than Allah, hard is the (way) to which you call them. Allah chooses to Himself those whom He pleases, and guides to Himself those who turn (to Him). (*Shura : 73*)

After that He said:

> And they became divided only after knowledge reached them, —through selfish envy as between themselves. (*Shura : 14*)

At another place, He has said:

> But only those people differed therein who were given the Book after clear teachings came to them out of spite among themselves. (*Baqarah : 273*)

When knowledge loses sincerity and becomes devoid of softness and love for the people, then how destructive it becomes ! How it tears the hearts and makes the sects quarrel among themselves. And it cuts all those relationships for joining which Allah had given command.

To have differences of opinion and to differ is not a novel thing, but this cannot be made the cause of mutual hatred and enmity. Enmity is generated when there are other factors also with that. The difference of views and ideas is used in an illegal way for personal aggrandisement.

If intentions are honest in debates and discussions, and if the parties are free from the selfish desires for achieving supremacy, fame, chairmanship and victory over others, then all those disputes can be decided which had filled our past history with tragedies and sorry spectacles.

We have seen with our own eyes that if to the differences political interests are attached, then the ordinary thing has been enlarged to mountainous proportions, and if the differences were merely of ideas, then even big problems are treated as minor things, and inspite of the differences of opinions no troubles occur.

> "As for those who divide their religion and break it into sects, you have no part in them in the least ; their affair is with Allah ; He will in the end tell them the truth of all that they did." (*Al-An'am : 159*)

Allah has warned Muslims that they should not be divided into sects like the people in the past in interpreting the religion, and they should not act against each other:

> Be not like those who are divided amongst themselves and fall into disputations after receiving clear signs ; for them is a dreadful penalty, on the Day when some faces will be (lit up with) white, and some faces will be (in the gloom of) black ; to those whose faces will be black, (will be said) : "Did you reject Faith after accepting it ? Taste then the Penalty for rejecting Faith. But to those whose faces will be (lit with) white, they will be in (the light of) Allah's mercy; therein to dwell (for ever)." (*Al-i-Imran : 105-107*)

The harmony of the heart and the feelings, and the unity of the objectives and the methods are the clear teachings of Islam, and making friends with the sincere Muslims has been declared as compulsory. Undoubtedly the Ummah can survive only with the unity in ranks, of identity and the kalima ; its rule can become everlasting and its message can achieve success. If the statement of Oneness of Allah is the gate of Islam, then the unity of thought and idea is the secret of its survival and progress, and also the foremost guarantee of meeting the holy Lord with bright faces.

Social Responsibility

According to the appearances, when a man performs a certain act alone, his reward is different, and when he performs the same act in company of others, then his reward *(sawab)* is quite different.

Take the two rakat prayer of the *fajr* or the four rakat of the *Zuhar* prayer, a man may say them alone or in the congregation, there is no difference in their preparation or performance, but the reward of the latter (congregational) prayer has been said to be twenty or twenty-two times more.

In reality it is an inducement that man should give up seclusion and aloofness and should live with the group. He should give up his aloofness and mix up with the society. In the sight of Islam it is very objectionable that a man should revolve round his own thoughts and ideas, and should be concerned with only his own loss and profit, cut off from the interests and concerns of the group and the group-life.

In the *hadith* it is stated:

> "There are three qualities against which there should be no rancour in the heart of a Muslim sincerity, well-wishing of the Muslims, and collectivism, because whoever will have these qualities, his prayer will be for the welfare of all individuals. (*Bazzar*)

In order to keep a Muslim attached with the Society, Allah has made five-times prayers with the congregation compulsory for a Muslim, induced Muslims to offer prayers in congregation, and for avoiding congregational prayers purposely they have been warned of punishments. Then the individuals of small villages and tubes have been enjoined to offer congregational prayers every week on Fridays. Then greater congregations have been fixed for the two Eids, which are to be offered outside the cities in the open, and in view of the social and religious advantages, all the individuals, even the women in menstruation, have been asked to gather in the *Eidgaahs*.

Then the programme of gathering all the Muslims from the East and the West in a magnificent gathering, by making Hajj compulsory on the eligible rich people, and its fixed place and time has been indicated, so that the different kinds of people, belonging to various races may make Hajj collectively.

Allah's messenger always warned against living alone and being cut off from the society. He always urged on having company while on journeys or staying at home.

Saeed bin Musayyab says that the Prophet (S.A.W.) has said:

> "Satan goes after one or two individuals, but when there are three persons, he is unable to harass them." (*Malik*)

Once Allah's Messenger found that when the caravan camped at a place, the people scattered around with a view to more comfort, as if they had no connection. The Prophet (S.A.W.) did not like this and disapproved of it.

Abu Sa'alba has narrated that when the people camped, they used to settle in different parts of the valley. Allah's Messenger said

> "This scattering of yours is a trick of Satan." After these instructions of the Prophet, when people stopped for resting, they used to remain near and hug each other, in such a way that if a big cloth were spread over them it could cover them. (*Abu Daud*)

This was the best example of the harmony of the feelings, exchange of love and compassion and unity in the ranks.

Good Manners

If people do not stick to truth, falsehood disrupts them. 1f the slaves of Rehman do not unite, the agents of Satan divide them into insignificant pieces. And if the eternal blessing of the Hereafter does not attract them towards itself, and if the spirit of collectivism is not roused in them, then they quarrel for small things. Therefore, it is said that fighting and war, hatred and hostility are the characteristics of the dark, non-Islamic (jahiliyah) days, or are the destiny of the unfaithful.

The Prophet (S.A.W.) has said:

> "After my death, do not adopt the course of action of the infidels and fighting among yourselves." (*Tirmizi*)

The clear meaning of this is that these bloody wars are the fate of the infidels, who are divided in various groups.

Islam has allowed differences of opinion and thinking, provided there is a sincerity for finding out the truth, and an urge to recognise what is right and to act on it.

The Prophet (S.A.W.) has said:

> "If the ruler takes a decision by himself, and it is a right decision then he is eligible to get double reward, but if his decision is wrong, then he deserves single reward." (*Bukhari*)

You can see that to the result of thinking and contemplation Allah's favour and blessing is attached, as it is attached to the intentions of welfare and virtue. Then why does the human mind think these affairs to be narrow when Allah's religion has made it wide? And why this series of mutual hatred and hostility, and oppression and tyranny?

When the Prophet commanded the *Mujahedeen* going out of Medina to offer the prayer of Asr in *Bani Quraiza,* some companions thought that he meant that if there were no fear of losing time, the prayer should be offered after reaching there. Accordingly, when they saw in the way that the time of Asr was running out, they offered the prayer in the way. As against this, the other group took the apparent meaning of his command, and they offered the prayer late *(qaza)* after reaching there. The Prophet (S.A.W.) acccepted the interpretation of both the groups and organised them in a single group against the enemy.

The same is the spirit of Islam in differences in academic matters, when it is not possible to avoid them and when the intentions of the intellect and conscience are sincere and the path is right. But if the purpose of the differences is of obtaining some material gains and to feed the flames of rancour and hatred, then the world is lost and first of all religion is done.

A learned man of religion was told that it is feared that in a certain mosque the worshippers might clash. He asked what was the matter. He was told that some worshippers want to offer eight rakat of Tarawih prayer while others think that twenty rakat are according to Sunnah (Masnoor). He asked them then what should be the answer ? They replied that they were waiting for his fatwa (opinion).

The learned man of the religion said that the fatwa is that the mosque should be closed, and no tarawih prayers be offered in that mosque, for tarawih is nafil (voluntary) prayer, and the unity of Muslims is compulsory *(Farz),* and for a nafil, farz cannot be given up in this kind of affairs, the noise and tumultous behaviour has nothing to do with sincerity and welfare.

To save the Ummah from the destructive effects of this kind of differences, the Ulema, with the help of the Islamic teachings, have given this fatwa (decision) that if there is a fear of a greater mischief *(fitna)* raising its head on performing the *farz* of preventing commitment of the forbidden thing (nahi and munkar), then this *farz* is not compulsory, because this forbidden thing is an evil, but the adverse outcome of this movement would be worse than this evil, and therefore the lesser evil will have to be tolerated. We know that the doctor performs a surgical operation only when the patient's body is able to bear it. When he finds that the sick person's body is not able to bear it, he does not operate, even if the disease continues.

The Prophet used to take the pledge from the Ansar that they will adopt the policy of listening, obeying and sacrificing in all conditions of paucity and plenty, happiness and anger.

It means that a righteous man should not be worried if he does not get enough material gains. If according to the decision of Allah he does not get high position, or plenty of wealth and property he should not grumble loudly and cry openly, for this kind of ugly manifestation of anger against the world is the habit of the hypocrites, about whom Allah has said :

> And of them is he who defames you in the matter of the alms. If they are given thereof they are content,

> and if they are not given thereof, behold they are enraged. (*Tauba: 58*)

If you study these divisiveness and groupism carefully, you will find that material love and blind selfishness are the real causes of these differences. Strength is in unity only. This principle is not operative in the case of humans only, but this is also the rule of the universe. A feeble strand combined with other strands becomes a strong rope, and this world is also a combination of the united particles.

A wise man wanted to teach his sons this wisdom, he called for a bundle of sticks and asked them to break the bundle. All of them combined together could not break it. Then he opened the bundle and gave each one of them a single stick, and in this way all the sticks were broken.

Mutual differences make a strong and big nations also weak, and drives the weak nations to the valley of total destruction. Therefore when the Muslims were successful in the Battle of Badr, .Allah gave them the first advice of having unity in their ranks.

When voices were raised on the distribution of the booty, Allah revealed the following verses:

> They ask you of the spoils of war. Say: The spoils of war belong to Allah and the messenger, so keep your duty to Allah, and adjust the matter of your difference, and obey Allah and His messenger, if you are (true) believers. (*Al-Anfal: 46*)

Then He explained to them that unity in action and deeds is the path to success and victory:

> And obey Allah and His Messenger, and dispute not one with another lest you falter and your strength depart from you. (*Al-Anfal : 46*)

And then warned them that in their greed and love for the world they should not adopt the course of action of those who do not expect any reward from Allah:

> And be not as those who came forth from their dwellings boastfully and to be seen of men, and debar (men) from the way of Allah. (*Al-Anfal* : 47)

Then in the battle of Uhad the Muslim received a great setback. Seventy great companions of the Prophet were martyred, and they had to face the disgrace of defeat and the taunts of the infidels. Why this happened, when their defensive passion was powerful enough to achieve victory? It happened because they differed among themselves and were guilty of disobeying Allah and His messenger:

> Allah verily made good His promise to you when you routed them by His leave, until (the moment) when your courage failed you, and you disagreed about the order and you disobeyed, after. He had shown you that for which you long. Some of you desired the world, and some of you desired the Hereafter. Therefore, He made you flee from there, that He might try you. (*Al-i-Imran* : 152)

At this critical turn of their history, if they would look at and take a survey of their conditions, the Muslims will see that the disgrace and frustration in which they have fallen today is on account of only one reason, and that is their rope (unity) has become loose and their aspirations are haphazard.

The assault of the cross in the modern times, and under its shadow the Zionist enemy have been able to raze the edifice of the Islamic community because they had distributed Muslims in different smaller nations and countries, among whom they were inciting hostility and rancour. To devour the East, the policy of the West has always been to divide and rule.

Islam is desirous of safeguarding its Ummah and of its survival, and therefore, it strikes at the roots of the differences with all the force at its command and considers it the responsibility of all the individuals of the Ummah that they should take it out of the mud of differences and hostilities, for "Allah's hand is over the Jamaat (group) and one who was separated from the society went to hell."

The enemies of Islam want that they should patronise a person who should be helpful to them and he should harm the entire community. There should be no wonder if such a man is rooted out of the society to save the entire society from his wicked deeds. Allah's Messenger has said:

> Various kinds of groups will be born. The person who would try to disrupt the affairs of this Ummah when it has been united, should be finished with the sword, whoever he may be. (*Muslim*)

The man who puts a spoke in the wheel of the unity in the Ummah comes under this command of Allah:

> And whosoever opposes the messenger and the guidance (of Allah) has been manifested to him, and follows other than the believer's way, We appoint for him that to which he himself has turned, and expose him to hell-a hapless journey's end. (*An-Nisa : 115*)

This warning should not astonish any one, because when the germs of difference generate, all those evils are created which push the Ummah into the pit of retrogression.

There are people who stick to their opinions at all costs for the whole life. When the signs of differences and disruption in the community become manifest, they sit silent, as if they are concerned with principles only, but the facts are different. That is why Allah's Messenger has said :

> "He who ran away from obedience and separated from the group, then he died, then he died a non-Islamic death." (*Bukhari*)

Another tradition has it:

> "He who advanced against our Ummah, beheaded the good and the bad, all people, did not care even for the true Muslims and broke his promise, then he has no connection with me nor have I concern with him." (*Muslim*)

It is the duty of the rich that they should give from their riches to the poor, and the well-to-do people should provide benefits to the Ummah. However learned, talented or wealthy a man may be, he cannot derive benefits from his accomplishments nor can he benefit others if he has the ambition of becoming the leader, because such a man is deprived of the grace of God. And the man who is deprived of the grace of God, is a failure and most unfortunate, even if he is a genius.

That is why Islam has deprived persons of high position and leadership, if they had the ambition of gaining leadership and high positions.

> Hazrat Abu Moosa (R.A.A.) narrates that he went in the presence of the Prophet, when two other persons from Banu Ami were also with him. One of them requested the Prophet (S.A.W.) : "O Messenger of Allah! (S.A.W.) Give me one of the responsibilities of the problems of which God has made you responsible." Similarly, the second man also requested the Prophet in the same way. The Prophet replied: "By God, we cannot entrust this work to a person who demands it or is greedy to get it." (*Bukhari*)

But the astonishing thing is this that what the principles of Islam had strictly forbidden, the same disease has sprung in the Ummah, and today individuals and families that are in love with leadership and supremacy, are continually breaking this principle.

If they have risen high on account of their leadership and power, then this thing cannot bring real progress and superiority, as explained by the Prophet (S.A.W.) . Then how can these bad-character people and the masters of the destinies of men can be considered deserving of these responsibilities?

Every Muslim must oppose such a deviation wherever he may see it, so that the unity of the Ummah may be strengthened.

EIGHT

Liberal Attitude

People react differently to the motivations and the occasions that generate feelings of sorrow and pain. Some people are provoked by ordinary things, and they become unmindful of every thing and in haste take a very unwise step. But there are also such persons as pass through various hardships and adversities and yet do not forget to behave with seriousness, wisely, with tolerance and good manners.

It is true that the original nature of a man and his natural temperament play a very big part in a man's being hot tempered or soft-hearted, serious or hasty, righteous or wicked. But there is a very deep relation between a man's selfconfidence and his solemn behaviour with others and in forgiving the errors of others. In reality, the more good-mannered and perfect a big man is, in the same proportion his heart will be big and the circle of his tolerance and forbearance will be wide. He will try to find the extenuating circumstances for the errors of others and will accept their apologies when offered. If anybody may attack him with the intention of injuring him, he will look at him as a philosopher looks at the children playing marbles on the roads, and will ignore him.

We have seen that anger makes a man mad. A man is disgraced in his own sight, when he feels that he has been put to great humiliation, and feels that this blot cannot be removed without shedding blood.

Can a man who has high moral character take such a step merely because he has to pass through sorrow and pain? Never. Those who indulge in inflicting insults on others are disgraced in their own eyes before insulting others.

This is what we understand from the tolerance and forbearance shown by Hud. He invited his nation to accept the belief of oneness of Allah. His nation greeted him with abuses, curses and accusations which he tolerated peacefully. The people of his nation said

> "Indeed, we see you in foolishness, and surely, we deem you of the liars. He said: 'O my people! There is no foolishness in me, but I am a messenger from the Lord of the Worlds. I convey to you the message of my Lord and am for you a true adviser'."
>
> (*Al-A'raf: 66-68*)

The abusing and the curses of the Nation of Hud did not provoke him, because there is a lot of difference between the two groups. On the one side is a man whom God has selected to be His Messenger. He is a representative of goodness and righteousness. On the other side are persons who are imbedded in ignorance and foolishness, and vying with each other in worshipping stones. On account of their foolishness they think that the stone idols are the masters of their destiny. How can a great teacher be disheartened by the misbehaviour of such a flock?

How Allah's Messenger imbibed the qualities of tolerance and forbearance to his companions can be understood from the following tradition, which shows the foolishness of an Arab and the love and serenity of the Prophet.

It is reported that a Bedouin came to the Prophet and asked for something, and the Prophet gave him something, and asked : "Did I treat you well ?" The Bedouin replied : "No, you have not treated me well." Hearing this, the Muslims got angry and advanced towards him. The Prophet made a sign to stop them. Then he got up and went to his house and gave him some more gift, and again asked : "Did I treat you well ?" He replied : "Yes, may Allah grant prosperity to your family." The Prophet said to him : "Whatever you have said to me, is alright in its place, but my companions are angry in regard to you, if you like you may repeat before them whatever you have said to me so that the anger from their heart may be removed." He said that it was agreeable to him. When the morning came, he came again, and the Prophet pointed towards him and said : "On what this Arab had said, I gave him something more, and now he says that he is happy and pleased. Is that so?" The Bedouin replied : "Yes, May Allah grant prosperity to your family."

Then Allah's Messenger said: "My example and that of this man is like that of a man whose she-camel has been lost and the people ran after her to catch her, but the animal was more startled; so that man told his companions : 'Leave me and my she-camel alone. I know her ways more and I can bring her to the right path.' Accordingly he lifted some grass from the ground in his two hands and showed it to the she-camel, it returned and sat near his feet. He tied the 'kajawa' on her back and rode her."

"If I were to leave you when he was using foul language, you would have killed him and he would have been sent to hell."

The kind Prophet was not provoked in the beginning from the misbehaviour of the Bedouin. He understood his nature and temperament, which was like that of the illiterates who are habituated to wild and foul language. If such people are summarily punished, then they will be destroyed and it would be unjust.

But the great reformers do not allow the errors of people reach such a sad end. They try to remove the ignorance and emotionalism of the people by their tolerance and forbearance, so persistently that they have to turn to rigorous things, and they become all praise for them.

The wisest of the wise intellectual and the wealthiest mad cannot reach his destination, however charitable and generous he may be. Of what use is that charity which meant for making people indebted to the giver ?

It is not unlikely that the Bedouin whose satisfaction was bought by giving him money might have become a wealthy man himself subsequently and he might have performed a great deed by giving his life willingly. In reality the wealth given by such great reformers is meant for such needy people, or in other words such a wealth is like the grass growing on the ground which is lifted in the hands and shown to the startled she-camel, and by means of it and by a little display of love the astray mounts are called near so that they may be used for travelling great distances.

The holy Prophet sometimes used to get angry, but he never crossed the limits of decency and the stage of pardon and forgiveness. How bright is this aspect of his character that he never took revenge for his own person, but he never hesitated in taking revenge from the man who violated the sanctity of Allah's laws.

Once when he was distributing the booty, one rough Bedouin insulted him by saying : "Deal with justice," because in the distribution of this booty only Allah's pleasure was sought. The Prophet did not say anything more than this : "Fie on you. If I will not deal justly then who else will ? If I did not do like this, then I failed, and I sustained a loss." With these words he gave an answer to his ignorance and also stopped his companions from killing the Bedouin, which they otherwise would have done.

Kindness and Patience

Once at the time of Asr (Middle prayer) in his speech to the people he said:

"Adam's sons have been created of different types. There are some who get angry late and very soon return to normal. Some people become wrathful soon and soon they return to normal, and some people become angry late and are also late in returning to normal, that is the return to normalcy is according to the speed of getting angry. Be careful. Some people get angry soon and they return to normal late. Listen, the best people among these are those who get angry late and immediately repent, and the worst among these are those who get angry soon, but are very late in coming to normal. Listen, among these there arc some who repay the loan in a better way, and also demand in a good way. Some people are lazy in repaying, but good in demanding. Some demand in a bad way and repay in a good way, i.e., they have one good quality and one bad quality. Some people prove to be bad in demanding and in repaying too. Listen carefully, the best among these are those who are good in demanding and also good in repaying, and the worst are those who are bad in both the things.

> "Keep in mind, anger becomes a spark in the heart of Adam's son. Do you not see that at the time of anger a man's eyes become red, and his nostrils become enlarged. If any one sees these sign in a man, he should be glued to the earth." (*Tirmizi*)

That is, he should sit in his place, he should not move so that the matter may not get worsened.

Because the flames of anger and wrath burn all matters. Intelligence and consciousness disappear from it, and man is imprisoned in the magic of passions. Then these affairs do not improve.

The above-quoted hadith explains the kinds of men and their achievements and value in greatness and morality. Wherever necessary, a faithful bends himself.

An angry man indulges into various kinds of foolishness. Sometimes he abuses the door if it does not open immediately for him. In his anger he breaks whatever machine or its part may be in his hand, and abuses the animal that is not brought under control.

> A man's sheet was flown away by the wind and he cursed it. Allah's Messenger said : "Do not curse it, because it is bound by the commands of God and it is under His control. He who curses a thing which did not deserve it then the curse returns on him." (*Tirmizi*)

There are many evils of anger, and their results are more devastating. It is therefore said that to keep the self in control at the time of anger is the proof of the praise-worthy power of control and the noble strength of toleration.

Ibn Masood has narrated that Allah's Messenger had asked:

> "Whom do you call a sandow ?" People replied : "One who is not knocked down by anybody is called a sandow among us." He said : "No, sandow is one who controls his self in his anger." (*Muslim*)

One man requested the Prophet: "Give me some advice, out not such a lengthy one that I may forget. The Prophet said : "Do not be angry."-(Malik). What reply could be better and shorter than this one?

Allah's Messenger always gave importance to the temperament and the environment of the individuals and groups in giving them instructions and training. He used to lengthen or shorten his speech according to the demands of the occasion.

The efforts which were made to remove the jahiliya had two foundations : One was ignorance against learning and the second against tolerance. The first ignorance he removed with the help of knowledge, understandding, sermons and advice, while the second was removed with the help of suppressing the rebellious desires and preventing mischief, etc. The Arabs of the pre-Islamic days were proud of their ignorance and wickedness. As an Arab Poet of the time says:

"Beware! None should show any ignorance and wickedness before us, else we will prove to be more ignorant and wicked than all"

When Islam came, it removed this intensity of feeling and emotionalism, and introduced the practice of pardon and forgiveness in the society. If one could not pardon, then one was given the command to act justly. This objective could be achieved only when anger and wrath could be kept under the control of the intellect.

There are a number of sayings in which the Prophet has given directions to the Arabs leading them to this ideal, so much so that the manifestations of tyranny, aggression, anger and wrath have been declared out of the circle of Islam. The things which unite a group and do not allow it to be disturbed, abuse, etc., has been declared to be the agent which breaks this unity:

> "Abusing a Muslim is wickedness, and his quarrelling and fighting is infidelity." (*Bukhari*)
>
> "When two Muslims meet, a curtain from Allah is hung between them. When one of the two says

> obscene things to the other he tears this curtain of Allah." (*Baihaqui*)

One Arab came to the Prophet to learn the teachings of Islam. Before this he had neither seen the Prophet nor did he know about his message. His name was Jabir bin Salim. He narrates : "I saw a man whose opinions are being copied by the people. If he says anything. people convey it to others. I asked them who this man was. They said that he is Allah's Messenger. I said to him : 'On you be peace (Alaik-as-Salam) O Messenger of Allah !' He said : `Do not salute like this. This is the salute of the dead ; but say Peace be on you (AsSalamu Alaik)'.

That Arab says : "I asked : 'Are you Allah's Messenger?' He replied : `I am the messenger of that Being whom you call in adversities, and he removes your adversities, and if famine catches you and you call Him, He grows grass for you; and if you lose your mount in the arid ground, then you call Him and He causes your mount to be returned to you."

> He says that I told him : "Advise me." The Prophet said: "Do not abuse anybody." Accordingly, thereafter I did not abuse any free man, slave, camel, goat. Then he said: 'Do not consider any virtue as mean, even if it is your brother's talking to you with a smile. This is also a virtuous act.' Then he said: 'If somebody reproaches you and makes you feel ashamed on any of your defects, do not make him feel ashamed on any of his defects, because this act of his will prove troublesome for him." (*Abu Daud*)

Rebuking and reproaching : There are also some people whose anger does not cool down. They are always in a turmoil, and this wrathfulness imprints a stamp of stone-heartedness and harshness on their face. If anybody clashes with them they spit fire like an oven. Anger, wrath, squeezing of the nostrils and reddening of the eyes, and then there starts a series of abusing and cursing. Islam is innocent of all these dirty qualities.

> Allah's Messenger has said: "A Momin does not taunt, does not curse and reproach, does not indulge in obscene talking and obscene acts." (*Tirmizi*)

Cursing and reproaching are the signs of meanness, and it is a quality of lowliness. Those who curse others far ordinary things, they put themselves to great ruin. It is the duty of a man that he should avoid this unseemly act, even if he is harmed considerably by his opponent.

As faith will be nourished in the heart, along with it will grow generosity, broad-mindedness, tolerance and forbearance, and there will grow hatred of anger for the usurpers of our rights and dislike for the desire for their destruction.

The Prophet was requested to invoke God's wrath against the polytheists and to curse them. He said:

> "I have been sent as a blessing (Rehmat). 1 have not been sent as a rebuker and reproacher." (*Muslim*)

A Muslim however much he would control his self, however much he would control his anger, would pardon others' errors, and however much would sympathise with others on their mistakes, in the same proportion his rank will be raised before Allah.

For this reason, the Prophet disapproved of Hazrat Abu Bakr when he cursed his slave, and said:

> "How can it be proper for a truthful man that he should rebuke and reproach." (*Muslim*)
>
> In another tradition it is mentioned that the Prophet has said: "It is not possible that you indulge in rebuking and reproaching and at the same time remain *siddique* (truthful) and straight." (*Hakim*)

Hazrat Abu Bakr, to atone for his error, freed his slave and went to the Prophet for apologising and said that he would not do such a thing again.

The reason for this is that rebuking and reproaching is such an evil as is more expressive of one's blind rage than the idea of punishing others. It is not at all proper to insult others by yelling at them.

> Allah's Messenger has said : "When a man curses somebody, then that curse rises up to the sky, but the the gates of the sky shut. Then it turns to the earth. Here also the gates are found shut. Therefore it wanders to the right and to the left, and if it does not find a proper place it goes to the man who was cursed. If he deserved well and good, otherwise it returns to the man who cursed." (*Abu Daud*)

Setting Scores

Islam has declared cursing and abusing, exchange of vulgar and obscene words and acts as haram (forbidden).

Many clashes occur in which people's honour is attacked and a series of exchange of accusations and fault-finding ensues. The reputation of the relatives, and the female folk of the household is damaged and attempts are made to rake up the dust of centuries. There is only one cause of all this dirty sinning, and that is man is overcome by anger and he washes his hands off all decency and good manners.

The entire responsibility for committing this low and mean type of sin goes to the head of the man who first put the spark to the combustible material. It is written in the hadith

> "The entire sin for mutual abusing and cursing will be on the man who first started it, except when the oppressed crosses the limit." (*Muslim*)

There is only one way of escaping these intense sins, and that is that tolerance and forbearance may be allowed to have an upper hand over anger and rage, and pardon and forgiveness may be allowed to rule over the passion of taking revenge.

There is no doubt that when a man's own personitv or that of his relative or friends is attacked and when he is made to suffer, and he has the means and sources for taking revenge, then he wants to avenge himself immediately and does not rest till he satisfies his passion for revenge.

Hardness be replied with softness : But in such cases another policy can be adopted which is much nobler and is liked by

Allah, which shows man's greatness and his regard for relationship and that is that he should control his anger, and should not indulge in abusing and cursing. He should restrain himself and should not be bent on taking revenge. He should consider the overlooking of the errors of the wrong-doers as a kind of gratitude to Allah, who has given him such a position that whenever he may want may take back his right.

Ibn Abbas narrates that when Ainia bin Hasn came, stayed in the house of his nephew Hur bin Qais, who was greatly respected by Hazrat Umar, because the readers of the Quran were the members of the Consultative Committee of Hazrat Umar, whether they were old or young.

The uncle asked the nephew to take him to the Amir-ul-Mumineen, Umar bin At-Khattab. Accordingly permission was sought, and when both of them went in the presence of Umar, he very harshly said to the Khalifa:

> "A pity on you, O son of Khattab! because you neither give us gifts nor do you deal with us justly." Hazrat Umar was enraged on this and wanted to punish him.
>
> The nephew, Hur, immediately intervened and said : "Amirul Mumineeen! Allah says to his Prophet : `Adopt the method of softness and forgiveness, advise for doing righteous deeds and do not clash with uneducated. This man is uneducated, he may be forgiven.'
>
> Accordingly, the Amir of the Faithfuls forgave him and did not deviate slightly from the teachings of those verses when it were recited before him and he was the true follower of the Book of Allah." (*Bukhari*)

Hazrat Umar was enraged because that Arab had come merely to provoke him. The idea of punishing him came to his mind because he had not gone there with the intention of giving right advice or reform. The only purpose of his going there was to rebuke the Amirul Mumineen and to receive rich gifts without working for them. But when he was told that the man was uneducated, he controlled his anger and allowed him to go scot free.

> It is written in a *hadith* : "He who controls his anger though he had the power to act on it, Allah will call him first of all on the Day of Judgment and will give him the authority to select whatever houri he likes."
> (*Abu Daud*)

Ibada bin Samit says that the Prophet has said:

> "May I not tell you those qualities for which Allah will give you tall buildings in the Paradise and He may raise your rank?" The people said: "Certainly, tell us O Messenger of Allah!" He said : "He who behaves with you in the manner of an uneducated person, you behave with him with tolerance, forgive the oppressors, and give to those who deprive you, and he who cuts away from you, try to join him."
> (*Tibrani*)

Quran has declared these decent habits and qualities as the path of welfare by which a man can enter the Paradise.

> "Be quick in the race for forgiveness from your Lord, and for a Paradise whose width is that (of the whole) of the heavens and of the earth, prepared for the righteous,-those who spend (freely) whether in prosperity or in adversity ; who restrain anger, and pardon (all) men ; for Allah loves those who do good."
> (*Al-i-Imran : 133-134*)

The excellent example : The way in which the Prophet ignored Abdullah bin Ubai, the leniency which he showed him, and the manner in which he overlooked his crimes, are instances whose example cannot be found in the entire human history. Abdullah bin Ubai was the worst enemy of the Muslims. He used to be always in search for finding out ways of inflicting injuries and damages to Muslims and he was in league with the devil against the Muslims. He never let slip any opportunity of harming Muslims, of defeating them and spreading a network of conspiracies against them. He cast aspersions on the chastity of the Mother of the Faithfuls, Hazrat Ayesha, and he incited some people to indulge in the whispering campaign against her and thus weaken the foundation of the Islamic society, as from the ancient times the eastern traditions had given a very high position of decency and nobility to women.

For this reason the Messenger of Allah and his dear companions were terribly distressed and were in great mental anguish. They were in a great dilemma on account of this blatant false accusation, till at last the verses of Surah Noor were revealed which refuted the charges of the hypocrites, vouchsafed the chastity and purity of Hazrat Ayesha and exposed the machinations of the enemies

> "Those who brought forward the lie are a body among yourselves ; think it not to be an evil to you ; on the contrary it is good for you ; to every man among them (will come the punishment) of the sin that he earned and to him who took on himself the lead among them, will be penalty grievous." (*Noor : 11*)

In this tragedy, those who had openly accused the Ummul Mumineen were punished, but the germ which had spread this disease was not touched, so that he might further go on with his nefarious activities of harming Muslims.

Allah blesses His Prophet and his armies with victory and glory. Islam refined the disorderly government of the centuries and reformed the corrupt society. The enemies of Islam were then found within the limits of the Islamic society. Abdullah bin Ubai was pining within himself till he fell ill and died, after leaving the bad and deadly odour of disruption behind him. His sons went to Prophet seeking his pardon for their father. He forgave him. Then the son requested for the Prophet's shirt for the shroud of his father. He gave it to them. Then they requested him to lead his funeral prayer and to pray for their father. The gracious Prophet did not refuse even this request of theirs. He stood up to pray for the salvation of the person who in the past had attacked his honour and reputation.

But Allah denied to grant all these concessions, and this verse was revealed

> "Whether you ask for their forgiveness or tot, (their sin is unforgivable); if you ask seventy times for their

> forgiveness, Allah will not forgive them ; because they have rejected Allah and His Prophet; and Allah guides not those who are perversely rebellions. (*Tauba : 80*)

In this tragic event of false accusation was also involved a near relative of Hazrat Abu Bakr, who was living on his help. This man did not hesitate to falsely muse the pure and chaste lady, whose father was giving him help and was sustaining him. He forgot the right of Islam, and did not care for the relationship, and tore to pieces the old custom. Hazrat Abu Bakr was deeply stirred and he swore that he would not give anything to this near relative of his and would not show any kindness to him as in the past. Thereupon the following command from Allah was revealed

> "Let not those among you who are endued with grace and amplitude of means resolve by oath against helping their kinsmen, those in want, and those who have left their homes in Allah's cause ; let them forgive and overlook; do you not wish that Allah should Forgive you ? For Allah is Oft-Forgiving, Most Merciful." (*Noor: 22*)

Accordingly, Abu Bakr restarted helping his relative saying: "I like that Allah may pardon me."

NINE

Kindness and Charity

Islam is a religion whose foundation has been kept on charity, generosity, and philanthropy. Narrow-mindedness, greed and miserliness are evils that shake its edifice. Therefore Islam likes that its followers should be generous and charitable. It has advised them to treat others kindly, to act righteously, to help their kinsmen and to do all kinds of good and virtuous deeds. It has stressed on its followers to make righteous living a permanent policy .

> "Those who spend (in charity) their wealth by night and by day; in secret and in public, have their reward with their Lord; there is no fear for them, nor shall they grieve." (*Baqarah: 274*)

It is the responsibility of every Muslim that in meeting his needs he should act in a balanced way, so that he may not spend all his wealth on his personal needs only, but that it is his duty that he should let others also partake of the blessings which Allah has bestowed on him, and that he should allot a part of his wealth for the help and assistance of the poor and needy persons.

> Allah's Messenger has said: "O Adam's son! Spend your wealth, it is good for you. And do not block it, it is bad for you, and the wealth according to the need cannot be reproached. Spend first for your family and dependents, and the raised hand is better than the lowered hand." (*Muslim*)

Quran has very clearly hinted at this subject when it has commanded the Muslims to spend for their kinsmen and the needy persons and prevented wasteful spending. A spendthrift wastes his wealth and indulges in foolishness. He spends his excess wealth for his personal pleasures, then what can remain with him for payment of the rights of others and the necessary assistance to the needy persons?

Allah has commanded:

> "And render to the kindred their due rights, as (also) to those in want, and to the wayfarer ; but squander not (your wealth) in the manner of a spendthrift. Verily, spendthrifts are the brothers of Satans, and the Satan is to his Lord ungrateful." (*Bani Israil: 26, 27*)

And after this, advice is given to be mindful of the sentiments of the needy and the people in want, and their feelings should not be hurt. If there is nothing that can be given to them, they should be refused softly and in a decent way:

> "And even if you have to turn away from them in pursuit of the Mercy of your Lord which you do expect, speak to them a word of easy kindness:" (*Bani Israil: 28*)

Islam's call to its followers to spend in the cause of Allah and for charity is famous and well-known. Similarly its war against miserliness, greed and narrowmindedness is as clear as the day.

> One *hadith* has it : "A giver of charity is near to Allah, is near to humans, and is near to Paradise and away from hell. And a miser is away from Allah, is away from humans, away from the Paradise and is near to hell. An uneducated giver of charity is liked more by Allah than a miserly worshipper." (*Tirmizi*)

There does not exist any system in this world, and there is also no possibility of its existence, in which all the people may be indifferent to and not in need of mutual co-operation. As long as there are power and weakness, wealth and poverty side by side in the human society, it is necessary for achieving peace and satisfaction and for ensuring the success and security of the society that the strong should be kind to the weak, and that wealthy should favour the poor and needy with gifts and donations.

If wealth and property are amassed as a result of the capabilities and striving of the people, then some people amass lot of riches and some people get only the bare necessities. And this cannot be objected to. The question regarding misfortune and ungratefulness arise when these people live a life away from the society, when they are concerned only with meeting their own personal needs and for providing for their own pleasures and luxuries, when Allah has caused the people to live together, and has declared this togetherness of theirs, instead of differences in their circumstances, a severe trial for them. This provides a test for their faith and an opportunity for proving their worth.

> "We have made some of you as trials for others. Will you have patience? For Allah is One Who sees (all things)." (*Furqan : 20*)

A community can be successful in this field of life only when the relationship among its individuals is strong and firm. No individual of the community should be so deprived that he may be facing a life of starvation and no wealthy man of the community should be so greedy that he may be spending his wealth only for his own personal pleasures and luxuries.

To achieve this high objective Islam has framed very strong laws. Peoples' hearts have been prepared to indulge in righteous and virtuous deeds, and they have been tempted to co-operate with each other, help each other and act righteously. It explained to them that the benefit of spending in the cause of Allah is not only derived by the poor and needy persons but the givers of charity also achieve the invaluable riches of peace and satisfaction; their hearts are protected from the earthquakes of rancour and jealousy, and they are saved from the adverse consequences of selfishness and narrow-mindedness:

> "Behold, you are those invited to spend in the way of Allah ; but among you are some that are niggardly. But any who are niggardly are so at the expense of their own souls. But Allah is free of all wants, and it is you that are needy." (*Mohammed : 38*)

Poverty destroys all charm : Poverty and want is a condition which causes a lot of trouble for men. It throws him down from the position which Allah had given him, and there is always a lurking fear that it may deprive him from that nobleness for which Allah has declared him the best of all the creatures.

Human nature does not like to see any person in dirty, torn and tattered clothes, that would expose a man's defects ; there should be no footwear to cover his feet, or his heels and fingers are dragging on the road, or he is hungry for a number of days ; he may be looking greedily at tasty and luscious food and be unable to taste it.

Those who see such sad and sorrowful scenes and are not moved by them at all, they are not humans : they are not Muslims. To feel disturbed and sorry by seeing the plight of the unhappy men is common human nature. One who is bereft of this basic quality is not a human ; he is a stone. As an Urdu poet says:

> "Man was created for sympathy (by Allah),
>
> Otherwise there was no dearth of angles for worshipping Him."

The question before faith is that it should frighten men from their Lord in relation to the condition of such helpless and poor people.

Once the Prophet of Islam saw such a scene the tears rolled out from his eyes, and he was very much perturbed. He gathered all the Muslims and delivered a very effective speech. He reminded them of the rights of men on men and their duties. He warned them of the punishment from Allah and the consequences in the Hereafter. His speech was so effective that the people who were present there, freely donated whatever they could, with the result that so much money was collected that the man whose condition had so moved the Prophet became a wealthy man from this spontaneous help from the companions of the Prophet, and all his defects were covered.

Jarir has narrated : "We were in the company of the Prophet in the morning. Some people came in his presence. They were ill-clad. Their sheets were torn from various places. Many of them belonged to the tribe of Bani Madhar. When the Prophet saw their starving condition, his face changed colour. He went into his house and then came out and asked Bilal to give Azan. He called the faithful to prayer and the Prophet led the prayer. Then he delivered a speech, and said

> "O People! Fear your Lord, who created you from a single person, created, of like nature, his mate ; and from them twain scattered (like seeds) countless men and women;-fear Allah through Whom you demand your (rights) of one another, and towards the womb (that bore you). Verily, Allah ever watches over you." (*An: Nisa:1*)
>
> "O People who believe ! fear Allah, and every person should see what he has prepared for his future." (*Hashr: 18*)

Then the Prophet said:

> "Every one should give in charity dinar, dirham, cloth, dates, wheat, etc." He went on till he urged : "Give, even if it is a stone of a date."

The narrator says that after this a man from Ansar brought a bag so full that it was slipping from his hand and it fell to the ground before he reached the Prophet. Other people also brought things to be given in charity, till there were two big heaps of eatable goods and clothes. At that time I saw that the face of the Prophet glowed with joy as if it was gold. Then he said:

"Anybody who inducted a good Sunnah in Islam, he will get its reward (sawab) and then also the reward of others acting on it, without there being any reduction in the reward of these who act on that Sunnah.

> And anybody who inducted a bad system in Islam, he will get the punishment for it and also the punishment of all those who will act on it, without there being any reduction is the punishment of those who act on it." (*Muslim*)

These eloquent words invite us to compete in matters of righteousness and we should try to vie with each other in performing virtuous deeds, e.g. social welfare work during inclement weather, or relief work after natural calamities, etc.

On the other hand these words warn those who introduce bad practices in the society, and by this they increase the problems and complications of the society, and they leave their successors to face the ill consequences of their acts.

***Charity* :** It is human nature to love wealth and to be greedy to get it. For this a man travels long distances and bears various kinds of troubles. The disease of selfishness and a tendency of giving preference to his own benefits over all other things are there in a man from the first day. He thinks about himself more and cares little for others.

If he is given the entire wealth of the earth, nay, even if he gets the treasures of the blessings of his Lord, he will not be prepared to spend from it willingly, and different kinds of diseases of selfishness will tie his hands.

> "Say (O Prophet!) If you get the treasures of my Lord in your possession, you would have blocked it from fear of it being spent. Verily, man is narrowminded."
>
> (*Bani Israil: 100*)

Islam has considered this kind of thinking and mentality as very cheap and mean, and it is to be resisted vehemently. It is to be counted with alertness and cleverness. Islam has very clearly stated that only that man can be successful in achieving the rewards in this and the next world who removes the motivations of narrowmindedness and niggardliness and nourishes charity and generosity

> "So fear Allah as much as you can ; listen and obey; and spend in charity for the benefit of your own souls; and those saved from the covetousness of their own souls,-they are the ones that achieve prosperity."
>
> (*Taghabun : 16*)

Heaps of silver and gold from which the rights of poor and needy persons are not met become the causes of their owner's punishment and disgrace in this world and in the next. Such wealth is like the snakes which are hiding in their holes and are waiting to bite men. Islam has clarified that this wealth will be turned into living snakes on the Doomsday, and this snake will be chasing for attacking and biting its owner.

> "The wealthy man who has not paid the rights of others from his wealth, his treasure will become a snake on the Doomsday, which will chase him with open mouth, then a voice will be heard: 'Catch hold of your wealth which you had concealed, and I am unconcerned with this.' When he will see that there is no escape, he will put his hand in its mouth, and it will bite him as a bull eats the grass." (*Bukhari*)

Islam explains to the man that his love for wealth leads him near destruction, and that if he ponders over the reality of wealth and its consequences he will realise that charity is better than selfishness and that gift is nobler than miserliness.

> "Man will say: my wealth, my wealth, although his wealth, was of three kinds : whatever he ate, drank and finished it ; or had spent on clothes and they were torn ; or he gave to others and stored for the Hereafter, and what was other than this has been finished or has been left for the people." (*Muslim*)

It is strange that what a man leaves for others, he expresses harshness in that? He will not use his wealth for bettering his own economic condition and for the welfare in the Hereafter, then from what else will he try to derive benefit?

> The holy Prophet disclosed this reality, when he said: "Who is there among you that likes the wealth of his inheritor more than his own wealth ?" The Companions replied: "O Messenger of Allah! We like our own wealth." The Prophet then said: "The wealth of each one of you is what he has sent to God, and the wealth of the inheritor is what each one of you leaves behind." (*Bukhari*)

In spite of this when the Prophet declared that he would collect the Zakat, he treated leniently and with softness the greed of men to hoard money and tackled them with great dexterity. He said:

> "Soon to you will come the collectors of Zakat. When they come, welcome them. Give them full liberty to collect whatever they want. If they act justly, they will do good to themselves. And if they are unjust, its evil will be on them. Keep them pleased, for the payment of your zakat will be completed by their pleasure, and they should pray in your favour." (*Abu Daud*)

If a man is successful in removing the obstructions that miserliness and narrow-mindedness place in the path of righteous feelings, then it is a perfect achievement in the eyes of Islam. Ordinarily a man is hopeful about his life, and his relationship with it is strong and firm, provided he is healthy and energetic and courageous about future. At such a time man spends his money moderately and he is always thinking of increasing his wealth, so that he may be re-assured about his future and that of his children. If in these circumstances a man controls all the factors, and keeps his hands open, spends his money open-heartedly and generously, he neither worries about poverty or want, nor is he afraid about his ruin, then such a man perfoms the act of great good.

One man went to the Prophet and asked him:

> "O Messenger of Allah ! What charity is the best rewardwinning ?" The Prophet said : "That you give in charity, although you may be healthy and in need of money ; you may be afraid of getting poor so also you may be hopeful of getting wealth and being free from want. Let it not happen that you should go on postponing to give in charity, till your last breath, then you start making a will to give this much in charity to this man and that much to that man."
> (*Bukhari*)

> "If you give charity openly even so it is good, but if you give it secretly to the needy, it is much better for you, and He will remove some of your illdeeds. And Allah is well aware of what you do." (*Baqarah: 271*)

> "If you loan to Allah a beautiful loan, He will double it to your (credit), and He will grant forgiveness ; for Allah is most Ready to appreciate (service), Most Forbearing,-Knower of what is hidden and what is open, Exalted in Might, Full of Wisdom"
>
> (*Taghabun : 17, 18*)

When a man commits a sin and he realises that there has arisen distance between him and his Lord, then the thing that brings back cleanness. light and gets him a shelter under the benevolence and pleasure of his Lord is spending his most loved wealth and property in the cause of Allah, and he should gladden the hearts of the poor and the needy with its help, and should try to achieve rank before the Most Gracious Being.

Hazrat Abuzar has narrated that the Prophet has said: There was a worshipper in the Bani Israil, who had worshipped Allah in a monastery for sixty years. One day there was rainfall and the whole area became green. When he saw from his hillside—monastery he felt—would it that he went down in the valley and recited Allah's praises and collected more virtue. Then he went down from the monastery. He had one or two loaves. In the meanwhile he met a woman, and talked to her and the woman also enjoyed, and suddenly he covered the woman and then slumber overtook him.

> Then he came for taking a bath to a lake, and a beggar asked him for alms. The monk then gave him both the loaves, and then he suddenly died. His sixty years' worshipping was weighed against the act of illegal sex, then the scale of the sin was heavier. Then in the scale of his virtue the two loaves were put, then the scale of the virtue became heavier, and he achieved salvation." (*Ibn Habban*)

> The effect of and the role that charity and generosity play in salvation and deliverance can be found in the best example that Allah taught to His Prophet so that he may convey it to his followers : "I command you to give charity. Its example is like that of a man who has been held by his enemies, his hands have been

tied to his neck, and he has been drawn near with the intention of being beheaded ; suddenly he inquires of the possibility of saving his life by giving money. Then he began giving whatever valuable things of little or more value that he had, till he was able to get himself free." (*Hakim*)

Zakat, charity and other generous acts are of great importance in this life and in the Hereafter. On its basis alone a Muslim's relationship with his religion either becomes strong or weak. There is nothing more depriving than miserliness in paying others' dues and nursing misgivings against God. And there is nothing more helpful for success and glory than confidence in Allah's favours and a man's charity and generosity.

Allah's Messenger has said: "The acts of righteousness and virtue save a man from the adverse consequences of the wicked acts. The charity that is given unobtrusively cools down Allah's anger, and kindness to kinsmen increases a man's age." (*Tibrani*)

Another tradition has it:

"Arrange for the cleanness by taking zakat out of your wealth. Arrange for the treatment of your sick by giving in charity, and fight the waves of adversity by praying to God meekly and humbly." (*Abu Daud*)

The heaviest blow to Satan, the most successful method to counter his tricks and the greatest shield against his distrusts is that man should give his wealth in charity, and spend his money in the cause of Allah. For this reason the devil inspires man to be weak and narrow-minded so that he may be prevented from giving generously and be involved in the entanglements of the material world:

"The devil threatens you with poverty and bids you to lewd conduct. Allah promises you His forgiveness and bounties. And Allah is All-Embracing, All-Knowing." (*Baqarah: 268*)

It is mentioned in the hadith:

> "When a man decides to give something in charity, a group of seventy devils clings to him and tries to put him off it." (*Ahmed*)

When a man distributes his salary or allots it to different items of expenditure, he allots its major portion to such items as are perishable. He thinks of them as if they are the dues from which there is no escape. Islam has informed that a man may consider the expenditure on his food and medicine as on perishable items, but the wealth which he spends in the cause of Allah is such that never perishes.

> Hazrat Ayesha narrates that they slaughtered a goat, and the Prophet asked : "How much of its flesh has remained?" They replied: "Nothing remained except the shoulder piece." The Prophet said: "Everything has remained except the shoulder piece." (*Tirmizi*)

This *hadith* is in accord with these words of Allah

> "Whatever is with you is perishable, and whatever is with Allah is permanent." (*Nahl: 96*)

In a *hadith-Qudsi* it is written

> "O son of Adam! Spend your treasure in the cause of Allah. With me there is no fear of its getting burnt, drowned or stolen. In its place whatever you would need, I will give it to you." (*Baihaqui*)

Equality for All

Sometimes a thought enters the mind that charity, reduces the wealth, and brings a man nearer to poverty, and takes away from him that peace and re-assurance that is available to him under the shadow of wealth. Such a thought is generated by Satan, who puts it into the minds of the hoarders of low and mean nature.

The fact is that charity is the means of nourishment and development. Donation of wealth is a long and wide road. A man who spends the gifts of Allah generously with his two hands, his hands are always full with the gifts of Allah. He is always surrounded by the favours and blessings of Allah.

In a *hadith* it is mentioned:

> "There are three men about whom I can take an oath. No man's wealth can be reduced by charity. Any man who shows patience in the face of oppression, Allah honours him. And a man who opens the door to begging, Allah opens on him the door of poverty and want." (*Ibn Majah*)

Man should display charity and generosity and should try to fill up the gaps found in society. Those poor and needy persons who may come to him for succour should not be returned by him disappointed, but instead he should satisfy them and should deal with them in such a way that he himself reaps rich benefits for the next world.

If today a little is spent in charity, tomorrow or day after tomorrow great advantages will accrue from that.

Allah has termed this generosity or donation as 'excellent loan,' which will be repaid in increased quantities, not two or three times-but many more times. He has encouraged His slaves to spend money in His cause and has very clearly informed them that this spending in the cause of Allah enables them to deservingly get limitless favours and blessing of Allah, which are everlasting.

It is mentioned in a *hadith Qudsi*:

> "O My slave ! spend, spend, it is your duty to spend. Allah's hand is full. The charity of the day and night cannot reduce it. What do you think, how much has He spent since He created the earth and the heavens? He never closed His hands, when His throne was on the water, in His hands was the balance which went down and went up." (*Bukhari*)

Allah says:

> "And whatever you spend (for good) He replaces it. And He is the Best of Providers." (*Saba: 39*)

Spenders in the cause of Allah remain in his sight and in his shelter in both the states of plenty and adversity. The angel sent Darud on them, and wish for increase in their wealth. As regards those who hoard money. very miserly, they wish their loss and ruin. And will they remain with their wealth or will the wealth remain with them for all time? The wealth has come to us from others, and will again go to others. Then why this pride and conceit about it? And for this reason why should one forget his position and manners.

The things with which man is attached in this world, will be left by him for the real inheritor of those things, and he will appear before his Lord in such a condition that he would have no wealth nor would he enjoy any rank or position. He will be totally emptyhanded, as he had first come to the world. The wealth and property about which he had acted miserly will become a load in his neck on the Day of Judgment. And it is not surprising because Allah will take revenge on such persons who forgot these realities and lived in this world unmindful of their duties. The only thought that troubled them was that whether a thing was beneficial for them or not they were thoroughly self-centred and in their selfishness they forgot what was really good for them.

> Allah's Messenger says : "Every morning two angels come down to earth. One of them says 'O Allah'. Give full recompense to the spender (for good cause).' The other one says : 'O Allah ! Ruin and destroy the miser'.
> (*Muslim*)

Eradication of Sufferings

A man is greedy for Wealth because he wants that he should leave behind him plenty of wealth and property for his children, so that they may be safe and secure after him. This is a good and virtuous intention. Islam considers it a duty of a Muslim that he should take care of his family and dependents, and keep them away from want and penury. If Islam wants you to be helpful in removing poverty and want from the homes of others, it also dislikes you to bring poverty and want in your homes.

It is mentioned in the *hadith:*

> "To leave your inheritors rich and wealthy is much better than leaving them poor and needy, and being forced to beg before others." (*Bukhari*)

Provision for the children and a guarantee for their future are duties of accepted importance. But how can it be proper if a man stakes his religion and character after these things? It is sheer foolishness if a man sacrifices his position, decency and Allah's pleasure only for the purpose of leaving his income for his children.

Islam shows that like all other good things a man's wealth and children are a trial for him. If he is entangled in their love and forgets his duties and does not offer the expected sacrifices, then these good things and gifts become a trouble for him, nay, they become more dangerous and destructive.

> "O you who believe! Truly, among your wives and your children are (some that are) enemies to yourselves; so beware of them ! But if you forgive and overlook, and cover up (their faults), verily, Allah is Oft-Forgiving, Most Merciful. Your riches and your children may be but a trial; but in the presence of Allah, is the highest reward." (*Taghabun: 14, 15*)

Yes, the man who does not go to *jihad,* because he likes the proximity of his wife, or the man who restrains his head from giving in charity because he wants to save his wealth for saving more and more for his children, he is showing ungratefulness to Allah for the good things of life that He has provided, and he thinks that they are really 'gifts' white actually they are a trial for him.

> Khaula Bint Hakim says: "One day the Prophet came out carrying his grandchild and he was saying: 'You (children) become the means of miserliness, cowardice, ignorance and foolishness. And you are also the fragrance of Allah." (*Tirmizi*)

It means that the person who preferred to be a miser, coward and fool on account of his child, he was in a loss, and a person who paid the dues of Allah and His slaves, he became successful.

However, being niggardly in paying the dues and for hoarding for the children, a man's poverty and need do not end, it also does not guarantee his becoming a wealthy person ; and such a man will not be able to proffer any excuse which will be acceptable.

Abdullah bin Masood narrates that the Prophet has said : "Allah has blessed two types of persons with plenty of wealth, property, and children. He will ask the persons of one of these groups: 'O Such and such man!' He will reply: 'We are present, O our Lord! we are present.' He will ask: 'What have you done with the wealth and property with which I had blessed you?' The slave will reply: 'That I have left for my sons, for I was afraid of his poverty'. The Lord will say : 'If you know the reality you will laugh less and cry more. The thing which you fear, I have sent it down on them."

> He will ask another person , 'O Such and such man!' He will reply: 'I am present, O My Lord! I am present.' He will ask: 'Had I not blessed you with plenty of wealth and property?' The stave will reply: 'Certainly, my Lord!' He will ask: 'What have you done with those blessings?'He will reply : 'I spent it in the path of your obedience, and I left my children to your Mercy, Kindness and Be nevolence.' Then God will say: 'Listen, If you know the reality, you will laugh more and cry less. The things on which you relied, I provided him with them'." (*Tibrani*)

Islam advises that man should first be kind to himself, then with his home people, then with his relatives and with all humans.

A man's being kind with himself means that he should meet all his permissible and proper needs by halal or permissible means, and should avoid *haram* or forbidden means. He should keep himself safe from the manifestations of poverty and starvation, for a man loses his dignity because of these conditions. The necessary standard of Muslim's honour is not maintained. But all these things should be done in between miserliness and wasteful spending. Muslims are allowed to keep so much wealth with them that it may suffice to meet their needs, and if they have not these swans then they are poor and needy.

> Abu Saeed Khudri narrates: "A man in a poor condition entered the *Masjid-i-Nabavi* (Prophet's Mosque). At that time the Prophet was commanding the people to give charity. When the people collected the donations, he gave two items of clothing to that man in poor condition. When for the second time the Prophet advised the people to give in charity, that needy looking man threw one item of clothing. The Prophet said in anger: 'See this shabbylooking man, I had given him two pieces of clothing, and when I again advised people to give in charity, he threw his one piece.' The Prophet reproached him considerably,"
>
> (*Abu Daud*)

The holy Prophet wanted to remove poverty, penury; to end want and obscenity from society, while some people did not care whether they were moving about without clothes or without footwear. If the people of this kind consider their such appearance as a manifestation of religious teachings, then it is not correct, because Islam makes it a duty for every Muslim to strive for so much wealth as may make him able to raise his head with dignity in society.

Jabir has reported : "A man came to the Prophet with a piece of gold with him and said to the Prophet that he got it from a mine and requested him to accept it ; that it was in charity and that he had nothing else which he could give in charity. The Prophet turned his face away. So he came from the right side, and again requested. This time also the Prophet turned his face away. So he came from the left side and pleaded. This time also the Prophet did not pay any attention. So he came from behind and repeated his request. The Prophet took it and threw it towards him so forcefully that had it touched him it would have been painful.

Then he said : 'Some of you come to give the entire property in charity. After this they go on begging before others, and the best charity is that which comes from a wealthy person'."

Who deserves first to partake of your wealth? : It is the duty of the Head of the family to find out what are the reasonable needs of his household-people, and he should meet them with generosity. It is not religiousness that a man should let his wife and children suffer for want of means and should spend his wealth for other purposes, however important they may be. Family relationships deserve more attention and preferable treatment over others.

> The Prophet has said : "One dinar is that which you spend in the cause of Allah, and one dinar is that which you spend for freeing a slave; and one dinar is that which you spend on your family. But of all these, the greatest reward will be given for the dinar which has been spent on the family." (*Muslim*)

In the discussion on Sincerity this hadith had been quoted:

> "What a Muslim spends on his family, for seeking the pleasure of Allah, is also counted as charity." (*Bukhari*)

By this clear guidance Islam wants that the allotment of the expenditure should be in proportion to the benefit to society; for. family is the foundation of a great society and the first brick of its edifice. Therefore, it is necessary to pay attention to it first and to pay its dues fully.

In this teaching there is a warning for those who spend heartily and squander money carelessly outside their homes among their friends while at home they become a picture of poverty and helplessness.

The people who deserve more to be benefited from the excess wealth of a person are his relatives and kinsmen. It is their right that when the hand should be raised for giving in charity it should first be extended towards them. It also appeals to a sound intellect that when there are needy and poor persons in the vicinity of a person, then where is the sense, in leaving them uncured for and extending the helping hand towards others? Such an action might generate a feeling of hatred and rancour in the hearts of the deprived persons, and they may feel that the ignorance shown in their respect is with a view to harming them and putting them to great loss. And if giving of pain and dissatisfaction is done consciously, then this kind of charity becomes troublesome for the giver.

> A *hadith* has it: "O Community of Mohammed ! By the Being Who has sent me with Truth, Allah cannot accept the charity of those persons whose relatives are in want of his kindness and help, and he is distributing it among others, lowing them. By the Being in Whose power is my life, on the Day of Judgment Allah will not look at such a man." (*Tibrani*)

The wife of Hazrat Abdullah bin Masood, Zainab Saqafiah says : "Allah's Messenger has said: 'O Group of ladies! Give in charity, even if you have to sell ornaments." She says: 'I went to Abdullah bin Masood and told him : 'You are a poor man and the Prophet has asked us to give in charity. You go to the Prophet and ask him whether this thing can be an alternative for charity, if so it is well, otherwise I will give in charity to others instead of to you.' Abdullah Ibn Masood said: 'You go and ask him.'

She says that on her way to see the Prophet, she met a woman from Ansar, who was also troubled with the same thoughts. They went together. As a precautionary measure they had to stop outside his room. When Hazrat Bilal came out of the room, she said to him: 'Go and ask the Prophet and tell him that two women have come to ask you whether looking after the husbands and nourishing their children can be an alternative to charity or not ? And do not tell him who the women are.'

> She says that Bilal went in the presence of the Prophet and asked him about her problem. The Prophet asked who the women were. He answered that one was a woman from the Ansar and another was Zainab. The Prophet asked: 'Which Zainab ?' He replied: 'The wife of Abdullah bin Masood.' The Prophet said: 'These

two will get the reward of the relationship and also the reward for the charity.' (*Bukhari*)

Allah's Messenger has said: "To spend on the poor is charity, and to spend on the relative gets the reward for double charity, one is charity itself, and another for kindness to relatives." (*Tirmizi*)

TEN

Mercy for All

Kindness is a basic quality of the human nature, which softens the heart when informed about the sufferings of the fellow creatures and makes one restless for providing relief to them. This quality makes a man feel sorry for the mistakes of others and causes him to guide them properly. This is a natural quality, because if this feeling of kindness dies, and it is not at all moved on occasions of happiness and sorrow, then a man falls to the level of animals, and all his virtues are vanished. This feeling is created by love and sympathy. Some times some vague feelings are created in animals too, on account of which they show some kindness to their offsprings, and for this reason hard-heartedness or cruelty is a trend which is lower and meaner than the tendency found in the animals. Nay, a cruel person is like the inanimate objects that have no feelings and no consciousness, and they are not moved by anything.

Kindness, in its highest and vast sense, is the attribute of the Almighty, God. His kindness is for all the existing things and covers the entire universe, wherever the ray of His knowledge (which encloses the entire universe) falls. The angels, in his praise, pray to him—

> Therefore, grant salvation to those who have repented and have followed Your path, and save them from the punishment of hell. (*Momin:7*)

It is narrated by Hazrat Umar bin Khattab (R.A.A.) that in the presence of the Prophet (S.A.W.) a female-slave was brought along with other prisoners. This woman was running here and there and trying to expel milk from her breasts. If she saw any child, she embraced it and suckled it. The Prophet (S.A.W.) saw this condition of the woman and said:

> "What do you think, can this woman throw her child into the fire?" They replied: "No, by God, this woman cannot throw her child into the fire." The Prophet (S.A.W.) then said: "Allah is more kind to His slaves than this woman is kind to her child." (*Bukhari*)

Most names of Allah carry the meaning of Kindness, Graciousness, Favour, Forgiveness and the like. A *hadith Qudsi* states:

> "My kindness surpasses My anger." (*Muslim*)

That is, to forgive humans for their lapses and errors is liked by Him more than to punish them, and therefore, He is more kind than the other people.

> O Prophet! Say : 'My Lord, pardon, and be kind, and You are the Most Kind of all the kind people'. (*Muminoon : 118*)

Today on this earth the blooming flowers of mutual love, good conduct, graciousness, and virtue that we see, are the reflections of the Divine Graciousness, only a small part of it He has placed in the hearts of His creatures. The most soft-hearted man among men is he who has received the greater portion of this kindness, and who has more sympathy with the life of the weak persons.

The cruel, the hard-hearted tyrants and the conceited persons of the nation will find their abode in the lowest part of the hell.

> The man who is cruel and hard-hearted will be the farthest away from Allah. (*Tirmizi*)

Allah's Messenger (S.A.W.) considered the dryness of the eyes and hardness of the heart as signs of ill-luck.

When Allah wanted to be gracious in view of the bad conditions on the earth and to send down a person who would remove the sorrow of the people of the world, who would tend to their wounds, who would sympathise with them on their lapses, who would inconvenience himself for their guidance, who would cause the strong to give the rights of the weak, who would fight for their rights and for their protection, who would convert the rebellious and tyrant men into kind-hearted human beings, He sent down, for all these purposes, Muhammed (S.A.W.) He placed treasures of knowedge and forbearance in his heart. He instilled in his character the light of virtue and righteousness. He made softness and kindness his second nature. He embellished his character with the qualities of charity and generosity. All these excellent qualities made Mohammed (S.A.W.) the most soft-hearted, kind, broadminded and generous of all the men in the world:

> It was by the mercy of Allah that you were lenient with them (O Mohammed), for if you had been stern and fierce of heart they would have dispersed from round about you. (*Al-i-Imran : 159*)

This quality was also seen in action it the Battle of Uhad when the polytheists were poised to kill him. He was thrown into a pit so that he may die there. He saw his companions dying around him. His remaining companions looked at him and found that there were scratches on his cheeks and some of his teeth were broken. On this crucial occasion, they pleaded with him to subject them to a curse. He prayed: "O Allah! Give guidance to my community, they know not what they are doing."

Pious men act in this manner only. The motivations of cruelty and tyranny do not excite their hearts. In the face of wrath and rage, tyranny and revenge, they always show mercy, forgiveness and kindness.

Cruelty is a very wicked thing for an individual to have. In the history of nations it has caused great upheavals. We should not be surprised to learn that Islam has warned us against it, and has declared it as a rebellion against God and deviation from the right path.

> Has not the time arrived for the believers that their hearts in all humility should engage in remembrance of Allah and of the Truth which has been revealed to

> them and that they should not become like those to whom was given Revelation aforetime, but long ages passed over them and their hearts grew hard ? For many among them are rebellious transgressors.
>
> (*Hadid : 16*)

Islam has commanded Muslims to be kind to all creatures and all humans, and has considered it a proof of perfect faith. A Muslim meets all Muslims. For them he has a feeling of love, sympathy and kindness in his heart. For them he extends his hand of co-operation and tries, as far as it is in his power, to remove their troubles and difficulties.

Allah's Messenger (S.A.W.) has said:

> "You cannot be a Momin until you are not kind among yourselves." The companions said that they were all kind. He said: "Kindness is not this that you sympathise with your companion, but kindness is this that you should think all men deserving of it."
>
> (*Tibrani*)

When a man meets his friends, sympathy is naturally created. When a man looks at his children, feelings of love and kindness are generated. This is a common thing. Bat for a Muslim it is certain that the sphere of his kindness is widest. He treats all humans with kindness and love and meets them with a smiling face.

There are many traditions in which this general kindness has been recommended for Muslims. The Prophet (S.A.W.) has said:

> He who does not show mercy to the people, Allah also does not show mercy to him. (*Bukhari*)

In another tradition it is said : "He who does not forgive others, Allah also does not forgive him."

Yet another *hadith* says:

> "How lucky is that man who adopts humbleness without having scarcity, who considers himself inferior without having to beg for anything, who spends his own earned money in the right causes without

> disobeying Allah, who is kind to the inferior and mean persons, and remains in the company of the learned men and the intellectuals." (*Tibrani*)

Allah has stated that the characteristic of the Muslim Society is that it is humble towards its own people and stern towards the others.

> Humble towards believers, stern towards disbelievers.
> (*Maidah : 54*)

At another place it is said:

> Hard against the disbelievers, kind among themselves.
> (*Fath : 29*)

Humble towards their own people and stern towards others : Here a question can be raised: What is the relevance of discussing hardness and sternness when the talk is about Rehmat and kindness? The fact is that Islam talks of general kindness and does not keep out any person, animal or bird from it, and the authorities quoted above, all support the exhortation for the general kindness. But some men and animals are such as are a cause of danger and a source of terror for others. In their cases the demand of the public benefit is that their evil should be cut short and their menace should be put a stop to. Sometimes sternness with a person proves to be beneficial to him and serves as a whip against his going astray.

Islam is entirely a religion of peace. It commands its followers to be gracious and kind to all mankind. Allah addresses His Messenger (S.A.W.) and says:

> "We sent you not save as a Mercy for the peoples."
> (*Ambiya : 107*)

All the Quranic Surahs are commenced with this verse:

> In the name of Allah, Most Gracious, Most Merciful.

But the human wolves act as obstructions in the path of this general Islamic kindness. They place rocks in its way so that the humanity may not derive benefit from its springs, and may die in the valley of bewilderment and ignorance by keeping away from it. It is necessary to remove these obstructions and it is inevitable that stern attitude should be adopted towards these social wolves. The day when their harassment would end their transgression and rebellion will be subdued, they will also come under the shadow of its kindness. Therefore, the fault does not lie with the kindness of Islam, but with these people, that they have kept themselves away from it. Allah's graciousness covers every thing, but a polytheist or an apostate cannot derive benefit from it:

> My Mercy embraces all things, therefore I shall ordain it for those who ward off (evil) and pay the poor-due (zakat) and those who believe Our Revelations, those who follow the Messenger, the Prophet who is unlettered. (*A'raf : 156-157*)

It can be illustrated in this way : A public hall has a capacity to seat one thousand persons, but there is a condition, of obtaining permission for admittance. If somebody refuses to get the required permission then he has deprived himself of admittance into the hall. The capacity of the hall is not affected by that.

The same sense is conveyed in this *hadith* in which the Prophet (S.A.W.) has said:

> "Every person of my Ummah will go to Paradise, save who denies." The people asked "Who can deny?" He said: "He who obeyed me will go to Paradise, and he who disobeyed me, denied." (*Bukhari*)

Sometimes kindness takes the mantle of sternness, but the reality does not change. Children are sent to school forcibly, and they learn their lessons after a little harsh treatment. If they are allowed to carry on according to their own sweet will, then they will never turn out to be good students or good citizens.

The doctor treats a patient in a similar fashion, and while performing a surgical operation has to cut the flesh, or sever the bones, and sometimes has to remove away a part of the body. This cannot be called unjust or harsh, on the contrary he is doing a favour to the patient by showing kindness to him.

Therefore, kindness does not only include comfort and convenience, it covers all rights and aspects. If a man is hanged, his body dangles from the gallows, his eyes become sightless, and his tongue protrudes. If on seeing this terrible sight, a feeling of sympathy is aroused in our hearts and the murderer is set free, then this whole world will be filled with anarchy and lawlessness. At such a time the real kindness demands that these kind of feelings should be suppressed.

> O you men of understanding! There is life for you in Qisas, so that you may fear to break His law (against murder). (*Baqarah : 179*)

The hard-heartedness which is considered objectionable and despicable in Islam is the name of dryness of the self and of the heart, which has no connection with intellect and logic, with justice and fairplay. It is the worst desire, which begins with pain-giving and trouble and spreads with selfishness and blind desires, but graciousness is a factor of the Divine Beauty, which is enshrined in the human heart. It induces them to be righteous and virtuous, and keeps their lives fresh and their breasts open in the hardest of times.

Allah's Messenger (S.A.W.) has said:

> "Allah has made hundred parts of kindness and has sent down only one part on the earth. With the help of that part the creatures sympathise with one another, even an animal removes away its hoof so that it may not hurt its calf. (*Bukhari*)

In another *hadith*, it is stated:

> "The day when Allah created the earth and the skies, He created hundred kindnesses. Every kindness or Rehmat is equal to the layer that is between the earth and the sky. Out of this, one layer of Rehmat He sent down on earth, as a result of which a mother loves her child, and animals and birds show kindness to one another." (*Muslim*)

As the intellect improves and develops due to various causes, similarly this Rehmat too grows and develops due to various causes. If it is allowed to die, then man will be liable to go to hell.

Hazrat Abu Huraira (R.A.A.) has narrated that he has heard the True and the Most Tustworthy Abul Qasim, the Prophet (S.A.W.) saying: "Rehmat (kindness) is snatched away from the cruel-hearted only."

Foremost Deserving of Kindness

Islam has shown that there are some who are the foremost among those who deserve our kindness and safeguard from us.

These are our kinsmen (Zawil Arham), who deserve our attention and our kindness more than others. Allah's Prophet (S.A.W.) has said:

> "Allah shows mercy to those who show mercy to others. Be kind to the people on the earth, the Master of the Skies will be kind to you. Kindness to the kinsmen is among the laws ordained by Allah, He who united the relations, Allah unites with him, and he who cuts them, Allah is separated from him.
>
> (*Tirmizi*)

Every Muslim has a duty to fulfil his responsibility towards his relatives, pay their dues, to strengthen the mutual relations with love, sympathy and kindness.

One's own parents are the most deserving of one's love, good treatment and favours.

> And lower to them the wing of submission through mercy, and say: 'My Lord I Have mercy on them both as they did care for me when I was little.'
>
> (*Bani Israil: 24*)

Then his own children are deserving of his mercies :

Barwa has narrated that Hazrat Abu Bakr (R.A.A.) came to his daughter, Hazrat Ayesha (R.A.A.) who had fever. He asked:

> "How are you my dear?" And he kissed her cheek.
>
> (*Bukhari*)

Rough and coarse people do not have much softness and kindness in their behaviour and their conduct expresses bitterness and meanness.

Abu Huraira (R.A.A.) has narrated that the Prophet (S.A.W.) kissed his grandsons Hasan and Husain (R.A.A.) . There, Aqra' bin Habisul Tamimi was also present, who said: "I have ten children, but I never kissed any one of them."

> The Prophet looked at him and said: "He who does not show mercy, will not to be shown mercy." In another tradition it is written: "May I understand that Allah has snatched away mercy from you heart?" (*Bukhari*)

> Anas (R.A.A.) narrates: "We went with the Prophet (S.A.W.) to Abu Saiful-Quin (R.A.A.) who used to feed milk to the Prophet's (S.A.W.) son, Ibrahim. The Prophet lifted his son and kissed him. Then again when Ibrahim was about to die we went with him for the second time. Owing to excess of sorrow, the Prophet (S.A.W.) shed tears, Ibn Auf was astonished and said: "You are crying O Prophet (S.A.W.) of Allah!" The Prophet replied: "O Ibn Auf ! This is a sign of mercy." Then again he said: "The eyes are shedding tears, the heart is bursting, but we will say whatever is liked by our Lord: O Ibrahim! we are sorrowful from your separation." (*Muslim*)

It is not permissible for a Muslim to close his heart, mind and his house to his relatives and to lead his life keeping away from them and severing relations with them, not to express sympathy in their difficulties, and to abstain from extending the hand of co-operation in their hour of need. Unconcern deprives a man of the Divine suspiciousness, and invites His wrath.

> Abu Huraira (R.A.A.) narrates that he has heard the Prophet (S.A.W.) as saying: "Kindness to kinsmen is within the commands of the Gracious God; it says: O My Lord! I have been treated with unconcern, and I have been maltreated, O my Lord ! I have been wronged." Then Allah replies: "Is she (kindness) not pleased that I unite with the person who unites with her and I separate from the person who cuts her off." (*Ahmed*)

Graciousness for the orphans : Orphans are also included in the list of those with whom dealing with mercy and kindness is enjoined. To treat them in an excellent manner, to be kind to them, to meet their needs, and to safeguard their future from ruin is an extremely purified kind of worship. Even the astray natures, by adopting these qualities, follow a policy of justice and moderation, and come to the right path.

> Abu Huraira (R.A.A.) narrates that a man complained to the Prophet (S.A.W.) about the hardness of his heart. The Prophet (S.A.W.) said : "Pass a hand of kindness over the head of an orphan and feed a needy person."
> (*Ahmed*)

The words of another tradition are like these: "A man went to the Prophet (S.A.W.) and described the hardness of his heart. Then the Prophet (S.A.W.) said:

> "Do you like that your heart should be soft and you should achieve your objective? Be kind to the orphan, pass a hand over his head, feed him your food, then your heart will be soft and your need will be fulfilled."
> (*Tibrani*)

The reason for this is that the heart becomes insensitive and dead in a society in which there is ample provision for pleasure and happiness; days and nights may pass but the people may not be able to see beyond their own luxuries and amusements. The men of wealth and power remain unaware of the difficulties and troubles of the common people, because the luxuries available to them close the gates of their hearts, so that they may not hear the sighs of the oppressed people. They veil their eyes so that they may not see the helplessness of the orphans and the needy. The common men are able to experience purified sensations and delicate feelings because they have to pass through hot and cold circumstances, and they taste both the happy and unhappy times. After this only they are able to know what is the meaning of helplessness and loneliness. How terrible is their defencelessness? And what is the plight of the wretched people?

Relief for the stricken people : The sick and the stricken people should be shown the best expression of kindness and mercy, because the means of livelihood are very limited for these people, for which reason they cannot take part in the race for life, and cannot meet the needs of their life. Allah Himself has declared them helpless and has forgiven them. It is not permissible for us to criticise them:

> No blame is there on the blind, nor is there blame on the lame, nor on one ill (if he joins not the war); but he that obeys Allah and His Prophet. —(Allah) will admit him to Paradise, beneath which rivers flow; and he who turns back, (Allah) will punish him with grievous penalty. (*Fath : 17*)

The sick person is in difficulties because of his sickness, and his life becomes very unpleasant and painful. If he shows patience, he achieves nearness to Allah and deserves to receive Allah's mercies. When on the pain of pricking with a twig a Momin's sins are forgiven, then what to say of the purification of the person who is constantly in pain in the form of sickness, and the worst types of pains are troubling him. This is the reason why such a person is directly under the protection of God. Therefore, we should abstain from illtreating, insulting and jeering at the sick persons, because it is the worst crime.

Kind treatment of the employees : Our servants and employees are also deserving of our mercy and kindness. We should give a proof of our good treatment of them. They should be entrusted with the work according to their capacity, and we should forgive their lapses. We should not make them conscious of our superiority over them, nor should we ridicule them, because when a man with the property and wealth granted by God adopts an attitude of cruelty and tyranny, then God takes back his property and wealth and makes him face adverse circumstances.

Abu Masood Badri (R.A.A.) narrates that he was whipping his slave, then suddenly he heard a voice from behind "Beware! Abu Masood!" He could not recognise the voice on account of his anger. When the voice came from near, he recognised it to be that of the Prophet (S.A.W.) , who was saying:

> "Listen O Abu Masood! The power you eaercise over this slave, Allah exercises more power over you than

that." He immediately replied: "For the sake of Allah's pleasure, I free this slave." The Prophet replied : "Had you not done this, the hellfire would have burnt you." (*Muslim*)

Another *hadith* says:

"The best wealth is that for which arrangement to develop it are made and ill-treatment of the creatures is a misfortune." (*Abu Daud*)

One man asked the Prophet (S.A.W.) : "How many times should we forgive a slave?" The Prophet (S.A.W.) replied: "Daily, seventy times."

There are many men and women who never lose an opportunity to take advantage of the weakness of the servants. They hurl them in different ways. Islam has warned against this misfortune and has declared definite punishment for such behaviour.

Feeling Pity for Creatures

Islam desires kindness to animals. Hazrat Umar (R.A.A.) saw that a man was dragging a goat by its feet for slaughtering it. He reproached him and said: "Fie on you, carry it properly."

One man told the Prophet (S.A.W.) : "O Messenger of Allah! When I slaughter a goat, I try to be kind to it." The Prophet (S.A.W.) said: "If you will show mercy on it, Allah show mercy on you." (*Hakim*)

Islam is very severe on those who are cruel to animals, and who have no hesitation in hurting them. It has been declared that if a man, however great he may be, ill-treats the dumb animals, he can even earn the punishment of the hell-fire.

Allah's Messenger (S.A.W.) has said:

"A woman was thrown into the hell, because she had tied a cat, which she neither fed nor set free, so that it could roam about and feed itself on insects, etc." (*Bukhari*)

He further clarified that the feeling of kindness generating in the heart, even if it is for a dog, washes away major sins. The Prophet (S.A.W.) has said:

> "One man was travelling in a desert. He got terribly thirsty. He saw a well, descended down it and drank to his heart's content. In the meanwhile a dog came to the well, thirsty, its tongue hanging out on account of the thirst. The man said to himself : "On account of thirst the plight of this dog is the same as was mine." Then he descended into the well, and filled his sock with water, and holding it with his teeth came out of the well. He made the dog drink that water. Allah appreciated this act of his and granted him salvation." The people asked "Is there reward for good treatment to the animals?" He replied: "There is reward for good treatment to every animate thing."

In one tradition it is stated:

> "A disobedient woman saw a dog looking down the well in extreme heat, and his tongue was hanging out on account of severe thirst. She felt kind towards it and she made it drink water by bringing it in her sock. Accordingly for this act of hers, she was granted salvation. (*Muslim*)

If this act of kindness of a disobedient woman with a dog can be the cause of her salvation, then surely the treatment of the humans with kindness can achieve wonders !!

ELEVEN

Celebrations

It is good to celebrate festive occasions which is a human urge and in commensurate with natural requirement. Islam being the religion of Nature realises the desirability of the celebration of joyous occasions with certain conditions. Islam does not desire that we should impose upon ourselves artificial reserve and seriousness not warranted by the occasion, and wear a pensive aspect all the time, killing all the attractiveness of our personality. Islam gives us full permission to celebrate all legitimate festive occasion so as to enbable us to remain fresh with ambitious desires, new and fresh hopes, and ever newer and fresher paths to tread. It is the ignorance of knowledge of Islam to assume that the celebration of festive occasions runs counter to the tenets of Islam.

If you have been privileged to fulfil some religious mission, i.e., Hajj; you or some of your close relation has achieved a high position in learning; you have been blessed with success in business or achieved' some monetary gains; you have a distinguished guest visiting your home; you have a marriage or birth in your house; you have heard the news of the recovery of a relation from long illness; have heard the happy news of the triumph of the Muslims, and, if there may be a feast in any ease, it is your natural right to celebrate such occasions, and Islam not only permits merry-making, but it considers it quite in conformity with it.

> Hazrat K'ab Bin Malik says, when Allah accented his atonement and he heard the good news, he immediately presented himself before the Holy Prophet (S.A.W.) greeting him. The countenance of

> the Holy Prophet (S.A.W.) was at the time glowing with cheer, and whenever he used to be happy, his face glowed like a part of the moon, and the companions would then understand from the glow of his countenance, that he was in an extremely happy mood. *(R iyaz-us-Salihin)*

On Festivals

Muslim festivals should be celebrated with an abundance and free play. The Holy Prophet (S.A.W.) when he arrived at Madina said: "You used to celebrate two feasts in a year. Now Allah has granted you two better days. that is, the Eid- and Eid-ul-Azha." Therefore, celebrate these two Islamic festivals to your heart's content and mingle with others to join on these festive occasions in a natural way. It is forbidden to fast during these festivals.

The Holy Prophet (S.A.W.) has further said:

> "These days are meant for feasts, mutual enjoyment and remembrance of Allah." *(Sharh Mani AlAsar)*

On the day of Eid take care for personal and environmental cleaning and washing. Don the best dress which your means may permit, apply perfume on your person and clothes, arrange for good and wholesome food. The children should be given every opportunity to please themselves with legitimate games and sports, and celebrate these occasions as they please.

Hazrat Ayeshah (R.A.A.) narrates that, one day on the occasion of Eid slave girls were singing couplets which the Ansars had composed during the Battle of Buas. (This battle was fought during the pre-Islamic era, between two Ansar tribes Aus and Khazraj). While the singing was going on, Hazrat Abu Bakr came and said: "Why this singing and sportiveness in the house of the Holy Prophet (S.A.W.)." The Holy Prophet (S.A.W.) thereupon said: "Let them, O Abu Bakr, celebrate. Each people have a day marked for their merry making and today we have the day of our Eid."

> Once on an Eid day few Negro jugglers were performing physical exercise. The Holy Prophet (S.A.W.) himself saw this performance and showed the same to Hazrat Ayeshah (R.A.A.) who witnessed the show from behind a cover. He was applauding the jugglers all the while. When Hazrat Ayeshah (R.A.A.) got, tired; he told her; "All right, you may go" *(Bukhari)*

Rejoicing in Keeping with the Spirit of Islam : While celebrating festive occasions, we should bear in mind the Islamic spirit and celebrate the event decorously. We must thank Allah for the same who has been the source of that pleasure and offer obeisance and submission to Him. Do not adopt an attitude that is at variance with the Islamic tenets. While celebrating such events, moderation ought never be lost sight of, and under no circumstances show pride and haughtiness to the exclusion of humility and submissiveness. The Holy Quran says

> "And do not strut upon having received those gifts from Allah. He does not like those who show themselves off and boast." (57 :23)

One should not get so much intoxicated by pleasure that he may become indifferent towards remembering Allah. The happiness of a Muslim lies in offering thanks to the Benefactor or Giver of happiness all the more, and to express his gratitude to Allah through his acts.

When you sight the Eid moon, after having fasted for the whole month of Ramazan, read the Quran and offered Tarawih prayers, you are immensely pleased. On realising the fact that you have carried out the command of Allah and through His Will have given a good account of yourself, you distribute a part of your wealth among the poor, so that if you have failed to carry out any of His commands with regard to prayers, or if you have tripped short of fulfilling your obligations or obedience to Him, this might make up for the same, and the poor and the indigent might also be able to partake in this collective merry-making. We then thank Allah for munificence on the morning of the Eid by offering two rakats of Eid prayers.

Similarly on the occasion of Eid-ul-Azha we offer prayers and alms to the poor to commemorate Prophet Ibrahim's and Prophet Ismail's (A.S.) unparalleled sacrifice and total submission to Allah's Will. We celebrate this occasion in remembrance of that event unsurpassable in its content of faith, and find our hearts over-flowing with sentiments of thanks-giving. Our cities and localities resound with Takbirs and recitations of prayers. When we eat good food and put on our best clothes, our activities, which are based on Shariah, become part of prayers to Allah.

Happy Occasions

When the expiation of Hazrat K'ab Bin Malik was graciously accepted, Muslims in large number went to him to offer their congratulation, and expressed their pleasure; Hazrat Talha's greetings moved him so much that he remembered Chem for the rest of his life. When Hazrat K'ab described the incident of this ordeal and repentance to his son, Abdullah, he especially mentioned Hazrat Talha with great pleasure, and said he could never forget the spontaneous joy that overflowed from him, and that it was an unforgetable experience.

When the Holy Prophet (S.A.W.) himself conveyed to Hazrat K'ab the tidings of the approval of his expiation, the former was very pleased and said:

> K'ab! This is the happiest occasion of your life."
>
> *(Riyaz-us-Salihin)*

Greetings at a Wedding. Hazrat Abu Hurairah says that, whenever the Holy Prophet (S.A.W.) greeted anyone on the occasion of his marriage, he used to say:

> "May Allah keep you prosperous and bless both of you, and you may gather happiness between you."

Greeting the Birth of a Child : Hazrat Husain-Ibn-Ali (R.A.A.) once told someone that the birth of a child should be greeted in the following words:

"May Allah bless you with prosperity in this gift and grace you with the ability to thank Him. Allah may enable your child to grow and enjoy youth, and he may be obedient to you."

Greetings on Return from a Journey : A relation or a friend on return from a long journey should be greeted, and pleasure expressed on his safe home coming and success in his mission. If he celebrates his return, one should participate in it. If you come back safely from a journey and celebrate it then invite all those near and dear to you, but do not spend beyond your means.

> The Holy Prophet (S.A.W.) on his return from the Battle of Tabuk, was received by the Muslim men and children at Sanniyat Al Wada. *(Abu Daud)*

When the Holy Prophet (S.A.W.) migrated to Madina and was entering the city from the south, the entire Muslim population came out to welcome him. The Ansar girls were singing the following verses in jubilation:

> "Tal'al bdro' alaina
> min Sanniyatil wada'i'
> Waja-bash shukro alaina
> Mada'a lillahe da'e.
> Ayyuhal mab'uso fina Jai'ta bit amril muta'i."
>
> (Today we have seen the full moon appear before us from the southern hill of Sanniyat Al Wada.
>
> It is incumbent upon us to offer thanks for the invitation towards Allah and enlightenment shown to us.
>
> O Prophet (S.A.W.) who has been sent to us, you have brought to us such a creed that we shall follow.)

Sanniyat Al Wada was a hillock on the south of Madina. The people of this city used to come to this place to see off their guests. Hence it got this name which means the Hillock of Farewell.

> Once when the Holy Prophet (S.A.W.) reached Madina from a journey, he celebrated his return with a feast, sacrificing a cow or camel. *(Abu Daud)*

Celebrate weddings with jubilation: Associate your relations and friends in these festivities. The Holy Prophet (S.A.W.) has permitted singing of some good songs and the bearing of cymbals, on such occasions. This helps expression of happy sentiments and also publicises the marriage.

> Hazrat Ayeshah (R.A.A.) married a lady of her family to an Ansar. When she was being sent to her husband's house, the holy Prophet (S.A.W.) remarked "Why not a slave girl was sent to accompany her to beat the cymbals and sing some songs." *(Bukhari)*

When Hazrat Rabi bint Moawwiz was being married, some girls sitting around her were playing the cymbals. They were singing verses praising their relatives who had laid down their lives in the Battle of Badr. A girl sang the follwing verse.

"We have among us a Prophet (S.A.W.) who knows what is going to take place tomorrow."

> The Holy Prophet (S.A.W.) having heard this, said: "Leave this. Sing what you were singing earlier". *(Bukhari)*

Entertaining the People at Weddings : In order to celebrate a wedding, arrangements should also be made to entertain relations amid friends with a dinner or some eatables. The Holy Prophet (S.A.W.) himself invited people to Walima (a feast arranged by bridegroom after wedding) dinners and has strongly recommended it to others. He has said:

"If you have nothing, then at least slaughter a goat and feed (your guests)."

"If one cannot participate in a wedding, he should at least send a message or greetings. Presents and gifts offered on such occasions, revive and revitalize relations and put friendship on more cordial footing. However, the gift should be in keeping with one's financial position, and within limits, avoiding extravagance and show.

When you come across a Muslim brother express your intimacy and happiness by saying Assalam-o-Alaikum (Peace be upon you)

The Holy Qur'an says:

> "O Prophet of Allah! And when those who believe in Our revelations come unto thee, say: Peace be unto you!" (6 : 54)

This verse is addressed to the Holy Prophet (S.A.W.) and the Ummah has been instructed indirectly to follow this principle. When a Muslim meets another, they should exchange these sentiments of love and pleasure for each other. And the best way in which this can be done, is that they should solicit Allah's mercy for each other. One of them should say As-Salam-o-Alaikum (Peace be upon you) and the other should reply by saying Wa-alaikum as—Salam (Peace be upon you too). This greeting is a step for increasing mutual love and sympathy.

The Holy Prophet (S.A.W.) has said:

"You people cannot enter Paradise unless you become Momin (True Believer) and you cannot become a Momin as long as you do not love each other. Why should I not tell you the way in which you can love each other? You can do this by making salutation a common practice among you."

Paying Regards

Whether meeting each other or in correspondence, greetings should be offered in the Islamic way, as laid down by the Holy Qur'an and not the expressions current in the contemporary society. The mode of greeting prescribed in Islam is both simple, meaningful, effective and a comprehensive prayer invoking good wishes. When we say *As-Salamo-alaikum* to a brother, it means that Allah may protect him and bless him. When we say *As-Salam-o-alaikum,* we condense all the prayers for the welfare and peace for the good of the person addressed. And, if we express these words consciously, what better words can there be for expressing sentiments of affection sincerity and good wishes? When you receive your Muslim brother with *As-Salam-o-alaikum,* you, in reality invoke Allah's blessings and mercies.

The source of all mercies and peace, that peace which is *As-Salam,* And only he can achieve peace and tranquillity whom

Allah may grant this, and he, whom He deprives of Peace, is deprived of it in both the worlds.

The Holy Prophet (S.A.W.) has said:

> "As-Salam is one of the names of Allah which He has bestowed upon (the inhabitants of the earth) for their benefit. Therefore widely publicise *As-Salam* amidst yourselves," *(Al-Adab Al-Mufrad)*

Every Muslim should be greeted, whether known or stranger. Indeed it is enough that he is your brother in faith, and a Muslim must cherish sentiments of love, sincerity and well being for another Muslim . . . .

> A man asked the Holy Prophet (S.A.W.) "What is the best act in Islam?" The Holy Prophet (S.A.W.) replied "To feed the poor and to greet every Muslim, whether you know him or not." *(Bukhari - Muslim)*

When one enters his own house, he should greet the people in the house.

The Holy Qur'an says:

> "But when ye enter houses, salute one another with a greeting from Allah, blessed and sweet." (24 :61)

> Hazrat Anas states that he was instructed by the Holy Prophet (S.A.W.) "My dear son. Whenever you enter your house, greet the inmates of the house first. The prayer for welfare is a prayer full of blessings and purity which has been taught by Allah." *(Tirmizi)*

Likewise when you enter another person's house, greet the inmates before entering the house.

The Qur'an says:

> "O ye who believe: Enter not houses other than your own, without first announcing your presence and invoking peace upon the folk thereof." (24 : 27)

> **Even children be saluted.** This is an excellent way of teaching them the practice of salutation, and it is also

> *Sunnah* of the Holy Prophet (S.A.W.). Hazrat Anas once passed by children, greeting them and said this was the practice of the Holy Prophet (S.A.W.)
>
> *(Bukhari - Muslim)*

Hazrat Abdullah bin 'Umar was so much particular in this respect that he used to write "Salam' even to children in his letters.

> **Women can greet men and vice versa.** Hazrat Asma Ansariya says that once she was sitting in the company of her female companions when the Holy Prophet (S.A.W.) passed by and greeted them.
>
> *(Al-Adab Al-Mufrad)*

You should cultivate the habit of generously and lavishly offering greetings. Exchange lavish and generous greetings among yourself. This increases mutual love and affection, and Allah protects against harm and loss.

The Holy Prophet (S.A.W.) says:

> "I may tell you a thing which may help to increase mutual love and affection among you. You greet each other as much as you can." *(Muslim)*

He (S.A.W.) also said "Exchange salam all over. Allah will keep you safe and sound,"

> Greeting is to be regarded as the right of your Muslim brother. One should be generous in the discharge of this right, as the Holy Prophet (S.A.W.) has said: "It is the right of a Muslim that when his Muslim brother meets him, he should greet him." *(Muslim)*

Hazrat Abu Hurairah says:

> "The most miserly person is one who is niggardly in greeting. *(Al-Adab Al-Mufrad)*

Always take initiative in greeting. Even if there may be differences of opinion. You should be the first person in greeting and making peace.

The Holy Prophet (S.A.W.) has said:

"The person who takes lead in greeting is closer to Allah." *(Abu Daud)*

And further :

"It is not proper for a Muslim to remain estranged with his Muslim brother and avoid meeting him for more than three days. He, who greets first, has precedence." *(Al-Adab Al-Mufrad)*

Someone asked the Holy Prophet (S.A.W.) who, of the two people who meet, should greet earlier. He said the one who is better in the eyes of Allah, would greet first. *(Tirmizi)*

Hazrat Abdullah bin 'Umar was so much meticulous in this respect that nobody could ever succeed in saluting him first.

Greet loudly. Greetings should be offered orally in a loud voice, so that the person greeted should be able to hear and respond. Sign of greetings may be made with the hands also if necessary. As for example if the person greeted, is deaf or is at such a distance that the greeting would not be heard by him.

Hazrat Abdullah bin 'Umar says: "When a person is greeted he should be made to hear the greeting as it is prayer pure and full of blessings from Allah." *(Al-Adab Al-Mufrad)*

Hazrat Asma bint Yazid says that the Holy Prophet (S.A.W.) passed by a mosque where some women were sitting. He greeted them with the signs of his hand. *(Tirmizi)*

This means that the Holy Prophet (S.A.W.) not only greeted with words but with the movement of his hands as wall. This is Confirmed by the tradition in Abu Land. Hazrat Asma says that when the Holy Prophet (S.A.W.) passed by us, he (S.A.W.) greeted us. However it is better to greet verbally, and only where necessary, with the movement of hands.

Be careful to offer greetings to your elders. When you ate walking, greet those who are sitting; and when in small group, greet the larger group. The Holy Prophet (S.A.W.) has said;

> "The younger should greet the elder, the pedestrian should greet the seated one, and the smaller group should greet the larger one." *(Al-Adab Al-Maufrad)*

Greetings by riders, pedestrians and smaller groups. If you are riding, salute those on foot, and those on foot should greet those who are sitting: and the party of smaller numbers may greet the one with larger numbers.

Greet on arrival and departure. When you go to meet somebody, or reach his sitting room, or pass by a gathering, or arrive at a meeting, salute on arrival at a meeting, salute on arrival as well as when taking leave.

The Holy Prophet (S.A.W.) has said:

> "When you join a meeting, greet them and when leaving them, greet them again; and remember that the first salam (on arrival) is not worthy of more recompense than the second one. This means that you may be equally particular about your first and second greetings." *(Tirmizi)*

Don't greet a person by name in a gathering. When you go to a meeting, greet the gathering as a whole and you should not greet any body in particular. Once Hazrat Abdullah was in a mosque when a beggar came and greeted him by name.

Hazrat Abdullah said:

> "What Allah has said is true, and His Prophet (S.A.W.) has fulfilled his mission." He then went home; while those who heard this could not follow the real meaning of what he had said. However when he came back, Hazrat Tariq asked him to elucidate what he had said. He replied; "The Holy Prophet (S.A.W.) has said that towards the advent of Doomsday, people would start greeting particular persons individually by naming them in a meeting." *(Al-A dab Al-Mufrad)*

Send greetings through post. If you get an opportunity to send greetings to your friend, relative or senior through a third party, do send your greetings.

> Hazrat Ayeshah says: "The Holy Porphet (S.A.W.) said to me; "Ayeshah! Gabriel is greeting you. I replied: Wa Alaikum us-Salam wa Rahmat Allah wa Barakatuhu. " *(Bukhari - Muslim)*

Greeting mixed gathering of wakefuls and asleep. If you go to a place where some people are sleeping and some are awake, you should greet wakeful ones in such a tone that those who are asleep may not get disturbed, while only those who are awake may hear you.

Hazrat Miqdad says:

> "We used to keep a little milk for the Holy Prophet (S.A.W.). When he came late at night, he greeted in such a way that those awake heard him and those sleeping did not feel disturbed. The Holy Prophet (S.A.W.) came and greeted (us) in his customary way." *(Muslim)*

Start talking only after salutation. When you meet somebody, do not start talking with him spontaneously; but greet him first with *As salam-o-Alaikum* and then start talking. The Holy Prophet (S.A.W.) has directed: "Do not reply to a person who starts talking before saluting."

No greetings are to be offered when:

(i) People are busy reading or teaching or listenting to Holy Qur'an or the Hadis,

(ii) When a person is engaged in delivering or listening to a Khut'bah (sermon),

(iii) When someone is calling for the prayers or announcing Takbir,

(iv) When an assemably is discussing religious matters or when somebody is explaining some theological matters to someone,

(v) When a teacher is busy in teaching; and

(vi) When someone is in the bathroom (lavatory).

And under the following situations you should not only avoid greeting a person but also show your indifference. abhorrence and dislike with tact:

(i) When someone is busy in acts amounting to licentiousness, blasphemy and anti-religous games and amusements and thus is insulting the faith.

(ii) When a person is uttering abuses and having filthy nonsensical and false dialogue and cutting indecent and vulgar jokes, thus ridiculing Islam.

(iii) When a man is busy propagating views against Islam and Sunnah and exhorting the people to abandon Islam and take up atheism.

(iv) When somebody is abusing Islam, its tenets principles and exhibiting his inner vile nature and hypocrisy.

The Holy Prophet (S.A.W.) has said that: "Do not take initiative in greeting the Jews and Christians. A believer should avoid all such acts that may reflect even an iota of adoration or respect for the Jews. In fact he should always adopt an attitude which would make the Jew understand that the ultimate result of hostility to the truth results in disgrace and ignominy.

> "The Holy Prophet (S.A.W.) has said: Never take a lead in offering salutation to the Jews and Christians. When you come across them on the road, see that they give way and move to one side." *(Al-Adab Al-Mufrad)*

> **Salute a mixed gathering.** When an assembly has both Muslims and non-Muslims, they be greeted with "Salam". The Holy Prophet (S.A.W.) once passed a gathering of Muslims and non-believers and he thus saluted them. *(Al-Adab Al-Mufrad)*

When you have to greet a non-Muslim, do not salute him in the conventional Islamic manner. Instead, words like Adab Arz,

Taslimat, etc (Respects to you) should be used or you can use western style of salutation like 'Good Morning,' Good Evening or simply how do you do, hello etc. No signs with your hands or head should be shown in a way that may be contrary to Islam.

When the Holy Prophet (S.A.W.) sent his message to Heraclius (Hiraql) the emperor of the Eastern Roman Empire, he greeted him as follows:

> "Greetings be upon him who follows the guidance (of Allah)."

> **After greeting, clasp the hands** of your friend or relative to express your happiness and affection. The Holy Prophet (S.A.W.) and his companions used to do this. When a group of persons from Yemen came to the Holy Prophet (S.A.W.) he told his companions that among all the visitors they (the visitors from Yemen) were more deserving of a cordial hand shake than others." *(Abu Daud)*

Hazrat Huzaifa bin Yaman reports the Holy Prophet (S.A.W.) as having said:

> "When two believers meet each other and shake hands after salutation, their sins are shed like dry leaves from a tree." *(Tabarani)*

According to Hazrat Abdullah bin Masud, the Holy Prophet (S.A.W.) said: "A complete greeting is that in which hands are also shaken after salutation."

> **On the return of a friend, relative,** or an elder from a journey, embrace him as well. When Hazrat Laid bin Harisa returned to Madina from a journey, he knocked at the door of the Holy Prophet (S.A.W.). He (S.A.W.) came out with the sheet trailing behind and embraced him, and kissed him on the forehead. *(Tirmizi)*

> Hazrat Anas narrates that when the august companions met each outer, they used to shake hands with each other followed by an embrace, if they returned from a journey. *(Trbarani)*

TWELVE

Prosperous Living

A great portion of Islamic teachings comprises the commands and directions concerning the special life of Muslims, so that their physical and spiritual training may be accomplished. The foundation of this training is most excellent and purified. These are the etiquettes and regulations which are concerned with their eating, earning, wearing, residing and satisfying all their needs, for which a man makes efforts in this world. There is in them neither a leaning towards asceticism, nor towards greedy materialism. Its foundation is on moderation and balance, and for these reasons the enforcement of the training is simple and pleasant.

In its teachings Islam keeps both the body and the spirit before it, and does not allow one to have the upper hand on the other. It arranges for their needs in such a balanced way that a man finds them very helpful in fulfilling the responsibilities of this world and the next. As against this, the wild philosophies which men have invented in the absence of the divine revelations, to shape their lives, have not been successful in meeting the needs of the body and fulfilling the demands of the two. In these philosophies balanced concessions have not been provided for the world, from which the journey starts, to the Hereafter, where every man perforce has to return.

Some ideologies are such as crush the demands of the body. Their idea is that the soul can reach perfection only when it is freed from the chains of the body, while other philosophies declare pleasures and luxuries only as their ideal, and they move all the machinery of life around these philosophies. They cannot see anything beyond the demands of the body.

But Islam is a religion which pays attention to the principles of nature and is a balanced faith and a religion of moderation. There is no room in it of that asceticism, which has no mercy for the feelings and urges of mankind, and the entire humanity feels constrained about it. Islam has also nothing to do with that animalism and pleasure-seeking, whose centre and axis is only man's belly and sex.

In this connection we should not lose sight of this reality that a Momin who confirms the belief in the life in the Hereafter and an infidel who considers this life only as be-all and end-all of everything, have a lot of difference in their ways of living.

Many people who destroy their chastity and strive their every nerve to seek as much pleasure as they can belong to the latter kind, if they do not give up their ways. About them Allah has said:

> "Verily, Allah will cause those who believe and do good deeds to enter Paradise underneath which rivers flow, while those who disbelieve take their comfort in this life and eat even as the cattle eat, and the Fire is their habitation." (*Muhammed:12*)

In Surah Hijr, He has said:

> "It may be that those who disbelieve wish ardently they were Muslims. Let them eat and enjoy life, and let (false) hope beguile them. They will come to know!" (*Hijr : 2, 3*)

As regards Momin, he keeps his wishes and desires spreading over both this world and the next world. He seeks virtue and welfare in the present as well as in the future. The holy Quran has informed us that the bliss and the good fortune of this world and of the next is in remembering Allah and reciting His words and praises

> "So when you have accomplished your Day rites, then remember Allah as you remember your fathers, or with a greater zeal. There are men who say: 'Our Lord! Give us in this world,' and they will have no position

in the Hereafter. And there are men who say: 'Our Lord! Give us good in this world and good in the Hereafter, and save us from the torment of the Fire.' To these will be given what they have earned."

(*Baqarah: 200-202*)

Quran has advised to work for both this world and the Hereafter, because this world is the means of achieving success in the next world, and if the means would be good, there would be guarantee of success, as in the desired results can be expected. That is why Allah had advised Quran .

"But seek, with the (wealth) which Allah lets bestowed on you, the Home of the Hereafter, nor forget your portion in this world; but you do good as Allah has been good to you, and seek not (occasions for) mischief in the world, for Allah loves not those who do mischief." (*Qasas : 77*)

Sustainable Development

On account of these principles Islam does not favour the idea of being a slave to the belly and the sex, and man should adopt the ideal of going all out for pleasures because life comes only once and should make living for eating as his purpose in life. All efforts in life should not be confined to the activities of eating and enjoying. If he gets delicious and rich food, he is happy otherwise he grumbles against luck.

Those who are fully occupied with eating to their hearts' content and meeting every demand of their carnal desires, they spend their days and nights only in activities which revolve round these things. They cannot work not any high ideals, and their cowardice and lack of interest comes in the way of jihad and sacrifice.

The Prophet has said:

"Those who are gluttonous eaters will be the most hungry on the Day of Judgment." (*Al-Bazzar*)

It is well known that many diseases are caused by indiscreet eating. Man goes on eating and his desire is not satisfied, and his stomach is unable to digest. That is why in the hadith it is mentioned:

> "Adam's children do not fill any vessel worse than the belly." (*Tirmizi*)

Mere worshipping and abstinence from irrelevant things cannot save a man from the disease of gluttony. The correct method is that man should fix a great ideal and should busy himself in reaching that ideal. By this he can be saved from pleasure seeking and gluttony.

It is said that an infidel once was a guest of the Prophet. The Prophet ordered a goat to be milked, and the guest drank all the milk. The Prophet then asked to get a second goat and it was also milked, and the guest drank all the milk. Even then his hunger was not satisfied. In all, seven goats were milked and the guest singly drank all the milk. In the morning he embraced Islam. The Prophet again asked a goat to be milked. One goat's milk was drunk by the guest, but he could not finish the second goat's milk, on which the Prophet of God said:

> "Momin drinks in one stomach while the idfidel drinks in seven stomachs." (*Muslim*)

The reason for this is that when a man comes from nonbelief to Islam and when he realises this new responsibility, his deep relationship with his Lord, the reckoning which he has to undergo in the hereafter, on account of the loftiness of his courage and elevation of his senses, all these things become insignificant for him and he is satisfied with eating merely whatever is available.

The fact of the matter is that all these excesses, carnal desires and amusements are of no value, because by involving himself in them man falls down and disgraces himself, and which we can see today all around us.

The Prophet has said: "Man's food has been made an example for the world, if it is mixed with condiments and made tasty. Just see how it ends."

In another tradition it is mentioned

"Whatever comes from man Allah has related it as an example for the world." (*Ahmed*)

From these verses and traditions like these many people are likely to fall into a misunderstanding. They think that a Muslim should remain aloof from the world and the matters of the world, and the things declared *halal* and permissible by Allah should also be given up, although this is not at all the intention of Islam. To make a *halal* thing *haram* is as big a crime as to make the *haram* thing *halal*. Allah has a right over every Muslim that he should be an epitome of patience. He should not make his forbidden (haram) things permissible (halal). He should adopt the attitude of gratefulness and should not make clean and permissible things forbidden.

To enjoy life and to receive benefits from it is his right

"On those who believe and do the deeds of righteousness there is no blame for what they ate (in the past), when they guard themselves from evil and believe,—and do deeds of righteousness,(or) again, guard themselves from evil and believe, (or) again, guard themselves from evil and do good, for Allah loves those who do good." (*Maida: 96*)

And we have seen our holy great grandfather, Hazrat Ibrahim rushing and placing a roasted calf before his guests:

"Then he turned quickly to his houeshold. brought out a fatted calf, and placed it before them. He said: "Will you not eat?" (*Zariyat : 26, 27*)

The holy Prophet and his companions used to act an this command of Allah :

"O you who believe ! Make not unlawful the good things which Allah has made lawful for you, but commit no excess for Allah loves not those given to excess." (*Maida : 90*)

There are certain requirements and demands of the body, and if they are not met, the intellectuals say that great harm will be done. The worship and the mysticism which prevent these lawful demands being met are not the concern of Islam. The attacks which it has mounted on materialism is mainly with the purpose of discouraging and preventing men from losing themselves in the forbidden carnal desires and unlawful pleasures.

Neither Excess nor Shortage

Islam commands that a balanced policy be adopted in the matter of clothing. It is unliked by Islam that man should either be proud and conceited in respect of his clothes. For Islam good clothing is not included in the quality of manliness or in excellent moral character, because many times a man dressed in tattered clothes proves to be much more valuable than the heaps of gold and silver.

> Allah's Messenger has said: "How many persons in wretched condition and dressed in rags are such that if they swear by Allah for doing something, they will accomplish that thing." (*Tirmizi*)

It will be a first degree foolishness if a man should clothe himself in costly clothes in order to display himself and his clothes, and should look upon them with pride and strut before others in vanity.

Here you will find innumerable young men who spend hours together in their homes to dress and make themhselves presentable. If they are asked to spend their valuable time in acquiring knowledge and in making efforts to awaken their religious consciousness, they will run away startled. According to them, dressing beautifully and appearing in a presentable form is the height of perfection, that is all!

Islam has stopped men from indulging in such acts very strictly, and has warned Muslims to avoid acting in this foolish manner. Allah's Messenger has said:

> He who puts on the clothes of fame in this world will be clothed in the clothes of disgrace by Allah on the Day of Judgment, and He will put the clothes afire." (*Ibn Majah*)

The fact is that the victims of this wickedness, men and women, when they find themselves wanting in etiquette and good manners and morals, they try to hide their defects in costly clothing and valuable dresses. A great pity on this kind of thinking!

> Abu Barida narrates that he went to Hazrat Ayesha and she showed a sheet of cloth having patches and a lungi made in Yemen and said swearing by God that Allah's Messenger breathed his last while wearing those two pieces of clothing. (*Bukhari*)

> Hazrat Jabir narrates that they attended the feast *(walima)* of the marriage of Hazrat Ali and Hazrat Fatima, and they did not see any better feast than that. They filled in the leaves of the palm in the bedding, and they ware presented with dates and raisins, *(munaqqa)*, and they ate them. Their bedding on the wedding night was the shin of a sheep.
>
> (*Bazzar*)

Avoiding wasteful spending and being satisfied with the necessities of life only are the signs of perfect morals and manners.

But it does not mean that Islam only likes poor and mean clothes, or wretched looks and ugly appearances are its favourites, or it desires that old, torn and patched up clothes should be worn, as some uneducated worshippers think. There is no room for such kind of thinking in the religion.

> One fellow asked Abdullah Ibn Umar as to what kind of clothes he should wear. He replied that he should wear such clothes which should not provoke the fools to taunt him and the intellectuals to consider objectionable. He again asked as to what should be its cost. He replied : "Between five dirham and twenty dirham." (*Tibrani*)

The prices mentioned were according to the conditions obtaining in the time of Hazrat Umar. In our times the prices will be higher.

> A man went to the Prophet. He was dressed poorly. The Prophet asked him : "Have you any wealth ?" He

> said: "Yes." He asked : "Of what kind ?" The man replied : "Allah has blesssd me with all kinds of wealth." The Prophet said "When Allah has given you wealth, then display the effect of Allah's benevolence and blessing." (*Nisai*)

There is another hadith

> "If a man is well to do, what will he lose if he would keep two pieces of clothing for Friday in addition to his working clothes." (*Abu Daud*)

You must have realised that Islam desires that its followers should put on good clothes and they should be clean and presentable. But there is a big difference. On one side is a man who conceals the real state of affairs and displays his wealth and spends his wealth on beautifying his body and clothes. On the other side how lofty is the behaviour of another man who safeguards his reality and perfects his morals and considers these things as the main purpose of his life, and in this abundance of duties and responsibilities, he does not miss the opportunities of displaying Allah's favours, good manners and good taste.

The world is moaning under the burden of the innumerable clothes and dresses for the different months of the year. Certain clothes are worn during the summer only while other dresses are put on during the winter months. And the clothes donned during the spring have different styles and different fashions. In the Kharif season there are altogether different dresses. Nay, we can see varied clothes during the different hours of the day. The clothes to be worn for work and during the waking hours should be diverse, and for the sleeping hours something else. This unnecessary formality and immitation is common in the societies of east as well as the west. The fair sex, and the youths running after them and men like them, are all tied in the same knot of custom and convention. Islam is unconcerned with this kind of selfish desires, and exhorts people fearing God to avoid them.

> Allah's Messenger has said : "There is ruin for the women covered with gold and coloured in the yellow colour." (*Ibn Habban*)

This warning is given to those women who are mad after ornaments and who are negligent of their duties and responsibilities.

These Islamic teachings are quite known that wearing gold and silk is haram (forbidden) for men. There is some room for other things, but it is against the dignity of men that they should use ornaments and should be always enveloped in seems. As regards women, they are allowed to use gold and silk, but they should not be entangled in beautifying and adorning themselves in such a way that it may result in waste of time and money.

Balanced in construction : Islam does not prevent from building strong forts and ramparts, from opening schools and universities, from constructing waiting rooms for travellers and hospitals, and from spending lakhs of rupees on them. The religion does not forbid these things, because generations terminate but the public welfare goes on, and therefore the necessity of tall and lofty structures is accepted, but how can this foolishness be explained that man builds, for his personal pleasure and luxuries, palaces and squanders money for these things like water?

Islam likes one to be generous and open-hearted is constructing one's house, but it advises its followers to desist from excesses, spending wastefully and undue formalities.

Qais bin Hazim narrates that they went to the sick bed of Khubab bin Al-Ars and saw that there were seven spots in his belly. He said : "Our companions passed away in such a way that the world did not harm them a bit, and today we are so sorry that its only use seems to be dust. Had Allah's Prophet not forbidden us to invite death. I would have prayed for it."

Then again we went in his presence, and saw him constructing a wall. He said

> "Whatever a Muslim spends on a thing, he gets his reward, however no reward is given for the wealth spent on this dust." (*Bukhari*)

This great companion of the Prophet was doing a work, but owing to his being greatly conscious about the duty of spending in the cause of Allah he thought that no reward would be given for the money he was spending on construction. It would have been so, had he been doing the construction with a view to profit making or satisfying his pride, and would have been negligent about the Hereafter, and would have been in love with the world, but if he was constructing the wall for his own security and maintenance, then he would definitely get its reward, and construction for this purpose is also a form of worship. (For details the discussion on Sincerity may be seen)

But about the personal property the commands of Islam are very clear and unambiguous. It has cut the roots of luxurious living and pleasure-loving in homes. It has forbidden to lead the domestic life in a grand style and squandering money for unnecessary things.

When Ma'az bin Jabal was sent as a governor of Yemen, the Prophet advised him:

> Avoid luxurious living, for Allah's slaves are not comfort- seeking." (*Ahmed*)

That is why Islam has forbidden to use utensils of gold and silver, bedding and floor-covering of harir and silk.

> It is enough for the people that they should have their utensils made from the usual and common materials, similarly their beading too. Hazrat Huzaifa narrates that the Prophet had forbidden them to eat or drink from the utensils made from gold and silver, and had prevented them from wearing Harir and silk, and from sitting on them. (*Bukhari*)

Sometimes people misunderstand that Islam is a symbol of harsh and strict living. Supposing that such an image of Islam is correct, then what is wrong with this ? However, it is surprising that life's softness and delicacy should be considered incomplete without the use of silk and gold.

For the entire humanity it is possible to live with satisfaction and happiness without using silver and gold and without wearing silk and Harir.

But Islam wants that the roots of luxurious living and wasteful spending should be thrown out from the individual as well as society's life, so that a strong community may be built up. It is the responsibility of the Muslim community that it should spend its life in the service of Allah's religion. It should strive continually for raising the word of Truth and for supporting the true religion, and it should keep clear its external and internal life from the mischiefs of the world and even from small amusements.

To be drowned in the carnal desires and to be contaminated with forbidden (haram) things is to run away from the responsibilities and to avoid putting in efforts and labour. It also amounts to losing the signs of decency and greatness. The community which is contaminated with evils inevitably loses its honour and decency.

> Allah's Messenger has said : "In my Ummah there will come people who will be eating different kinds of colourful foods, will be drinking various kinds of drinks, and will be putting on varied types of clothes ; and they will be talking by opening their mouth widely. These will be the worst people of my Ummah." (*Tibrani*)

If you want to see the picture of this hadith, then have a glance at the conditions of those people who consider religion as a philosophy, and have made it a means of amusement and pastime. They were lost in the world, and the reality of their religion was lost in between them. As a poet has said

> "The reality is lost in the stories.
>
> This community is lost in the absurdities."

Sustainable Consumption

Allah has condemned those who were lost in the pleasures of the world and were drowned in their amusements, those who had employed all their abilities in satisfying the demands of their bodily pleasures and carnal desires, and were seekers of mean and lowly things

> "And on the Day that the Unbelievers will be placed before the Fire, (it will be said to them): "You received your good things in the life of the world, and you took your pleasure out of them ; but today you shall be recompensed with a penalty of humiliation; for that you were arrogant on earth without just cause, and that you (ever) transgressed." (*Ahqaf* : 20)

And when they will be punished, they will be reminded that this is happening on account of their lack of balanced living and moderation and for their losing themselves in waywardness and carelessness.

> "This is because you exulted in the earth without right, and because you were petulant." (*Mumin* : 75)

The fact of the matters is that because of the disintegration of the Islamic government the greater portion of the Muslim population is lacking in moderation and balanced living, is drowned in pleasures and carnal desires, though they were warned by the Messenger of Allah against this disruption and waywardnes:

> Abu Barzah has narrated that Allah's Messenger has said : "I have fears about you from the waywardness of your bellies and sex and the carnal desires." (*Ahmed*)

The advent of Islam began with poor and helpless men ; so poor that they were unable to meet even their proper requirements, what to speak of their eating delicious things to their hearts' content. And they served Islam in this simple and Bedouin type of living.

> Abu Huraira has reported that he had seen seventy 'Ashab-i-Suffa', but none among them had sufficient clothes to cover the body ; either there was a lungi or other piece of cloth which they used to throw around their necks; some cloth could reach the middle of the calf and in some cases up to the knees ; they used to adjust it with their hands from fear of exposing their private parts. (*Bukhari*)

Poverty is a troublesome adversity. It is the responsibility of the people that they should try to be relieved of this adversity. Islam itself declares the grandeur and magnificence of the world as the right of the Faithfuls. The Prophet was apprehensive that when Islam will be in power and its principles will be spread to the four corners of the world, this severe lack of wealth might show its reaction. Accordingly the condition which was likely to follow after his death, he warned about it and said that if the lack of material wealth is bad, then to be involved in its mischiefs and to be entangled in its trials is worse than that.

Moderation is the outcome of greatness. Here moderation means that the life and the conditions of living should be brought under control so that they may be used for reaching the high ideal, and not for collecting and hoarding worldly good, and nor is total deprivation of material goods is right which makes a man helpless and useless.

This was the meaning of the following saying of the Prophet (S.A.W.)

> "By God, I am not afraid of your poverty, but I fear that the world will spread its net over you, as it had spread it over the people who preceded you. Then you will also compete in world-seeking, as they had begun doing it. So it will also destroy you, as it had destroyed the people before you." (*Bukhari*)
>
> And Allah's Messenger has said: "Beauty of form, seriousness and moderation are among the twenty four parts of prophethood." (*Tirmizi*)

THIRTEEN

Professional Life

Always try to sit in the company of well behaved and virtuous people. Take lively part in the deliberations of the gathering. To sit tongue-tied with a gloomy face is a sign of diffidence, while sitting quiet with wrinkles on the forehead reflects pride. When the companions of the Holy Prophet (S.A.W.) held discussions in company, the Holy Prophet (S.A.W.) used to join them in those parleys. Therefore, never wear a dour face in an assembly. Sit with a smiling face.

Sit wherever you find a place. Do not rush or push others in order to reach the front line, This is an obnoxious practice and causes inconvenience to those who are already sitting there, and makes the person doing this, look haughty.

Do not try to snatch a seat from a person already seated from his seat in a meeting. This will not be tolerated by any body and will send a wave of resentment and hatred for you among those present there. It will, by the way, indicate as if you are somebody big and important.

Don't behave ridiculously while sitting in a meeting. If people are sitting in a circle, do not sit in the empty space, in the centre. This is extremely rude and absurd. The Holy Prophet (S.A.W.) has expressed his dislike for such people.

Do not occupy the place of a person who has left the meeting temporarily. Let it remain reserved for him, and occupy it only if you know for certain that he will not come back.

If two persons are sitting close to each other, do not try to separate them, as they may be sitting there for some good reason. Segregating them, would make them feel hurt.

Do not try to sit on a distinctive place in a meeting unless you are invited to do so. Take care not to sit with your legs spread and calves exposed.

Do not try to sit near the master of ceremonies of the meeting and take your seat in such a way that the people coming later, are not obstructed. Incoming persons should be accommodated without any grumble.

Improper Way of Courtesy : Do not stand in front of or around somebody even if it may be as an expression of courtesy. This way of courtesy is contrary to Islamic teachings.

When in a company, two persons should not whisper to each other. Others would feel that they have not been taken into confidence or that they are being talked about.

Don't Show Off in a Meeting : If you have to say anything, say it with the permission of the sir, and do not adopt an attitude in the course of discussion or questions and answers, which may indicate as if you were the Chairman or somebody important. This may be taken as if you wanted to show off. This may also be considered as an insult to the chair.

One person should speak at a time, and everyone should have a chance to be heard with attention. Those present should not lose patience and start speaking simultaneously, creating confusion and chaos in the meeting.

Maintain Secrecy : If secret matters have been discussed in the meeting, they should not be disussed elsewhere. The assembly owes it to its members that its deliberations and decisions are not divulged.

Another suject should not come under discussion while a subject is already being discussed. Also do not interrupt another speaker. However, if the situation demands that you should speak then and there, seek the permission of the person who is already speaking.

The Chairman of the meeting should be fair in giving all the members equal chance to express their opinion freely, and he should have his eyes all over the assembly.

Prayer at the End of the Meeting : Offer the following prayer before the assembly diperses:

> "O Allah! Grant us capacity to fear Thee which may help us to save ourselves from sin. Vouchsafe us Thine obedience which may help us to reach Thy Paradise. Give us that firm faith before which all our losses may the world pale into insignificance. O Allah ! As long as Thou keepest us alive, grant us the capacity to derive full benefit from our sense of hearing, and bodily energy and keep this good in operation after us, Wreak revenge upon our oppressors and grant us victory over our enemies. Do not, O Allah, test us in our faith nor make the world our goal. Make not the world as the optimum of our knowledge, nor make us over to a person who pities us not."

Business Manners

The Best Earning : Work hard with enthusiasm to earn your living from your business and don't be a burden upon others. Once the Holy Prophet (S.A.W.) was asked as to what was the best way of earning. He said:

"The earning which is earned through one's own efforts, and the business which is free from falsehood, and cheating."

Be Truthful in Your Business : To develop your venture always speak the truth, and shun falsehood in any form.

The Holy Prophet (S.A.W.) has said:

> "On the Doomsday Allah shall not speak to, nor look at, nor purify the person and admit him into Paradise who promotes his business through false oaths."
>
> *(Muslim)*

> He (S.A.W.) also said: "Eschew false oaths for increasing your business, for, although in the short term, they look like promotion, but ultimately it loses blessings and profit." *(Muslim)*

> ***Be always honest and trustworthy*** in your dealings. Do not pollute your *Halal* (Lawful) income through black -marketting or supplying poor quality goods. The Prophet of Allah (S.A.W.) has said in this context; "Allah will raise an honest and reliable tradesman with the Prophets, Siddiqs (Friends of Prophet) and Martyrs on the Day of Judgement." *(Tirmizi)*

Always try to supply the best possible Goods to the customer. If your are not certain about the quality of the goods, do not sell the same to the customer. If customer seeks your advice, be honest in giving him the best advice.

Try to win the confidence of the customers, so that they may regard you as their well-wisher and trust you. The Holy Prophet (S.A.W.) has said:

> "The person who subsisted on rightly-earned earnings follows my Sunnah, and did not harm the people in any way is a person destined for the heaven." The Companions said: "O Prophet of Allah; "Such people are in great number in these days." He said: "Even after me such people will abound." *(Tirmizi)*

Always be punctual and reach your shop or office in time, and work there patiently and steadily. The Holy Prophet (S.A.W.) has said:

> "Go in search of your livelihood early in the morning as the business conducted in the morning brings blessings and abundance." *(Tabarani)*

Work hard yourself and see that your employees also work hard. But they should be treated well and sympathetically. Don't treat them curtly or express anger or suspicion.

The Holy Prophet (S. A.W.) has observed in this context: "Allah does not grant piety to the people among whom the poor are not given their due share."

Be always polite with the customers; you should neither be harsh with them nor be inflexible when demanding return of loan.

The Holy Prophet (S.A.W.) has said: "May Allah have mercy upon the person who in matters of business and recovery of debts deals with sympathy and courtesy." *(Bukhari)*

He (S.A.W.) also said: "Anyone wishing to be saved from the worry and suffocation on Doomsday, should give latitude to the debtor who is empty handed, to enable him pay his debt, or to take off the load of debt from his shoulders." *(Muslim)*

You should avoid passing defective goods as wholesome. The buyer should be explained the defects of the product if there be any. The Holy Prophet (S.A.W.) once passed by a stock of grain. He touched it and fell moisture inside the stock. He asked the stockist what it was. The merchant said: "O Prophet of Allah (S.A.W.), rains poured upon this stock." The Holy Prophet (S.A.W.) remonstrated: "Then why did you not place the wet wheat over the rest of the stock, so people could see it for themselves. Any one practising deception has no relationship with me."

Do not hold back and hoard food grains expecting a risk in price so that you may earn excessive profits. This amounts to harrassing Allah's creatures. Holy Prophet's (S.A.W.) injunction on this issue is clear. "He who hoards is a sinner."

Be Fair in Measuring and Weighing : The buyer should be given full measure what he has paid. The same measure should be observed both for sale and purchase. The Holy Prophet (S.A.W.) has warned such merchants: "You have been made responsible for two such things which (if mishandled) have led earlier nations towards destruction." The Holy Quran says:

1. Woe unto the defrauders:
2. Those, who when they take the measure from mankind demand it full,
3. But, if they measure unto them, or weigh for them, they cause them loss.
4. Do such (men) not consider that they will be raised again.
5. Unto an awful Day,

6. The day when (all) mankind stand before the Lord of the Worlds ? (83 : 1-6)

Make Amends for Lying and Wrong Acts : You should make it a point to make up for the acts of omissions and commissions in the course of your business, through Sadaqah and alms as Kaffarah (expiation). The Holy Prophet's (S.A.W.) directive in this connection to tradesmen is as follows:

"O ye, who deal in trade! In business transaction there are chances of lying and commiting worng. Therefore, you should invariably give Sadaqah from your wealth."

One should always bear in mind that trade, which will salvage us from dire punishment in the next world, and which gives in return not material wealth, but everlasting triumph, pleasure and tranquillity, as the Qurna has said:

> O, ye who believe! shall I show you a commerce that will save you from a painful doom? You should believe in Allah and His messenger, and should strive for the cause of Allah with your wealth and your lives. That is better for you, if you did not know. (61 : 10 - 11)

In Times of Distress

How to Behave in Emergencies : Whether due to the fear of killing, bloodshed, looting, atrocities or widespread disturbances by the anti-Islam forces or apprehension of large scale devastation brought about by natural phenomena, in any case, as a Muslim you have to give a good account of yourself. You should try to find out the real causes of such happenings instead of wasting time on shallow measures and take steps as laid down in the Holy Qur'an and the Sunnah.

The Qur'an says:

> "And the mishaps that have visited you, are the results of your misdeeds. And Allah does forgive many of your misdeeds." (42 : 30)

And further the Holy Qur'an has shown the remedy in these words:

> "And turn to Allah, all of you together, O Muslims, so that you may succeed." (24 :31)

Taubah means to 'Turn to' to 'Revert to'. When the Ummah engulfed in the whirlpool of sins feels repentant on its sins, returns to Allah with all humility, and washes its sins with the tears of repentance, renewing its pledge of faithfulness and obedience to Allah, such an act is designated as *"Taubah"* by the Holy Qur'an and it is this *"Taubah"* or repentance that is the best remedy against all kinds of fears and trepidetion.

Do not yield or surrender to the enemies of your religion, as a result of your fear of their atrocities. Do not beg for mercy from the merciless. Do not smear your national image with the spots of cowardice. Instead, we should brace up and cultivate that courage for want of which we are losing ground to the enemies of Islam.

Cause of the Downfall of the Muslims : The Holy Prophet (S.A.W.) has already anticipated that:

> "A time will come when other nations shall fall upon my (Ummah) like hungry people jostling for food. Some one enquired, "O! Prophet of Allah, will our population be so small that other nations would gang up to swallow us." "No", replied the Holy Prophet (S.A.W.), "Your number will not be small : but you will be weightless like the sticks or straw carried by a river in spate. The enemies will not be afraid of you, as your hearts will be filled with cowardice. On being asked by a person as to why the Ummah would lose courage, the Holy Prophet (S.A.W.) said, "This would be due to the Muslims' love for the world and their distaste for death and avoiding to die for a just cause."
>
> *(Abu Daud)*

We should constantly carry on Jihad against collective maladies which cause panic and fear within the society, and poverty, famine, and bloodshed become all too common; such a situation is the ideal compost on which tyrants grow and hold the people in the vice of ear. Hazrat Abdullah-ibn-Abbas has said:

"A people among whom the habit of misappropriation becomes rampant, Allah will make them suffer from fear of the enemy. And a society in which adultery is common is doomed to perish; while persons practising short measure, shall invariably suffer from famine and starvation; and a place where judgments are unjust shall suffer from murder and killing; and a nation that betrays and turns its back on solemn affirmation, shall be subjugated by the enemy. *(Miskhat)*

Courage in the Midst of Ordeals : However shocking be the circumstances, we should always ,support the truth. To die in the cause of truth is better than to live a life devoid of faith and honour. Even if beset with the severest trial and danger, we should not abandon truth. If somebody threaten us with death, we should smile and, if the occasion for martyrdom comes, we should welcome it. The Holy Prophet (S.A.W.) has said:

"The wheel of Islam is in rotation. Turn to the direction shown by the Quran. Beware! The Quran and the (secular) power (state) shall soon separate. Beware! Lest you leave the Quran. There will be rulers who would make decisions about you. and if you submit to them, they would deflect you from the right path; and if you refuse to obey them, they may kill you." A companion asked: "Then what should we do?" The Holy Prophet (S.A.W.) said: "Do what the disciples of Christ did. They were sawed alive and crucified but they did not falter. It is far better to die in obedience to Allah than to live a miserable life in disobedience to Him."

Prayers for Safety from Enemies : When there is fear from enemies, the following prayer is to be recited:

"Allah! we make Thee our shield against these enemies, and seek Thy protection against their mischiefs."

"O Allah! cover my defects and grant me peace and immunity from fear and anxiety."

How to Act When Over-taken with Fear and Panic : The following prayer is to be recited when you are over taken with fear and panic.

"Pure and Sublime is Allah the real King, free from all blemishes. Lord of Angels and Jibrail. Thou hast covered the Heavens and the Earth with glory and might."

God willing, fear will be banished and you will receive peace of mind. According to Hazrat Baraa-bin-Azib: "This prayer was prescribed by the Holy Prophet (S.A.W.) to a person who complained of dread haunting him. He recited this prayer and the dread was dispelled. (*Mujam Al Tabrani*)

How to React on Seeing a Hurricane : When there is high wind or storm, it is natural that one should feel anxiety and fear.-Hazrat Ayeshah (R.A.A.) says that she never saw the Holy Prophet (S.A.W.) laugh so as to make his mouth open widely. He would smile only. And whenever there was a thick cloud or high wind, he used to feel anxious and started praying. He (S.A.W.) would get up and sit down, and this restlessness persisted till it rained. Hazrat Ayeshah (R.A.A.) says, she asked the Holy Prophet (R.A.A.) "O Prophet of Allah, I see people turn cheerful when they see the rain-laden clouds, but I see uneasiness and anxiety on your face, when you see thick cloud". The Holy Prophet (S.A.W.) replied "O Ayeshah, how can I feel immune from anxiety, when I know that the people of 'Aad were visited by similar clouds, which they thought would rain water over them, but they brought catastrophe. (*Bukhari - Muslim)*

On such occasions recite *Surah Al Falaq* (Chapter 113 and *Surah An Nas* (Chapter 114) of the Holy Quran:-

Translation of Chapter 113 is given below:

"Say: I seek refuge in the Lord of day-break, from the evil of that which He, created, from the evil of the darkness When it is intense and from the evil of the malignant witchcraft, and from the evil of the envier when he entreth.

Translation of Chapter 114 is given below:

"Say: I seek refuge in the Lord of mankind, the King of mankind, the God of mankind, from the evil of the sneacking whisperer Jinns and menkind.'

According to Hazrat Ayeshah, the Holy Prophet (S. A.W.) recited the following prayer when he saw high wind rising:

O Allah! I ask Thee the good of this wind and the good of whatever is in it; and good for the purpose for which it has been sent. And I seek Thy protection from the evil of the wind, from the evil of that, which is in it, and from the evil of the purpose for which it has been sent. *(Muslim)*

When there is apprehension of danger due to heavy rains, the following prayer is to be offered:

"Allah! let it rain around us, not upon us. Let it rain over mountains, hillocks, valleys, fields, and on places where vegetation grows." *(Muslim)*

When there is roaring of the clouds and thunder, all conversation should be stopped and the following Ayah of the Holy Qur'an be recited:

"The Thunder hymneth His praise and sends the angels for awe of Him." (13 : 13)

Hazrat Abdullah Ibn Zubair, used to stop talking on hearing the roaring of the thunder and started reciting this *Ayah*. *(Al Adab Al-kufrad)*

Hazrat Ka'b says anyone who recites this Ayah thrice, shall be safe from the ill effects of the roaring of the clouds. *(Tirmizi)*

When the Holy Prophet (S.A.W.) used to hear the roaring of thunder, recited:

"Allah kill us not with Thy wrath; destroy us not with Thy punishment and take us in Thy protection before the advent of such an adverse moment."

When fire breaks out, 'Allaho Akbar' should be recited continuously alongwith strenous efforts to put it out. The Holy Prophet (S.A.W.) has said: "When there is a fire, recite 'Allaho Akbar', this extinguishes the fire."

When there is eclipse either of the sun (kasuf) or the moon (khasuf), prayers should be offered and alms be given to the poor. As a result of these supplications, Allah will ward off all catastrophies and miseries.

Hazrat Mughirah ibn Shu'bah says that the Holy Prophet (S.A.W.) once remarked:

> "The sun and moon are simply two signs of Allah. The two planets do not come under eclipse due to the death or birth of an individual. When you see them under eclipse, solicit Allah's mercy and pray till such time as the sun or the moon gets cleared."
>
> *(Bukhari - Muslim)*

How to Pray : When there is solar eclipse, prayers should be offered in congregation in the mosque, but there should be no call for prayers Azan or Iqamat. Only people should congregate and offer prayers. When there is a lunar eclipse, Nafils (optional prayers) should be offered individually and not collectivity.

Continuous Nafil Prayers During Eclipse : When there is a solar eclipse, two Nafils should he offered, and the recitation (during the Qiyam) should be longer than usual. Prayers are to be continued till the eclipse is cleared. Verses from the Holy Qur'an should be recited a bit loudly.

> There was a solar eclipse during the life time of the Holy Prophet (S. A.W.). Incidentally Hazrat Ibrahim, the infant son of the Holy Prophet (S.A.W.) died on that very day. People began to attribute the eclipse to the death of Hazrat Ibrahim. When this was brought to the notice of the Holy Prophet (S.A.W.) he collected the people and offered a two-rakat prayer, with a long qirah during the qiyam, reciting Surah Al-Baqarah. He knelt (Ruku) and prostrated (Sajdah) for a longer spell. By the time the prayer was over, the sky was

clear. The Holy Prophet (S.A.W.) then told the worshippers that solar and lunar eclipses are two signs from Allah and the same is not due to the birth or death of anyone. He exhorted the people to take recourse to prayers and contemplation on such occasions, and to offer prayers and charities.

(Bukhari — Muslim)

Hazrat Abdul Rahman bin Samurah has this to say about a solar eclipse.

"A solar eclipse took place during the blessed days of the Holy Prophet (S.A.W.). I was practising archery outside Madina. I threw the arrows and at once left for the city to see for myself as to what the Holy Prophet (S.A.W.) does on this occasion. As such I presented myself before the Holy Prophet (S.A.W.). I saw that with his hands cupped and raised, he was praying and supplicating to Allah. He then offered a two-rakat prayer, reciting two long surahs. He remained thus engaged till the eclipse was cleared."

Which Surahs are to be Recited : When the prayer is for the solar eclipse, Surah Ankabut (The spider) is to he recited after Surah Fatihah in the first Rakat and Surah Rum in the second Rakat. It is better to recite these Surahs although the same is not compulsory; other Surahs can also be recited.

If women desire to participate in congregational prayers held for solar eclipse, they may be allowed to do so. Children should also be encouraged to join such a congregation so that the concept of monotheism takes roots in their hearts from the very beginning and no contrary impression takes root.

As laid down by the Shariah prayers are not to be offered at sunrise, sunset and when the sun is at its peak. If the solar eclipse has occurred during these hours, prayers should not be offered, only recitation of supplications and verses from the holy Qur'an together with distribution of alms and charities be done. If the eclipse persists even after these prohibited hours prayers can be offered.

FOURTEEN

Freedom from Evils

What would be a better way of giving comfort to hearts, of removing sorrow and of providing coolness to the eyes than that man should live the life with a healthy and peaceful heart. His bosom should be free from the disturbances of rancour, jealousy and ill-feelings for others. He should be glad to see others enjoying the comfort of life, and should consider it as a favour of Allah and think that all slaves are dependent on Him. He should remember the saying of the Messenger of Allah:

> "O Allah! The gifts that you have bestowed on me or on any other creatures, it is only on account of your favour, in which none is associated with You. All praises and all thanks are for You." (*Abu Daud*)

And when a man should find some other person in difficulty, and sorrowful, he should sympathise with him, and pray to Allah to remove his difficulties and to pardon his sins, and he should remember that prayer which the Prophet had made to God:

"O Allah ! If you are the Forgiver, then forgive the sins of all creatures. And no slave of Yours should be in difficulty."

A Muslim should live in such a way that he should be a sympathiser of the people and a sharer of the woes of humanity. He should be content and thankful for his life and should be happy with whatever Allah has given him. His self should be rree from the feelings of jealousy and rancour. The corruption of heart from rancour and jealousy is a fatal disease from such a heart faith disappears immediately, like the liquid that flows down from the hole in its container.

Islam pays special attention to heart, for a black heart tarnishes righteous acts, it disfigures its attractiveness, and it stains and mars its brightness.

And if the heart is glowing, then Allah bestows prosperity even on a small act of righteousness, and towards it every good rushes speedily and makes its place in it (heart).

> Abdullah bin A'mar narrates : "The Messenger of Allah was asked as to what people were great (in virtue). The Prophet replied: 'One whose heart is neat and clean, and whose tongue is truthful.' He was told : `We are aware of the truthful tongue but what is the meaning of neat and clean heart.' He replied: 'One that fears God, is free from evils, there is no sin in it, neither insubordination, jealousy nor rancour'."
>
> (*Ibn Majah*)

Therefore, in reality the Muslim society truly is that which is based on mutual lout, friendship, brotherhood, the feeling for mutual co-operation and straight dealings. There is no room for an ungrateful person in that society, no place for a person nursing jealousy and rancour in his bosom ; on the contrary his condition should be like this:

> "And those who came after them say : 'Our Lord! Forgive us, and our brethren who came before us into the Faith, and leave not in our hearts rancour (or some injury), against those who have believed. Our Lord! You are indeed full of Kindness. Most Merciful'."
>
> (*Hashr : 10*)

Keep away from mutual enmity **:** When the quarrel intensifies and its roots go deeper, and its thorns become branches and branches increase in number, then the freshness of the fruits of faith is adversely affected. Softness, sympathy, satisfaction and peace which are encouraged by the Islamic teachings receive a setback. Performance of worship loses its righteousness, nor does the self get any benefit from it.

Many times the mutual quarrels perturb the persons who claim to be wise. In this they take a recourse to the lowly and superficial things, and sometimes indulge in such dangerous acts which only increase difficulties and bring troubles. When a man is displeased, his eyes become prejudiced and ignore the camel and object to gnat. Such eyes do not appreciate the beauty of the peacock, for they only see its ugly feet and claws. If a slight defect is present, it turns the molehill into a mountain. And sometimes the internal rancour and jealousy affect them so badly that no hesitation is felt in inventing imaginary stories. Islam disapproves of all these manifestations of ill-feeling and advises to abstain from them. It declares their avoidance as the most virtuous form of worship.

> The Prophet has said : "Listen, may I not tell you something more important than salat, fasting and charity?" The people requested him to do so. He said : "To keep the mutual relationship on the right footing, because the defect in the mutual relationship is a thing which shaves a thing clean, I do not mean that it shaves the hair, but that it shaves (removes) the religion." (*Tirmizi*)

Many times Satan is not able to persuade wise men to worship idols, but since he is very keen on misguiding and ruining open, he manages to succeed in driving them away from God, so much so that these wise men become more indifferent in respecting the rights of God than the idolaters themselves. The best method adopted by the devil for this purpose is to sow the seeds of enmity in the hearts of the people. When this enmity develops into a fire and open hostilities result, he enjoys the scene. This fire burns man's present and future into ashes and totally destroys their relationship and virtues.

> The Messenger of Allah has said : "The Satan has been disappointed that he would not be worshipped in the Island of Arabia, but he has not been disappointed from kindling the fire of fighting among the people." (*Muslim*)

It means that when wickedness takes roots in the hearts, and people start hating love and brotherhood and when these are destroyed, people revert to cruelty and enmity, and break all those relations and connections for joining which Allah has given command; and thus they spread corruption on this earth.

Do not sever relations : Islam is fully alert in respect of the destructive causes of aggression and excesses, and tries to remedy them before they may go beyond the limit. It is common knowledge that men differ from one another in their nature and temperament. If their mutual contact does not result in clashes and estrangement, then inevitably there will appear narrowness and perturbation. For this reason Islam has formulated such principles as may keep the Muslims away from disruption and mischief, and as may generate in their hearts the feelings of love and friendship. For this purpose Islam has forbidden its followers from severing relations and mutual enmity.

In human life it so happens if the slightest excess is experienced from some other persons, then it causes us pain, and immediately we sever our relations.

But Allah does not like that the mutual relationship among Muslims should be subjected to such adverse consequences.

> Allah's Messenger has said : "Do not sever relation. Do not, indulge in mutual enmity. Do not entertain rancour and jealousy against one another, and do not be jealous of others. Be brethren among yourselves and become Allah's slaves. It is not permissible for a man to have severed his relations with any of his brethren for more than three days." (*Bukhari*)
>
> In another tradition it is mentioned : "It is not permissible for a Momin to have no connection with another Momin for more than three days. After three days have elapsed and he happens to meet him, he should salute him. If he answers the salute, then both will share the rewards (Ajr), and if the other person does not answer the salute, the sin will be on him, and the Muslim will be innocent of the sin of severing relations." (*Abu Daud*)
>
> In this *hadith* the period of three days is kept so that during this period the intensity of anger will be

> reduced and his wrath will be cooled. After this it will be the responsibility of every Muslim to restore his relationship with his brethren and to revert to his old routine, as if the severing of relation was a cloud that had gathered due to some causes, till the wind blew and drew away the cloud and cleared the atmosphere.

In every dispute or quarrel, a man is necessarily in one or the other condition, he is either an oppressor or the oppressed. If he is an oppressor, he has usurped the rights of others, then he should give up this wrong policy and should reform his character. He should understand that his opponent can abandon his hostility and rancour towards him only when he takes a satisfying and pleasant step in this regard. In such a condition Islam has commanded that he should request his opponent to come to a peaceful settlement and he should please him.

> The Prophet has said: "He who has harmed his brother's rights or has hurt his honour, then he should please him today, before the day comes when there will be neither dirham nor dinar with him. If he would have virtues, then they would be taken in proportion to the agression that he had committed. If there would be no virtues in his record, then the evil deeds of the oppresed would be thrust into his (oppressor's) account." (*Bukhari*)

This is Islam's advice for the oppressors, but those who are the oppressed and whose rights have been harmed-for them the advice of Islam is that when the oppressor may ask for their pardon and may seek his Lord's forgiveness, then he should pardon him and should show softness. In such circumstances, to reject the request for pardon is a great sin.

It is mentioned in the tradition:

> "A Muslim brother apologises to another Muslim, and the latter does not accept his apology, then on him will be the same sin as is on the person who collects a tax which is not due." (*Ibn Maja*)

> "If a person pleads his innocence to the other, and the other one rejects it, then he will not be brought to the water-tank." (*Tibrani*)

In this way it brings the Muslim society on the high level of a life full of love, friendship and justice.

Islam considers it a meanness of the human nature and lowliness that the hatred should take roots in the hearts and may not come out, but continue to burn inside like a volcano.

Those who nurse rancour and hatred against others in their hearts are always in search of opportunities to vent their inner hatred. They feel satisfied only when they shout in anger at the top of their voices and indulge in abuses. They hurt the feelings of others and spread corruption and mischief on the earth.

> It is narrated by Ibn Abbas : "Allah's Messenger has said : May I not show you the sign of the wicked people ?" The people said : "If you are pleased, you may tell us." He said : "The most wicked person among you is he who keeps himself aloof, is harsh on his slave, and does not give any gifts to others. May I not tell you of another person more wicked than this ?" The people said "Definitely, O Messenger of Allah ! If you are pleased." He said: "He who has rancour against the people and the people have rancour against him." Then he asked : "May I not tell you of a more wicked person than this?" The people said "Definitely, O Messenger of Allah ! If you are pleased." He said : "He who does not pardon the errors of others, does not accept their apologies, and does not forgive their crime." Again he asked : "May I not tell you of a more wicked person than this ?" The people said : "Definitely, O Messenger of Allah ! If you are pleased." He said: "He from whom no good may be expected, and from whose wickedness there may not be security." (*Tibrani*)

The wicked tendencies covered by this hadith are the different stages of rancour and hatred, which occur in proportion to the defect and disease. This is not a strange thing, because from the olden times the people knew about them. Even in the pre-Islam days (Jahiliyah) rancour was considered to be the lowest stage of the wicked conduct, and decent people always avoided it. A poet of that period, Antara says:

"People of high position do not have rancour in their heart,

"One who has ancour in his nature cannot reach high position."

Roots of Sin

There are many evils in the society about which Islam has warned. If we think seriously, it will not be difficult to find out their source.

Inspite of all these evils having different shapes and forms, they revolve round only one basic disease, and that is rancour and enmity.

False accusation of innocent people is a crime, the real cause of which is ill-feeling and hatred. Since it is extremely effective in mutilating the realities and to condemn the innocent persons, Islam has declared it to be the worst kind of falsehood.

Hazrat Ayesha narrates that Allah's Messenger asked his companions: "Do you know what is the worst aggression?" They said: "Allah and His Messenger know it better:" He said : "Before Allah the worst aggression is to make halal (permissible) for oneself the honour of another Muslim." Then he recited the following verse of the Quran:

> "Those who have caused pain to the Momin men and Momin women without any fault of theirs, surely they pure earned the (consequences of) false accusation and open sin." (*Al-Ahzab*)

Undoubtedly the tendency to unnecessarily search out defects in other people and to foist it on them is the proof of meanness and wickedness. For being guilty of falsely accusing any person, Islam has decreed punishment in this world also, and it is difficult to imagine the punishment that the perpetrator of this sin will receive in the next world.

> Allah's Messenger has said: "He who, in order to find fault, says something about a person which was not there, Allah will throw such a man in hell till ha tastes fully what he had fabricated." (*Tibrani*)

In another tradition it is mentioned: "If a man spreads a rumour about another person of which he was innocent in order to bring him into disrepute, then it is Allah's task to melt him in fire on the Doomsday till he gets the full taste:"

Abstain from backbiting : The meaning of the cleanness and purity of the bosom is this that if a man does not work for the good of others, then at least he should wish well of others. But if a man who does not see any defects in others, and yet he accuses them of those defects and tries to entangle them in baseless charges, such a man is a liar, a deceiver and shameless. Allah has said:

> "Those who want that obscenity may spread in the group of those who believe, for them there is very severe punishment in this world and in the next world. Allah knows and you do not know." (*Noor : 19*)

This is a great favour of Allah on His slaves that He approves of covering the defects of the creatures, even if those defects are present. And it is not permissible for a Muslim that he should feel pleased by condemning another Muslim, even if his condemnation may be correct, because men of healthy mentality feel pain when they see others in pain, and they wish for their recovery and welfare. As regards having pleasure from the disgrace suffered by others, from relating others' defects, and from uncovering their evils, this cannot be the course of action of a true Muslim.

Because of this Islam has declared backbiting as *haram* (forbidden), for in this the latent rancour gets a chance to come out and man is deprived of grace and blessing.

Abu Huraira has narrated that Allah's Messenger has said : "Do you know what is backbiting ?"

> The people said: "Allah and His Messenger know better." He said: "You remember your brother in a

> way that may be disliked by him." He was asked: "If my brother has the defect which I am relating, then is that also backbiting ?" He replied "If that defect is in him, then it is backbiting; and if the defect stated by you is not in him, then it is a false accusation." (*Muslim*)

The etiquette and principles formulated by Islam for the security of friendships and for a safeguard against divisive tendencies includes the forbidding of telling tales. (backbiting), because it creates ill-feeling among friends, and it destroys the cleanness of the hearts.

> The Prophet used to restrain his companions from saying things which could hurt the feelings of others. He has said : "None of you should convey to me any hurtful thing about my companions, for I want that as long as I may come to you my bosom should be clean in respect of every one of you." (*Abu Daud*)

If some one hears a wrong thing about some other person, then he should not widen the hole of the torn cloth by putting his finger in it. Many evil gossips die their own death, if they are left to themselves, and many statements give rise to wars, because large numbers copy them and encourage them. They are like sparks which fly carrying destruction with them.

> Allah's Messenger has said : "No tell-tale can enter Paradise." (*Bukhari*)

In another tradition, the word "Qattat" has been used. Ulema say that `Qattat' and 'Nammam' have the same meaning. But there is also a contention that Nammam is one who hears some people talking and then goes on quoting them, and Qattat is one who eavesdrop other people talking and then goes on quoting them here and there.

> In the *hadith* it is stated : "Telling tales and rancour will go to hell. These two things cannot gather in the heart of a Muslim." (*Tibrani*)

The essential outcome of enmity and rancour is that man should be under a wrong impression, should be in search of defects of his adversary, should grieve internally on seeing others in good position and well-placed. Islam has severely disapproved of all these things.

> The Prophet says : "Any one who knows about the defect of his another Muslim brother and he has concealed it, then Allah will cover (his defects) on the Day of Judgment." (*Tibrani*)

> In another tradition, it is said : "He who has veiled the defect of a Momin, he has acted as if he has revived a girl placed in a grave." (*Tibrani*)

The majority of persons who are always in search of the defects of others commit more abominable crimes than those committed by the professional criminals. The hearts of such people are miles away from their Lord. To be in search of a crime in order to give it publicity is more reprehensible than actually committing that crime.

What a mean difference is there between these two feelings and attitudes? One feeling is that there is consideration against the things forbidden by Allah and concern for safeguarding it, while on the other side there is rancour against Allah's slaves and wish and desire to disgrace them.

The first feeling may even reach the limit, but it is not so bad as the second feeling, which secures pleasure and satisfaction from the ruin of the fellow-creatures it waits for their faltering, and laughs in their adversities.

• ***Walk away from rancour :*** The safety of a Muslim's bosom and its purity is such a good gift that does not allow to attach his life to his fate or fortune or his sensibilities to the people, because many times he fails to achieve something, when others succeed. Sometimes he remains among the 'also ran' in the race of life, and others go ahead.

But this would be a very mean and uncivilized thing if a man is overcome by the feeling of selfishness and wishes others to sustain loss and setbacks only because he himself has not been able to forge ahead and derive benefits.

Then a Muslim must be broad-minded, a benefactor of humanity and a sympathiser of the people. He should look at all things from the viewpoint of public good. He should not keep his own selfish gain in view.

Generally people entertain the feelings of rancour and enmity because they see that their wishes and desires are not being satisfied, while others are having more than their share of the spoils. This is the trouble which does not allow them to rest awhile.

In the ancient times, the Devil had seen that the rank and position which he himself wanted had gone to the share of Adam; therefore, he decided that he would not allow Adam to enjoy these blessings

> "Because You have thrown me out of the way, lo! I will lie in wait for them on the straight way then will I assault them from before them and behind them, from their right and their left, nor will you find in most of them gratitude (for your mercies):"
>
> (*A'raf* : *16-17*)

This Satanic tendency develops in the nature of the spiteful people and destroys their hearts. Islam has severely warned people to keep away from this forbidden tendency, and to give place to tranquillity and satisfaction in life.

Anas bin Malik narrates that we were sitting with the Prophet when he said : "Just now a man of Paradise is coming to you." Immediately a man from Ansar came there. His beard looked dishevelled from the water of ablutions (Wuzu), and he was carrying in his left hand his shoes. On the second day also the Prophet repeated the same words, and the same man again appeared before them, in the same condition. On the third day also the Prophet repeated the same thing and the man of Ansar again appeared in the same condition.

When the Prophet stood up, Abdullah bin A'mar went after that man, and said to him : "I have had a quarrel in my house for three days. If you give me shelter, it would be most desirable." He said : "It is all right."

Anas says that Abdullah bin A'mar says that he spent three nights in the company of that man, but he did not find him praying in the night, but whenever he went to bed, he used to remember Allah till he used to get up for the prayer of the morning. But Abdullah bin A'mar says that he did not hear anything from his mouth except words of goodness. Abdullah says:

"When three nights passed and in my eyes his conduct did not hold any importance, I told that man : 'O slave of God! I have neither quarrelled with my father, nor have I severed relation with him. The fact is that I have heard the Prophet of Allah saying that a man of Paradise is coming before us, three times, and you appeared before us. Then I desired to stay with you and to see what act of yours is that-so that I may follow the same, but I did not see you doing any extra-ordinary work. What is the reason that the Messenger of Allah has said such a nice thing about you ? He replied

> "The reality is what you have seen." When I was returning he called me and said : "The reality is the same that has been witnessed by you ; however, I do not keep any spite against any of my Muslim brethren, and if Allah has blessed someone with any good thing, I am not jealous of him. Abdullah bin A'mar said: "This quality of yours must have reached the Prophet of Allah." (*Ahmed*)

In another narration the words of the hadith are as follows:

> "The thing that you have seen is correct. O my nephew! I do not pass a night keeping spite against a Muslim." (*Bazzar*)

Islam has declared jealousy as *haram* (forbidden). Allah has commanded his Messenger to seek shelter from the mischief of jealous people, because jealousy is a spark that burns inside the bosom and hurts the jealous person as well as others.

The man who wishes that the good things of life should be destroyed, he becomes a source of trouble for the society. His conscience is not satisfied with anything. Allah's Messenger has said:

> "In the stomach of a man, the dust flying in the path of Allah and the flames of hell cannot be together, nor can the faith and jealousy dwell together in the stomach of a man." (*Baihaqui*)
>
> In another tradition it is mentioned: "Keep away from jealousy, for jealousy eats up virutes in the same way as fire eats up wood." (*Abu Daud*)

The person who hates the rewarded person or the one deserving Allah's favours and wishes that they should have been deprived of those things, for such a man there are a number of causes which repel him from the realities of life.

The first cause is that he is imprisoned by the world and the lure of the wealth of the world. He fights against it, and he sheds tears for not achieving his material goat, and he entertains feeling of jealousy against those who are successful in this world. He is angry with them.

This is a great misunderstanding about comprehending both the worlds ; and the fact is that he has completely ignored the next world and has closed his eyes from the necessity of making preparations for that world. This negligence on his part has resulted in his reaching this condition. It is necessary that every man should prepare for the next world, and should be sorry for losing opportunities to do so.

> "O mankind! there has come to you a direction from your Lord and a healing for the (diseases) in your hearts, and for those who believe, a guidance and a mercy. Say: 'In the bounty of Allah, and in His mercy,- in that let them rejoice; ' that is better than the (wealth) they hoard." (*Yunus : 57-58*)

The man who is jealous is weak of determination helpless, forgetful of his Lord, and unaware of his Lord's principles operative in this world. For this reason. when he fails to achieve something, he conspires and schemes against the successful people. As an Arabic poet says:

"People became jealous of the young man because they could not reach up to his successes. So every one appears to be his enemy and opponent."

The proper thing for him was to turn to his Lord, to seek His favours because his treasures are not limited to or reserved for any single person. After this he should again strive for his objective. It is quite likely that what he could not achieve in his first attempt could be available in the second. Undoubtedly this is much more desirable than nursing spite and rancour in his bosom.

There is a very big difference between jealousy and high ambition, in jealousy and desire and envy, in jealousy and not desiring any deviation in straight dealing, and in charity and in expressing displeasure against contamination. It is obvious that these two things cannot be placed together.

Ambition is the name of the desire for reaching the high pinnacle and of achieving it, and this is the quality of Allah's faithful slaves. Hazrat Sulaiman prayed to his Lord thus:

> "My Lord ! Forgive me and bestow on me sovereignty such as shall not belong to any after me. Surely, You are the Bestower." (*Sad: 36*)

A quality of the slaves of the Most Gracious that has been mentioned is that they pray to their Lord thus

> "Our Lord! Vouchsafe us comfort of our wives and of our offspring, and make us patterns (leaders) of the righteous." (*Furqan: 74*)

To achieve Allah's blessings it is necessary to strive for it and primarily to have a sincere desire for it. To grieve internally over another person's achieving His blessings is an abominable tendency. There is a great difference between these two.

Envy is the name of the desire to have those gifts which Allah has bestowed on others. But since nursing such a desire and envy can also open the gateways of mischiefs, can encourage the inclination towards wrong desires, and can also incite for achieving that which is apparently beneficial but in the ultimate analysis harmful. Islam has, therefore, fixed the norms for the things for which a man can have desire and for which competition is permissible. Allah's Messenger has said : "Excepting two things, in no other thing jealousy is permissible: one—it is permissible to be jealous of the man who has been given wealth by Allah and who is spending it in the cause of truth unhesitatingly, and second, that man whom Allah has blessed with wisdom, in whose light he takes decisions and imparts education in it to others."

The sense in which the word jealousy has been used in the hadith does not include the desire for bringing to an end the blessing or the favour, but it means the efforts to achieve that blessing and having envy for that blessing has been termed as jealousy.

The idea is that the thing which a man should make his objective should be great and magnificent. It is lack of ambition or courage that a man should desire for small things, and should entertain expectations from them. There are many things which do not yield anything but distress and sorrow, and the spite against other people is generated because they think in an unhealthy manner as to why other people have achieved those things from which they are deprived.

About such things Allah says:

> "In no wise covet those things in which Allah has bestowed His gifts more freely on some of you than on others ; to men is allotted what they earn. And to women what they earn ; but ask Allah of His bounty ; for Allah has full knowledge of all things."(*Nissa: 32*)

As regards disliking the unstraight dealing in general conditions and matters, this is the rightful demand of justice and assertion. It has nothing to do with despicable jealousy.

If we feel angry that some person has earned a lot of benefits from a little labour, or has obtained a highranking position, then such an anger is understandable and praise-worthy. This is a kind of public welfare which has nothing to do with jealousy.

Islam has been hearing and watching individuals at intervals, so that it may clean them of the impurities of spite and enmity, and may nourish in the hearts of the general people clean and pure feelings for their good, and for itself also. Every day, every week and every year arrangements are made for the cleaning of the individuals, so that their dirt and filth may be removed, defects may be done away with, and even the slightest trace of spite and rancour may not be found in the faithful heart.

About the daily *Farz salat* (compulsory prayer) it has been clarified that its reward will not be given to a Muslim unless his heart is not found free from ill-will against others, and is not bereft of all disputes, quarrels enmity and rancour against the people.

> Allah's Messenger has said : "There are three persons whose prayer does not rise even a fist above their heads. One is that man who leads the prayers of others who do not like it. Second is that woman who spends her night in such a way that her husband is displeased with her. And third are those two brothers who have severed their relations with each other." (*Ibn Maja*)

Self-assessment

Every week the acts of Muslims are evaluated. Allah sees every week what a Muslim has collected for the next world, and what feelings are hidden in his heart. If his bosom is free from spite and rancour, then he is saved from destruction, and if it is filled with the feelings of displeasure, jealousy and ill-will then he remains backward in the field of action.

> Allah's Messenger has said : "Every Monday and Thursday men's acts are placed before Allah. On these days Allah forgives the sins of everybody, except the polytheists. However, if there is a person who has spite and rancour against his brother, He says about them : 'Leave these two alone in their condition till they come to a settlement." (*Muslim*)

It is not correct for a Muslim that the days and nights may pass off and he should be shackled for the whole year in the chains of enmity and spite, and tied with the handcuffs of rancour and ill-will. Allah grants gifts to those who are sincere and broad-minded. In the *hadith* it is mentioned:

> In the night of the 15th of Sha'ban, Allah acquaints himself of the conditions of His slaves. So He forgives those who seek His pardon, bestows mercy on those seeking mercy, and leaves the spiteful people alone." (*Baihaqui*)

Even after this much cleansing if a man leaves this world carrying the dirt and filth of spite, rancour and jealousy, then he deserves to be burnt in the fire of hell. The man whose cleansing has not been possible by the Shariah, the fire of hell will reach him and it will not be helpless in burning his sins and his enmity.

Spite and jealousy and the diseases which were created by them have been condemned by Islam, and they have developed and progressed because man is a prisoner of the world and the desires to achieve it, and the longing to enjoy the pleasures and luxuries of life to the utmost keep him in trouble.

But if some one is hated for Allah, if a man gets angry in the cause of truth, or if tumultous enthusiasm and liking is displayed to achieve righteousness and virtue, then this is quite a different matter.

It is no sin for a Muslim if he severs his relation till the end of his life with such persons as disobey the commands of Allah, or who cross the limits of Shariah. If he hates such persons or declares his enmity towards them, then he cannot be blamed for that; on the contrary it is a sign of his perfect faith, selflessness and sincerity.

Allah has commanded us that we should keep away from His enemies, even if they may be our relatives:

> "O you who believe ! Choose not your fathers nor your brethren nor friends if they take pleasure in disbelief rather than faith. Whosoever of you takes them for friends, such are wrongdoers."
>
> (*Taubah* : 23)

Or whose company is bad, who has the habits of meanness and of talking glibly and endlessly, to keep away from such a one is necessary.

And one who has committed a wrong against Allah, to punish such a one there is nothing wrong if that one is boycotted for a fixed period, because the Prophet had severed his relation with some of his wives for a period of forty days and Abdullah bin Umar did not have any relation with one of his sons till his death, because he had rejected one command of the Messenger of Allah. His father, Abdullah bin Umar narrated a hadith in which women were allowed to go to the mosques, but his son had rejected this *hadith*.

FIFTEEN

Intellect and Scholarship

Islamic temperament makes it a duty of every Muslim that he should be an educated man, and that the Society should consist of educated and civilized people—there should be a majority of educated people and the proportion of the uneducated people should be very small or, if possible, there should be no uneducated people in that society.

Because the basic and other principles of this religion do not concern themselves with the external appearances which a son gets from a father as a heritage or they are not like talisman and amulets that by their use or by such other mumbo jumbo some spirit may be instilled in them. They are such realities which are derived from the holy Quran and the Prophet's traditions (Sunnah). The manner of their derivation is not that they should merely be recited, but that the people should have the right kind of understanding, high ideals and purified character. The Islamic method of education undoubtedly can create an atmosphere of proper and correct understanding of the Shariah and Fiqh on the basis of right and wrong acts and rights and duties in every nation or community,and can create such an atmosphere of collective behaviour and regulations as would be conducive to encourage the right acts and prevent the commitment of the wrong ones. This can be done with the help of the rightful discussion in the spirit of proper understanding and sincerity. And all the problems which have been evading solution in every age and all the complicated matters which have been baffling the people in the past can be solved in the light of the Islamic principles.

Therefore, I say that all these problems crop up in such an atmosphere where the plant of Islam has withered, and the leaves of its plant have suffered the onslaught of the autumn, like the trees of the regions where there is no water and where the growth of trees is a very difficult task.

After a serious consideration of the universe around us it is agreed upon by all that the Quranic Verses and Commands are the first foundation of a firm and strong faith. This contemplation, thinking and search have provided the conveniences and comforts of the modern civilization. The veils from the secrets and mysterious things of the universe have been removed, and they have placed all those things at the disposal of men, who did not know about them in the past. Then Islam ordained to follow the Truth and argued and discussed over its minutest details and points in a scholarly way, and disapproved of the blind surmises, baseless thoughts and their pursuit, and closing of the ears, eyes; mind and heart. It guarantees the formation of such a society as is free from absurdities, above superstitions and tomfoolery—not a society where amulets and talisman are encouraged, where these absurd things rule over the people for which there is no authority or argument from Allah.

Attainment of Knowledge

Learning is as much necessary for Islam as it is for the human life. And this religion can find a place in the hearts of only those people who have solid learning and possess a healthy intellect. That is why Allah says:

> This is a clear message for mankind in order that they may be warned thereby; and that they may know that He is only One God, and that man of understanding may take heed. (*Ibrahim : 52*)

Quoting the talk of the people of hell, the Quran says:

> Had we been wont to listen or have sense, we had not been among the dwellers in the flames. (*Mulk : 10*)

Describing the example of those whose sensitivities are dead, the windows of whose mind are closed and whose abilities are frozen, the Quran says:

> Those who disbelieved are like the cattle which hear nothing, except a shout and a cry, when they are called. They are deaf, dumb and blind, and therefore they do not understand anything. (*Baqarah: 171*)

When a person reaches the age of understanding and maturity, and his abilities and energies are developed, and when he becomes capable of absorbing the best teachings and the progressive civilization, Allah blesses him with the knowledge about Islam. This helps him to shape his life in such a way as to achieve progress and perfection, and by following the path of Islam the venues for achieving success in the material world are also thrown open for him.

Take the example of salat (prayer), which is the first form of worship in Islam. If you think over it, you will find that its performance and its announcement are such that appeal to the intellect. The call for the prayer (Azan) taps the intellect, awakens the heart, declares Allah's greatness and His Oneness, and invites men for attaining success. It is not the sound of the bell that rings and creates some vibrations in the atmosphere, and which probably stirs some vague feelings.

Similarly the prayer consists of the verses and prayers that have come from a Book which is full of righteous teachings virtuous lessons and best of guidance. The prayer is accepted by God only when it is performed in the correct way, and when its real meaning and sense is understood by man's intellect.

The fact is that a man attains high position owing to his intelligence, ability to derive benefit from his experience, and the consistency of his nature, in the same proportion in which these qualities are found in him, and he achieves distinction among Muslims. But those who lack this gift from God, i.e. intelligence and whose mentality is sick, they cannot hope to achieve any distinction in this religion.

Consider the first verse of the holy Quran:

> Recite, (O Prophet!) in the name of your Lord, who created; created man from the clot of congealed blood. Recite and your Lord is very Gracious, Who taught

> knowledge with pen, taught that knowledge to man which he did not know. (*Alaq : I-5*)

This is the first voice which tells about the value of the pen and declares a war against ignorance and negligence. It considers reading and learning as the the first brick for the making of a great human. Allah has elevated the position of the ulema (learned men) to such a high degree that for giving a witness to His oneness and to affirm His justice he has placed Himself, the angels and the learned men in the same category:

> Allah (Himself) is a witness that there is no God, save Him. And the angels, and the men of learning too are witness. Maintaining His creation in justice, there is no God save Him, the Almighty, the Wise.
> (*Al-i-Imran : 18*)

It is not surprising because how can foolish and narrowminded people absorb the light of the Brightest Being? How can a man, who loses himself in the pleasures and luxuries of the world, find a way to understand anything about the Wisest Ruler? Or how can he see His great attributes and great signs?

That is why Allah has declared the learned men to be respectable and honoured men, and has given them preference on account of their knowledge and learning. Allah's Messenger has said: "On the Day of the Judgment, when Allah will sit on judgment, He will address the ulema and say:

> "I had placed My learning and forbearance at your disposal because I wanted to forgive your lapses, I have no care about any thing except this." (*Tibrani*)

Hafiz Manzari (R.A.A.) says that Allah's words 'learning and forbearance' merit consideration. "If you ponder over these two attributes, you will realise that here the learning of our times which is bereft of sincerity and forbearance is not meant."

By mentioning forbearance the idea is to point out that the learning should be such which should not encouarge internal differences and it should be able to control the carnal desires of man.

Learning superior to worship : For Allah the best knowledge is better than that act which is performed with hesitation and confirmed learning is better than that worship which is performed with ignorance and lack of understanding.

Allah's Messenger (S.A.W.) has said:

> "The superiority of knowledge is greater than the superiority of worship." (*Bazzar*)

> "Less knowledge is better than much worship which is performed with ignorance." (*Tibrani*)

> "Systematic religious thinking is the best worship." (*Tibrani*)

> O Abuzar! As soon as it is morning, learn a verse from Allah's Book. It is better than performing hundred rakaat of prayer, and that you should learn a chapter of knowledge daily, whether you may or may not act. It is better than your saying one thousand rakaat of prayer. (*Ibn Majah*)

The secret of this command is that the worship performed by the ignorant people is as useless as their friendship, on the contrary they put themselves to a loss but they think that they are doing some useful work, as they become a source of loss to their friends due to their ignorance while their intention is to benefit them. Ignorant worshippers very vigorously perform the external manifestations of the religious worship, and they have very strong feelings about that, but on account of conceit and false pride their attitude is so harsh that it many times causes a loss. But for the men of learning their light of knowledge paves the way for them and guides them to the good of all concerned, although their acts maybe less, but there is abundance of light and straightness in their acts.

For this reason, Allah's Prophet (S.A.W.) has said:

"One *Faqih* is more over-powering for Satan compared to a thousand worshippers."

Another *hadith* is:

> "A learned man has the same superiority over a worshipper which I have over an ordinary man from amongst you." (*Tirmizi*)

In another tradition, it is mentioned:

> "A learned man has a superiority of seventy degrees over a worshipper, and between every two degrees is the distance equal to the running of fast horses for seventy years, because Satan puts into circulation innovations among the people and a learned man sees it and tries to stop it, when the worshipper is busy in the worship of his Lord, and he cannot turn his attention to that innovation nor can he know about it. (*Isbahan*)

The Importance of learning can be seen from this verse of the holy Book:

> As for these examples, We coin them for mankind, but none can grasp their meaning save the men of learning. (*Ankabut : 43*)

Allah has made it clear that only that conscience turns to righteousness, avoids evil, and is greedy to seek Allah's pleasure which is rich with the treasures of knowledge and learning, and has received the illumination from his Lord:

> "Is one who worships devoutly during the hours of the night, prostrating himself or standing (in adoration), who takes heed of the Hereafter. and who places his hopes in Mercy of his Lord (like one who does not) ? Say : "Are those equal, those who know and those who do not know ? It is those who are endued with understanding that receive admonition." (*Zumar : 9*)

Education for Success

The learning, to which a Muslim turns and to open the gates of which he tries his utmost, is not confined to 'Albidya' and

'Qaduri' (religious books), but every branch of learning which widens 'the thought and opens the closed windows of the intellect, may guide him to real knowledge, which may open the new avenues of discoveries and inventions, and which may teach him the secrets of the world leadership, which may give him a control over the hidden secrets of energies, are all included in the list of learnings, the achieving of which is the duty of a Muslim. It is the responsibility of every Muslim that he should take away his share of knowledge from this treasure. A number of verses and traditions are witnesses to this wide sense.

The traditions which encourage the tendency of deriving benefits from every kind of learning are innumerable, but a few are quoted here:

> "He who walks for achieving and in search of knowledge, for him Allah makes the path to Paradise easy." (*Muslim*)

> "No earner can earn anything better than that knowledge the superiority of which guides a learned man of religion towards the right guidance or turns him away from waywardness ; and no man's piety can be right unless his intellect is right." (*Tibrani*)

> "It is not permissible to envy anybody except two men, first that man whom Allah gave wealth and he distributed it in the cause of Truth and second that man whom Allah blessed with wisdom, with which he gives his decisions and teaches it." (*Bukhari*)

> "Allah, His angels, and all the creatures of the earth and the skies, even the ant in its hole and the fish in the sea, pray for the man who teaches righteousness to the people." (*Tirmizi*)

In these holy traditions the words knowledge and learning have been used for every art, science or technique which can be the cause of good and by wisdom is meant that learning which protects from harmful things and encourages turning to useful things. 1t is not necessary to confine learning to any special culture. It is like saying a particular portion of property as wealth and to refuse to call the remaining portion as wealth, for no food reason.

There is no doubt that at the head of the list there should be that learning which teaches Allah's rights over humans and the knowledge of mutual rights and duties among humans themselves, because even today the teaching of right guidance and virtuousness play an important role in the formation and organization of societies and in guiding a country's politics. But it would be very imprudent if we would think that the learning has been exhorted to be achieved in the Quran and a hadith is merely *Fiqh* and *Hadith* and the branches of learning allied to these, and that the position of the other worldly learning is unimportant, the achieving of which or otherwise is left to the individual's sweet will, and for which there is no responsibility on him.

This is a very serious misunderstanding, for the learning or the sciences about the universe and life, the discussions about the control over the earth and the heavens and their effects are not less important than the pure worldly branches of learning. And sometimes the outcome of the study of the modern sciences proves, in connection with the understanding of Divine nature and understanding of the self, to be more effective than diving into the religious learning.

In this connection the guidance of the holy Quran is sufficient for us. When it describes the greatness of learning and the superiority of the learned men, its allusion by this knowledge is the understanding which is the outcome of thinking about and contemplating over the vegetable and the animal worlds and other physical things, and by ulema or the learned men are meant those persons who comprehend the greatness of the Creator by understanding the greatness of the creatures and the creation.

> Do you not see that Allah sends down rain from the sky ? With it We then bring out produce of various colours. And in the mountains are tracts white and red, of various shades of colour, and black intense in hue. And so amongst men and crawling creatures and

> cattle, are they of various colours. Those truly fear Allah, among His servants, who have knowledge; for Allah is Exalted in Might, Forgiving. (*Fatir: 27-28*)
>
> And of His signs is the creation of the heavens and the earth, and the difference of your languages and colours. Verily, herein indeed are portents for men of knowledge. (*Rum: 22*)

In order to serve the religion and to disclose the secrets of the realities of the life, the learning of the worldly sciences and knowledge is not less important than the learning of the religious teachings. The difference is only this that learning of the physical sciences requires a lot of time and labour, while learning of the religious instruction is comparatively easier, provided a few months are earmarked for that. However for learning minor details of religious teachings and its branches more time and study would be needed, but this long period and time depends, like other collective and social interests and advantages, on the needs of the government. It is for the government to decide whether the required time and labour be spent on that project or not. The study of the rights and the law according to religion, in itself, is not more important than the learning of the worldly sciences, like medicine, etc., even if a person attains the prominence attained by Imam Abu Hanifa(R.A.). The person will gain importance and superiority only on the ground that he had attained that knowledge for the sake of Allah and how much he is successful in imparting it to the people and making it beneficial for them for the purpose of Allah's pleasure only.

Aims of Education

The difference between the pure religion and specific world is very ordinary, and also very big, but as we have stated we will have to make the purity of purpose and the ideal as the real deciding factor, because a thing, which becomes a major sin on account of the carnal desires, is considered as a jihad (striving) in the cause of Allah, if it is performed with the sincerity and purity needed.

In the Quran, it is stated:

> The wealth and children are an ornament of the worldly life. (*Kahaf* : 46)

It is so, if they are exclusively treated as such, but these resources also help in helping the cause of jihad and Allah has called the abundance of wealth and progeny as sources of his assistance:

> Then We gave you superiority over them, and helped you with wealth and children, and increased your numbers. (*Bani Israil*)

Abundance of wealth and children only helped this Ummah to revive after a collapse. After its downfall, it has stood up to rise to the heights destined for it. It has attained the pleasure of Allah after having lost it earlier.

Same is the case with learning. If a man obtains proficiency in the science of fertilisation and with its help makes Allah's land more fertile and greener, then his reward will not be any less, and it is quite likely that if he believes in Allah and follows the righteous path, he will probably get better rewards from Allah than the worshipper who pays during the night and is very keen to offer prayers regularly.

Islam has given a very honourable position to the men of learning, and has always been appreciating their efforts. It has given them the glad tidings of countless rewards.

Ma'az bin Jabal (R.A.A.) says:

"Seek knowledge, because to seek knowledge for the sake of Allah is righteousness, to pursue knowledge is worship, to hold discussions on it is remembering God. Research and striving for it is *jihad*. To impart education to those who are ignorant is charity. To spend it on the deserving people is the means of nearness to God, for it teaches one about what it is *halal* and *haram*. It sheds light on the paths of the people of the Paradise. Knowledge is the companion of the loneliness, a friend of the stranger; it converses in the privacy and points out good and bad conditions. It is a weapon against the enemies, and a means of ornamentation in the gathering of the friends. Through it Allah raises nations and makes them leader and guide, that are followed and are obeyed, and whose advice is sought. The angels wish to have them as friends, and pass their wings lovingly over them. All the creatures of the land and the sea pray for their salvation. The fishes in the sea and the insects, the beasts of the forests and the animals pray for them, because knowledge revives the hearts from the death of ignorance, it is a tower of light in the darknesses. A man reaches to the high rank of the noble persons, and achieves glory in this world and the next. Thinking and contemplation in the cause of knowledge is equivalent to observing fasts. The duty of learning and teaching is equivalent to offering prayers during the night. Through this, relationships are united; through it, a distinction between halal and haram is made. It is the leader of the activity and controller. Fortunate people attain it and unfortunate ones are deprived of it."

Mastering the Languages

Learning of other languages is among the things recommended in the traditions of the Prophet for every Muslim to achieve. Allah's Prophet stole a march towards achieving knowledge from this aspect. He commanded his copyist, Zaid bin Sabit, to attain proficiency in the Suryani language. Zaid says that he was commanded by the Prophet (S.A.W.) to learn it and accordingly he learnt to correspond with the Jews in the Suryani language. The Prophet (S.A.W.) said:

> "By God, I am not satisfied with the Jews that they would correctly copy my letter." Zaid says that before half a month passed he attained proficiency in the Suryani language and then he started writing letters to the Jews on behalf of the Prophet and replying to them on his behalf." (*Bukhari*)

To learn the different languages is among the needs of Islam, because the message of Islam is for all the peoples of the world, and it is impossible for all the peoples to learn any one single language, when the difference of languages is among the signs of Allah. "Therefore, it is easier and more reasonable to translate the Islamic teachings in all those languages which the people speak and understand than to teach the Arabic language to all the peoples. Allah has said:

> "And We never sent a messenger save with the language of his folk, that he might make (the message) clear to them." (*Ibrahim : 4*)

The commentators in explaining this verse write that the Prophet of Allah was born in Arabia, speaking the Arabic language, but the representatives that he sent to the places around his country were asked to translate his message in other languages and they conveyed his message in the language of the people concerned. The commentators write that either the Quran should have been sent in all the languages of the world, or only in one language. The first thing is useless because by translation that purpose can be achieved, but the Arabic language was selected because at that time many were conversant with it and the fear of changes of the message in that language was much less.

From this discussion, one thing that comes out very clearly is that it is enjoined upon Muslims that they should learn other languages, otherwise they will be considered to have been dishonest with the treasure (message) of which they have been made the trustees, and they will be held responsible for keeping the people unaware of and unaquainted with that message knowingly.

This fact also should not be lost sight of that knowledge or learning has no native place, nor is limited to any race. If we study the sources of the learning of the ancient and the present times, then we will be able to drink from the springs of knowledge. There had been many nations that had remained unlettered and uneducated, and paradoxically it has also happened that uneducated forefathers brought up a generation full of researchers, scientists and learned men. Europe itself was in the darkness a few centuries ago. It was ignorant. But today it is the protector of the heritage of ancient civilizations. Muslims are enjoined to travel far and wide for seeking knowledge, from whatever source it may be obtained or in any city it may be available.

> Allah's Messenger has said: "A Momin cannot be content with good (knowledge) which he hears, until he goes to Paradise." (*Tirmizi*)
>
> "Wisdom is a Momin's lost property; he is the most deserving to obtain it wherever he may find it." (*Tirmizi*)
>
> "Any man who sets out to seek knowledge is in the path of Allah till he returns home." (*Tirmizi*)

To learn and to teach is the spirit of Islam. Without it neither its essence can remain nor can a guarantee be given about its future. In the eyes of Islam the position of the individual is that either they are students, seekers of righteousness and guidance, or they are learned men, but seeking further knowledge. Besides this there is no value of other kind of individuals in its eyes. Allah's Messenger (S.A.W.) has said:

> "The learned teacher and the taught are both participants in righteousness, and in the remaining people there is no aspect of righteousness." (*Ibn Majah*)

SIXTEEN

Time and Space

Every lost thing can be regained. The lost game can be rewon. But the time which has passed away, it is useless to hope for its return. That is why in all the possessions of man, time is considered to be the most valuable and most precious. Man should spend his time in such a way as a greedy man spends his money. He does not show the slightest carelessness in spending even the smallest amount, and he considers everything compared to wealth insignificant and of no value.

When a man thinks about his existence and contemplates over his past life to count the months and the years that have flown by, he is unable to give much time to this sort of thinking, because he cannot have the correct estimate of his correct timings. Then days and months pass away, and the accidents and events of these days and months pass from his sight, and he feels that the whole life had been spent in one day, and all the accidents and events had taken place in a single day.

An Urdu poet says:

"We had come with a long life of four days, which we had begged,

Two days passed away in wishing, and two days in waiting."

This feeling a man has in this world. What would be his feelings on the Day of Judgment, when there will be reckoning?

> "And on the day when He shall gather them together, (when it will seem) as though they had tarried but an hour of the day, recognising one another."
>
> (*Yunus: 46*)

"Murmuring among themselves, You have tarried but ten (days). We are best aware of what they utter when their best in conduct say: You have tarried but a day."
(*Taha : 103-104*)

"On the day when they behold it, it will be as if they had but tarried for an evening or the morn thereof."
(*Nazi'at : 46*)

This feeling is very auspicious. And those who realize their own reality that they are made of the dust and are to mix with the dust one day, they will be uncomfortable with this feeling. This is a great and right feeling, provided the life in this world is compared with the life in the next. But this very feeling becomes a means of straying and misguidance for those who are not moved by the passage of time, being totally lost in a luxurious and sinful life. They are ignorant of their past and future, but when their last moments come, their eyes become helplessly sightless, the darkness of death is approaching, at that time they may suddenly wake up from their slumber, and may feel sorry and cry. But at such a time of what use this crying and feeling sorry would be for them. What is the use of crying over spilt milk!

In this world the position of man and his affairs is very strange. He is busy in amusements and pleasureseeking, and the destiny is busy with its work. He is totally lost in his luxuries and his every act and thought is being entered in the records:

On the day that Allah will raise them all up (again) and show them the Truth (and meaning) or their conduct. Allah has reckoned its (value), though they may have forgotten it, for Allah is Witness to all things.
(*Mujadla : 6*)

A true Muslim values the time very dearly, because time is his life and if he loses it, he will he digging his own grave.

Man is rapidly running towards Allah. Every revolution of the heaven that brings a new morning is a stage in this path, in which there is no stop-over and no staying. Is it not wise that man should not forget this reality, and that he should always keep it before his eyes. The past and the future should always be kept by him in his sight. It is only a deception of the sight that a man travelling by train should think that all the things outside are travelling or running in the opposite direction at a fast pace, and that he himself is stationary. The fact is that the time is advancing towards its destination taking man with it. It cannot leave him.

Time as Wealth

Islam is such a religion as recognises the importance and value of time. 'It gives to its followers this valuable advice with full emphasis : "Time is like a sword; if you will not cut it, it will cut you." It considers it a sign of faith and righteousness that man should understand this reality and in this light should lead his life

> Verily, in the difference of day and night and all that Allah has created in the heavens and the earth are portents, verily, for folk who ward off (evil).
>
> (*Yunus*: 7)

Those who are careless of the future, intoxicated with the present and are under the spell of the glitter of the world have been called by Islam as foolish and the losers.

> Verily, those who expect not the meeting with Us but desire the life of the world and feel secure therein, and those who are neglectful of Our revelations, their home will be the Fire, because of what they used to earn. (*Yunus* : 8, 9)

Islam has distributed its important forms of worship in the various parts of the day and the different seasons of the year. The five times' prayers cover the whole day, and their timings correspond with the passage of the passing day. The Archangel Jibril came down from the heaven so that the proper timings of the beginning and the end may be fixed, through which a firm system to regulate the Islamic life may be brought into being. Accordingly from the dawn to the dusk, the various hours have been fixed for prayers and remembrance of Allah:

> So glory be to Allah when you enter the night and when you enter the morning-Unto Him be praise in the heavens and the earth! -and at the sun's decline and in the noonday. (*Rum: 17-18*)

A limited sight can only see the perceptible manifestations and the limited signs. It is confined to the world's accidents and events, the festivities and the tragedies, while Time makes the conceited tyrants eat the dust, tramples the wishes and aspirations of men, and completely destroys even such civilizations whose achievements make men gasp in wonderment. It is Time itself that alerts the intelligent and prompts them to proceed towards righteous deeds and collecting profitable materials for the next world :

> Blessed is He Who made constellations in the skies, and placed therin a lamp and moon giving light; and it is He Who made the night and the day to follow each other, for such as have the will to celebrate His praises or to show their gratitude. (*Furqan: 61-62*)

The night follows the day, and then day appears with the movements of the skies. This coming and going of the day and night has not been arranged by Allah without any purpose. It will be extremely foolish if man thinks that this organised life of his is purposeless.

This is a field of competition for man, and in it only that person takes part who recognises his Lord, is aware of His rights, is thankful for His gifts, and who thinks that the continuity of the months and years is for putting in efforts and labour, so that final grand relief and comfort may be obtained.

Those who are ignorant of the realities, and run after their own worldly ephemeral benefits, are fools. They cannot take advice from any wise example and no lesson is beneficial for them:

> See they not that they are tried every year once or twice ? Yet they turn not in repentance, and they take no heed. (*Tauba : 126*)

Life is a gift given by God, about which every man will be questioned on the Day of Judgment as to where did he spend it and in what work did he utilise it ? Allah's Messenger says: "On the Doomsday no person will be able to walk a step further before answering four questions : In what acts did he spend his life ? In what did he spend his youth? From where did he get wealth and where did he spend it? And to what extent did he act on the knowledge that he attained?"

In many of its do's and don'ts, Islam has taken into consideration the importance and value of time. For example when it says that to abstain from sinful amusements is the sign of faith, in reality there is a wise move hidden in this that steps should be taken against those who invite each other for wasting time in sinful amusements. Do these idiots know that it is a game with life and that wastage of time in this way is destructive for the individual and the society both?

Time is short and Duties are Countless : The common people do not know this secret that "Duties are many and the time is short," and "The time is never impartial, either it will be the closest friend or the fiercest foe."

It is a saying of Hasan Basri (R.A.): "With the appearance of the dawn a caller from God declares: 'O Son of Adam : I am a new creature and a witness for your arms. Through me collect righteous deeds, because I cannot return again till the Doomsday."

These valuable advises are extracted from the spirit of Islam and are charged with the great lesson of considering the worldly life as a sowing field for reaping the produce in the Hereafter. And this is only the favour of Allah that man spends a portion of every age in righteous deeds and gets ready for launching new acts of virtue with fresh vigour:

> Of His mercy has He appointed for you night and day, that therein you may rest, and that you may seek His bounty, and so that you may be thankful.
>
> (*Al-Qasas : 73*)

It is a pity that the common people are not careful about wasting their time. With this they are also guilty of committing another great crime, and that is they also waste the time of others. They interfere with the men who work and disrupt their work by making them turn to purposeless and useless amusements. How truthful had been the Prophet of Allah:

> "There are two gifts about which people are mostly dishonest: one is health and the other is leisure."
>
> (*Agreed upon*)

For the correct use of time, Islam has suggested that the work should be done continually, though it may be small and ordinary, and doing abundant work at one stretch should be avoided as its continuity is broken, because if the small work is done with consistency, then with the passage of time it becomes quite big, of which man had no idea in the beginning.

If a desire takes hold of man for being immediately fulfilled, he is tempted to commit excesses and after the passing away of the time and subduing of the passions he feels fed up, and in this way the work he had undertaken, is abandoned by him. Islam dislikes this way of working. There is a *hadith:*

> "O People! Perform only those acts of which you have the strength, because Allah is not afraid of giving rewards until you are fed up. Allah likes that act best which is done consistently, even if it may be ordinary."
>
> (*Agreed upon*)
>
> Hazrat Ayesha narrates that the Prophet of Allah went to her and a woman from the Banu Asad tribe was sitting with her. He inquired who she was. Hazrat Ayesha replied that she was such and such lady and said that she offered prayers during the whole night. The Prophet (S.A.W.)said : "Wait, only that much quantum of work is enjoined for doing which you have strength, and Allah likes that piety which has consistency in it."
>
> (*Muslim*)

For safeguarding time, Islam has ordained its followers to rise early in the morning, and it has induced them to start their day's work with full determination and enthusiasm. If in the beginning of the day there is a determination that full benefit is to be derived, then man will always take care to see that his time is not wasted.

The Islamic system starts its day with the dawn, and declares it compulsory that man must be fully awake before the sunrise. On the other hand that kind of night watching is disliked which comes in the way of performing the morning prayer later than its traditional time. There is a tradition of the Prophet :

> "O Allah! Make the rising in the morning of my ummah auspicious." (*Abu Daud*)

It is great deprivation and negligence that people should continue sleeping much after the sunrise. The sun may rise and they may sleep wrapped up in warm covers, while others may be busy going to earn their living or busy in earning for the Hereafter! Hazrat Fatima(R.A.A.) bint Muhammed(S.A.W.) narrates

> "Allah's Messenger passed by me and I was lying. He stirred me with his foot and said : 'O my daughter! get up and behold the gift of your Lord, and do not be neglectful, for Allah distributes livelihood from the appearance of Fajr (dawn) to the sunrise. (*Baihaqui*)

This is the time when the lazy and the active persons are distinguished from one another. And Allah gives to every man from the good of the world and the Hereafter according to his capacity.

Lesson is for the Intelligent : As this worldly life is full of troubles and difficulties that befall men, similarly it is full of those decisions and commands which Allah ordains in respect of His slaves. Those who take interest in these decisions can only take a lesson from them

> Verily, Allah causes the revolution of the day and the night. Verily, herein indeed is a lesson for those who see. (*An-Nur : 44*)

People see the accidents and the events, but forget or are neglectful of the One who causes them. They enjoy good times and suffer during hard times, but remain unaware of the Being who is the source of everything. Therefore, if in any case they are surrounded by difficulties, they start abusing the time or the world. This is a proof of the ignorance about Allah and of being negligent of the destiny. Allah's Prophet(S.A.W.) has said:

> Allah says that Adam's son hurts Him; he abuses the time, although I am Myself time, in My hand is the rein of all affairs; I cause revolution of the day and night. (*Abu Daud*)

That is the time itself does not involve anybody in good or bad conditions, so that people may be pleased with it or may be sad. All this is done by the Creator of the Time and Space, the Almighty Allah.

> Every soul must taste of death, and We try you with evil and with good, for ordeal. And to Us you will be returned. (*Ambiya: 35*)

Allah is describing all these different conditions so that the learned men may think over them, may contemplate over them, and from that their faith may be strengthened.

> He does regulate affairs, explaining the signs in detail, that they may believe with certainty in the meeting with your Lord. (*Ra'ad:* 2)

But those who are foolish and unintelligent, they see the good and bad conditions in the world, but do not derive benefit from them. In the *hadith* it is stated:

> "When a hypocrite gets ill and then recovers from his illness, his example is like that of a camel, whose master ties it to a stake and then frees it, but it does not know why was it tied and why was it freed'.
>
> (*Abu Daud*)

It is correct that a person cannot be a Momin if the experiences do not make him civilised and the passage of time does not teach him anything. Difficulties and adversities befall a man so that the ignorant may become learned, the neglectful may become alert and the transgressor may become righteous

> We have already sent to peoples that were before you, and We visited them tribulations and adversity, in order that they might grow humble. If only, when a disaster came on them, they had been humble!
>
> (*Al-dn'am* : 42-43)

It is human nature that man remembers God is adversity. Why he is Surrounded by various kinds of difficulties, and when all the sources of worldly support vanish, he seeks Allah's refuge. A wise man's attitude should be like this that when in difficulties he turns to Allah, in other days of comfort also he should make his relationship with Him firm and strong, because it will be sheer meanness that man should feel independent of Him and should deny His immense favours to him.

Defaulters, who deny higher values and are careless of accidents and events, seek the refuge of Allah in danger, and during the peaceful days run away from Him .

> And when his misfortune touches a man he cries to Us, (while reclining) on his side, or sitting or standing, but when We have relieved him of the misfortune he goes his way as though he had not cried to Us because of a misfortune that afflicted him. This is what they do make (seeming) fair to the prodigal. (*Yams:* 13)

This is a very abominable act, which does not become a decent man.

Anthropological Studies

One way of learning a lesson from the world is to study the history of the peoples, and Allah's signs should be sought in the skies and men ; the conditions of the nations should be reflected upon as to how some reached the peak of progress and how others became subject to decline and fall. What were the causes of the progress and the downfall ? Allah wants that people should see the different periods and stages of the past, and should try to derive benefit with the help of alert conscience:

> Have they not travelled in the land, and have they hearts wherewith to feel and ears wherewith to hear?

> For indeed it Is not the eyes that grow blind, but it is the hearts, which are within the bosoms, that grow blind. (*Hajj : 46*)

A man can have two conditions, either he has some specific experiences with the help of which he will correct and strengthen his faith, or he will have no knowledge. In the tatter case, he should listen to others and try to derive benefit from the experiences and learning of others. If he sees the events of the world, but does not take any lessons from them, then it is called darkness, blindness and way wardness, which does not become a Momin.

Life is very short, and the condition in which a man is breathing is very straitened. Being confined to this sphere, life cannot provide to man intellect, survival and provisions for progress. It is necessary that access should be achieved to the higher spheres and everlasting times.

On consideration of the realities and the events of this world and the next, of the past, present and the future times, a vast treasure of ideas, stories and opinions would be available, which would acquaint us with the world. 1t will help us to understand correctly the knowledge about the Lord of the worlds. On these foundations of discussion and research, thinking and reflection, experiences and discoveries, the edifice of a strong and firm faith is built.

For this reason Islam commanded its sons to undertake long journeys and distant travels and considered the covering of the distances of the east and west as an approved act. But this covering of long distances should not be for amusements and pleasure seeking but should be for deriving benefit and for acquiring knowledge. It should not be for passing away time or for sport but for research, fact-finding and discovery, and for learning a lesson from the histories of the dead and the living

> Systems have passed away before you. Do but travel in the land and see the nature of the consequence for those who did deny (the messengers). This is a declaration for mankind, a guidance and an

admonition to those who ward of (evil).

(*Al-i-Imram : 1.17-138*)

Have they never travelled in the earth that they might see the consequence of those who had preceded them. They were stronger than them and have left greater heritage in the earth. Then Allah grasped them for their suns, and there was home to save them from Allah.

(*Madyan : 21*)

In this way the holy Quran directs to reflect on the past civilizations and the causes of their downfall so that the coming generations may be saved from the lapses, which the earlier people had committed. How many wonders can come to light from the study of the history!

The world itself is a sign, whose reality is not possible to be discovered. However we can recognise it only by studying its signs and symptoms, because the secrets of the ephemeral and everlasting life are buried in that

He it is Who has sown you broadcast on the earth, and to Him you will be gathered. And He it is Who gives life and causes death, and His is the difference of night and day. Have you then no sense ?

(*Almuminoon : 79-81*)

The thing necessary to understand is this that this life of ours is not useless, and that Allah has not made it without any purpose. When we will get to know this secret, the world will not be able to destroy us ever.

Bibliography

Ahmad, Aziz, *Studies in Islamic Culture in the Indian Environment,* Oxford, 1964.

Aiyer, Sir Sivaswamy *Evolution of Hindu Moral Ideals,* (Calcutta University Press, 1935).

Antony G.N. Flew, *'Wants or Needs; Choices or Commands', in Fitzgerald, Human Needs and Politics.*

Arberry, A.J., *The doctrines of the Sufis, tr., of Kalabadhi's Kitab alta, Aruf,* Cambridge, 1935.

Arnold, Sir Thomas, *The Calilhate, rev. edn.,* London, *1965.*

Asborn Eide, *"Human Rights in World Society"*, Oslo. 1977.

Baral, Lok Raj *"Regional Migrations, Ethnkity and Security"*, The South Asian case, (1990).

Basu, M. Introduction to the Indian Constitution (New Delhi: Rejhi Publishing, 1960).

Bagley, R.R.C. (tr.) *Ghazali's Book of Counsel for Kings,* Oxford, 1964.

Boyle, J.A. ed., *The Cambridge History of Iran,* Cambridge, 1968.

Burckhardit, Titus, *Introduction to Sufi Doctrines,* Lahore, 1959.

Chimni B.S. "*The Legal Conditions of Refugees in India*" journal of Refugee Studies, Vol. 7.

Corbin, H, *Avicenna and the Visionary Recital, tr.,* W. Trash, New York and London, 1960.

Dagmar Hellmann-Rajanayagam, *Tile Tamil Tigers: Armed. Struggle for Identity,* (Stuttgart: Franz Steiner, 1994).

De Laet, *Description of India* and *Fragment of Indian History,* tr., J.S. Hoyland and annotated by S.N., *The Political Systems of Empire,* New York, 1963.

Dogra, Bharat *"Developmefttal Refuges: Displaced Forever"*, Frontier, August 31, 1991;

E. Zolla (ed.), *Eternitá e storia. I valori permanenti nel divenire storico,* Florence, 1970.

F. Schuon, *Islam: the Perennial Philosophy,* London, 1976.

Faris, Nabith A., *The Book of Knowledge,* tr., of a chapter of Ghazali's Ihya', Lahore, 1962.

Faruqi, Bherhan Ahmad, *The Mujaddid's Conception of Tauhid, Lahore,* 1940.

Field, Cland H., *Al-Ghazali : The Alchemy of Happiness,* London, 1910.

Foster, W., *The English Factories in India,* 13 Vols., Oxford, 1906-27.

Francois Bernier, *Travels in the Mogul Empire,* 1656-58, tr, *A. Constable,* ed. V.A. Smith, London, 1916.

Frykenberg, R.E. (ed.,) *Land Control and Social Structure in Indian History,* Wisconsin, 1969.

Gaur K.D., *"Poor Victims of Uses and Abuses of Criminal Law and Process in India"*, Journal of the Indian Law Institute (JILI) (New Delhi), Vol. 35, (Part II) (1993).

Gairdner, W.H. Temple *Al-Ghazzali's Mishkatu'l-anwar, The niche for lights,* London, 1915.

G. Durand, 'Défiguration philosophique et figure traditionnelle de 1'homme en Occident', *Eranos-Jahrbuch,* Vol. XXXVIII, Zurich, 1971, pp. 45-93.

Gibb, H.A.R, *Islamic Society and the West,* London, 1960.

Halepota, A.J, *Philosophy of Shah Waliu'llah,* Lahore.

Haqq, En'amul, *Muslim Bengali Literature,* Karachi, 1957.

Hasrat, B.J., Dara Shikoh : *Life and Works,* reprinted, New Delhi, 1982.

H. Corbin, *LKe livre des pénétrations métaphysiques,* Tehran-Paris, 1964.

Hodgson, *G.S. The Order of Assassin,* The Hague, 1955.

Husaini, S.A. Q. *The Pantheistic Monism of Ibn al-'Arabi,* Lahore, 1970.

Ikram, S.M., *Muslim Civilization in India,* New York. 1955

Iqbal 'Ali Shah, Sardar, *Islamic Sufism,* London, 1933.

Irfan Habib, *The Agrarian System of Mughal India,* Bombay, 1963.

Jalbani, G.N., *Teachings of Shah Waliyullah of Delhi,* 2nd edn., Lahore, 1973.

Jois, M.R., *Human Rights and Indian Value* (National Council of Teacher Education), Revised Edition, New Delhi, 1998.

J. Servier, *L'homme et l'invisible,* Paris, 1964.

Khushwant Singh, *A History of the Sikhs* Vol. I, 1469-1839. Princeton, 1963.

Lings, Martin, *A Sufi Saint of the Twentieth Century,* London, 1971.

Lord Northbourne, *Religion in the Modern World,* London, 1963.

Luckner, R.C., *The Bhagvad Gita,* Oxford, 1969.

Manucci, N., *Storia do Mogor,* 1653-1708, tr. W. Irvine, London, 1907-8, reprint, New Delhi, 1980.

Mayne, P. *Saints of Sind,* London, 1965.

Mathew Thomas *"Political Economy of Etimic Conflict in Bhutan",* School of International Studies, Jawaharlal Nehru University, New Delhi.

McCarthy, R.I., *The Theology of al-Ash'ari,* Beirut, 1953.

Mir Valiuddin, *Love of God,* Hyderabad, Deccan,1968.

M. Lings, *Ancient Beliefs and Modern Superstitions,* London, 1965.

Mohan Singh Diwana, *An Introduction to Punjabi Literature,* Amritsar, 1951.

Mole Marigan, Les *Mystiques Musulmans,* Paris, 1965.

Moreland, W.H., *India at the Death of Akbar,* London, 1920.

Mujeeb, M., *The Indian Muslims,* London, 1969.

Mukherji, Partha Nath *"The Great Migration of 1971"* Vol. IX, No. 10.

Murthy, T.S. *Assam: The Difficult Years,* New Delhi: Himalayan Books, 1983).

Nasr, Seyyed H., *Three Muslim Sages,* Cambridge, Mass., 1964.

Nayar, Kuldip *"No Decision Yet on Lanka Tamils"*, the Statesman, 6th October, 1992.

Nicholson, R.A., *The Mysteries of Islam,* London, 1914.

Nyberg, H.S., *Kleinere Schrifteu des Iban 'Arabi,* Leiden, 1919.

Padwick, C.E., *Muslim Devotions,* London, 1960.

Petersen, E.L., *'Ali and Mu'awiya in early Arabic Traditions,* Copenhagen, 1964.

Qanungo, K.R., *Dara Shikoh,* Calcutta, 1935.

Rafiqi, *A.Q. Sufism in Kashmir,* Delhi, 1977.

Raverty, H.G., *Selections from the Poetry of the Afghans,* London, 1862.

Riazu'l Islam, *Indo-Persian Relations,* Tehran/Lahore, 1970.

Richards, J.F. *Mughal Administration in Golkonda,* Oxford. 1975.

Rizvi, S.A.A., *Muslim Revivalist Movements in Northern India in the Sixteenth and Seventeenth Centuries,* Agra, 1965.

R. Guénon, *The Reign of Quantity and the Signs of the Times,* trans. by Lord Northbourne, Baltimore, 1972.

Russel, Ralph and Khurshidu'l Islam, *Three Mughal Poets,* Cambridge, Mass., 1968.

Sadarangani, H.I., *Persian Poets of Sind,* Karachi, 1956.

Sadiq, M., *A History of Urdu Poetry,* London, 1964.

Saksena, B.P., *History of Shahjahan of Dilli,* Allahabad, 1958.

Saran, P., *Provincial Government of the Mughals,* Allahabad, 1941.

Saxena, K.P. ed. *Human Rights: Perspective and Challenges in 1990s and Beyond* (New Delhi: Lancers Books, 1994).

Sharma Sastri R., *Kautilya's Arthasastra* (Mysore: Raghuveér Press, 1951).

Singh M.P., *"Position of Aliems in Indian Law"*, Heidelberg Colloquim *"The Legal Position of Alliens in Nation and international Late"*, September 1985.

Singh, Nagendar *Human Rights and International Cooperation* (New Delhi: S. Chand & Co., 1969).

Sonwalkar, Prasun *'Exodus of Bangladeshis to India'*, The Times of India. 6 December, 1991.

Schacht, J., *The Origin of Muhammadan Jurisprudence*, Oxford, 1950.

Schimmel, A., *Islamic Literatures of India, Sindhi Literature, Classical Urdu Literature, in J. Gonda, History of Indian Literature*, Wiesbaden, 1973-75.

Sharif, M.M., *A History of Muslim Philosophy*, 2 Vols., Wiesebaden.

Sharma, S.R., *Mughal Government and Administration*, Bombay. 1951.

Shehadi, F., *Ghazali's Unique Unknowable God*, Leiden, 1964.

Shejwalker, T.S., *Panipat: 1761*, Poona, 1946.

Shemesh, A.B., *Taxation in Islam*, Leiden, 1958, 1965.

Sherwani, H.K., *The Bahmanis of the Deccan*, Hyderabad-Deccan, 1953.

S.H. Nasr, *The Encounter of Man and Nature, The spiritual Crisis of Modern Man*, London, 1968.

Siddiqi, M.Z., *Hadith Literature*, Calcutta, 1961.

Smith, M., Rabi'a *The Mystic and her Fellow Saints in Islam*, Cambridge, 1929.

Sorley, H.T., *Shah 'Abdu' i Latif of Bhit : His Poetry, Life and Times, 1940*, reprint, Oxford, 1966.

Spear, P., *Twilight of the Mughals*, 2nd edn., Cambridge, 1969, reprint, New Delhi, 1970.

Subhan, J.A., *Sufism : Its Saints and Shrines*, 2nd edn., Lucknow, 1960.

Sufi, G.M.D., *Kashmir*, Lahore, 1940-9.

Tarachand, *Influence of Islam on Indian Culture*, 2nd edn., Allahabad, 1963.

Tavernier, Jean-Baptiste, *Travels in India*, 1640-67, tr. V. Ball, ed. and revised by W.Crooke, London, 1925, reprinted, New Delhi, 1977.

Temple, R.C., *Legends of the Punjab,* London, 1893-1901.

T. Burckhardt, *Alchemy,* trans. by W. Stoddart, London, 1967.

T. Izutsu, *The Concept and Reality of Existence,* Tokyo, 1971.

Thomas, R.C., *Legends of the Punjab,* London, 1893-1901.

Thomas, W.F., *Mutual Influence of Muhammedans and Hindus in India,* Cambridge, 1892.

Titus, M., *Indian Islam,* Milford, 1930, reprinted, New Delhi, 1979.

Tod, J., *Annals and Antiquities of Rajasthan,* Oxford, 1920.

Trimingham. J.S., *The Sufi Orders in Islam,* Oxford, 1971.

Tripathi, R.P., *Some Aspects of Muslim Administration, 2nd* edn., Allahabad, 1959.

Tritton, A.S., *The Caliphs and their non-Muslim Subjects,* Oxford, 1930.

Underhill, E., Mysticism : *A Study in the Nature and Development of Man's Spiritual Consciousness,* Paperback, New York, 1956.

Vaudeville, *Charlotte, Kabir,* Vol. I., Oxford, 1974.

Wahed Husain, *Administration of Justice during the Muslim Rule in India,* reprint, Delhi, 1977.

Waheed Mirza, *The Life and Works of Amir Khusrau,* Calcutta, 1935.

Walker, B., *Hindu World,* London, 1968.

Watanmal, L., *The Life of Shah' Abdul Latif,* Hyderabad, Sind, 1889.

Watt, M., *The Faith and Practice of Al-Ghazali,* London, 1953. *Muslim Intellectual : A Study of al-Ghazali,* Edinburgh, 1959.

Yusuf Iblish and Peter Lambron Wilson, *Traditional Modes of Contemplation and Action,* Tehran, 1977.

Zaehner, R.C., *Hindu and Muslim Mysticism,* London, 1960.

Ziadah, N.A., *Sanusiyah : A study of a Revivalist Movement in Islam,* Leiden, 1958.

References

Amery L.S. "Thoughts on constitution", Oxford, 1956.

Dorothy Pickles, "Democracy", London, 1960.

Douglas, William O. "Bunyadi Insani Huquq Ka Mas'lah" (Urdu translation) Lahore, 1965.

Fennessy R.R., "Burke, Paine and the rights of man", Martiness Nijhaoff Hague, 1965.

Hanson, D.W. "From Kingdom to Common-Wealth," Princeton, London, 1970.

Henderson J.J. Craik, "Parliament—A Survey", George Allen and Unwin London, 1965.

Jennings, Sir Ivor, "Approach to Self-Government", Oxford, London.

Kernig C.D. "Marxism Communism and Western Society", New York 1972.

Mcllwain Charles Howard, "Constitutionalism".

Phillips, O. Hood, "Reform of the constitution," London, 1970, p. 120.

Scarman, Sir, Leslie, "English Law—The New Dimensions", Stevens and Sons, London, 1974, p.18.

Index

□□□